PATERNOSTER BIBLICAL MONOGRAPHS

Between Horror and Hope

Paul's Metaphorical Language of Death
in Romans 6:1-11

PATERNOSTER BIBLICAL MONOGRAPHS

A full list of all titles in this series and
Paternoster Theological Monographs
appears at the close of this book.

www.ingramcontent.com/pod-product-compliance
Lightning Source LLC
Chambersburg PA
CBHW071447150426
43191CB00008B/1258

Graham J. Watts
Revelation and the Spirit
A Comparative Study of the Relationship between the Doctrine of Revelation and Pneumatology in the Theology of Eberhard Jüngel and of Wolfhart Pannenberg

The relationship between revelation and pneumatology is relatively unexplored. This approach offers a fresh angle on two important twentieth century theologians and raises pneumatological questions which are theologically crucial and relevant to mission in a postmodern culture.

2005 / 1-84227-104-0 / xxii + 232pp

Nigel G. Wright
Disavowing Constantine
Mission, Church and the Social Order in the Theologies of John Howard Yoder and Jürgen Moltmann

This book is a timely restatement of a radical theology of church and state in the Anabaptist and Baptist tradition. Dr Wright constructs his argument in dialogue and debate with Yoder and Moltmann, major contributors to a free church perspective.

2000 / 0-85364-978-2 / xvi + 252pp

Paternoster
9 Holdom Avenue,
Bletchley,
Milton Keynes MK1 1QR,
United Kingdom
Web: www.authenticmedia.co.uk/paternoster

July 2005

Scott Swain
God According to the Gospel
Biblical Narrative and the Identity of God in the Theology of Robert W. Jenson
Robert W. Jenson is one of the leading voices in contemporary Trinitarian theology. His boldest contribution in this area concerns his use of biblical narrative both to ground and explicate the Christian doctrine of God. *God According to the Gospel* critically examines Jenson's proposal and suggests an alternative way of reading the biblical portrayal of the triune God.
2006 / 1-84227-258-6 / approx. 180pp

Justyn Terry
The Justifying Judgement of God
A Reassessment of the Place of Judgement in the Saving Work of Christ
The argument of this book is that judgement, understood as the whole process of bringing justice, is the primary metaphor of atonement, with others, such as victory, redemption and sacrifice, subordinate to it. Judgement also provides the proper context for understanding penal substitution and the call to repentance, baptism, eucharist and holiness.
2005 / 1-84227-370-1 / approx. 274 pp

Graham Tomlin
The Power of the Cross
Theology and the Death of Christ in Paul, Luther and Pascal
This book explores the theology of the cross in St Paul, Luther and Pascal. It offers new perspectives on the theology of each, and some implications for the nature of power, apologetics, theology and church life in a postmodern context.
1999 / 0-85364-984-7 / xiv + 344pp

Adonis Vidu
Postliberal Theological Method
A Critical Study
The postliberal theology of Hans Frei, George Lindbeck, Ronald Thiemann, John Milbank and others is one of the more influential contemporary options. This book focuses on several aspects pertaining to its theological method, specifically its understanding of background, hermeneutics, epistemic justification, ontology, the nature of doctrine and, finally, Christological method.
2005 / 1-84227-395-7 / approx. 324pp

Hazel Sherman
Reading Zechariah
The Allegorical Tradition of Biblical Interpretation through the Commentary of Didymus the Blind and Theodore of Mopsuestia

A close reading of the commentary on Zechariah by Didymus the Blind alongside that of Theodore of Mopsuestia suggests that popular categorising of Antiochene and Alexandrian biblical exegesis as 'historical' or 'allegorical' is inadequate and misleading.

2005 / 1-84227-213-6 / approx. 280pp

Andrew Sloane
On Being a Christian in the Academy
Nicholas Wolterstorff and the Practice of Christian Scholarship

An exposition and critical appraisal of Nicholas Wolterstorff's epistemology in the light of the philosophy of science, and an application of his thought to the practice of Christian scholarship.

2003 / 1-84227-058-3 / xvi + 274pp

Damon W.K. So
Jesus' Revelation of His Father
A Narrative-Conceptual Study of the Trinity with Special Reference to Karl Barth

This book explores the trinitarian dynamics in the context of Jesus' revelation of his Father in his earthly ministry with references to key passages in Matthew's Gospel. It develops from the exegeses of these passages a non-linear concept of revelation which links Jesus' communion with his Father to his revelatory words and actions through a nuanced understanding of the Holy Spirit, with references to K. Barth, G.W.H. Lampe, J.D.G. Dunn and E. Irving.

2005 / 1-84227-323-X / approx. 380pp

Daniel Strange
The Possibility of Salvation Among the Unevangelised
An Analysis of Inclusivism in Recent Evangelical Theology

For evangelical theologians the 'fate of the unevangelised' impinges upon fundamental tenets of evangelical identity. The position known as 'inclusivism', defined by the belief that the unevangelised can be ontologically saved by Christ whilst being epistemologically unaware of him, has been defended most vigorously by the Canadian evangelical Clark H. Pinnock. Through a detailed analysis and critique of Pinnock's work, this book examines a cluster of issues surrounding the unevangelised and its implications for christology, soteriology and the doctrine of revelation.

2002 / 1-84227-047-8 / xviii + 362pp

Jim Purves
The Triune God and the Charismatic Movement
A Critical Appraisal from a Scottish Perspective
All emotion and no theology? Or a fundamental challenge to reappraise and realign our trinitarian theology in the light of Christian experience? This study of charismatic renewal as it found expression within Scotland at the end of the twentieth century evaluates the use of Patristic, Reformed and contemporary models of the Trinity in explaining the workings of the Holy Spirit.
2004 / 1-84227-321-3 / xxiv + 246pp

Anna Robbins
Methods in the Madness
Diversity in Twentieth-Century Christian Social Ethics
The author compares the ethical methods of Walter Rauschenbusch, Reinhold Niebuhr and others. She argues that unless Christians are clear about the ways that theology and philosophy are expressed practically they may lose the ability to discuss social ethics across contexts, let alone reach effective agreements.
2004 / 1-84227-211-X / xx + 294pp

Ed Rybarczyk
Beyond Salvation
Eastern Orthodoxy and Classical Pentecostalism on Becoming Like Christ
At first glance eastern Orthodoxy and classical Pentecostalism seem quite distinct. This ground-breaking study shows they share much in common, especially as it concerns the experiential elements of following Christ. Both traditions assert that authentic Christianity transcends the wooden categories of modernism.
2004 / 1-84227-144-X / xii + 356pp

Signe Sandsmark
Is World View Neutral Education Possible and Desirable?
A Christian Response to Liberal Arguments
(Published jointly with The Stapleford Centre)
This book discusses reasons for belief in world view neutrality, and argues that 'neutral' education will have a hidden, but strong world view influence. It discusses the place for Christian education in the common school.
2000 / 0-85364-973-1 / xiv + 182pp

Gillian McCulloch
The Deconstruction of Dualism in Theology
With Reference to Ecofeminist Theology and New Age Spirituality
This book challenges eco-theological anti-dualism in Christian theology, arguing that dualism has a twofold function in Christian religious discourse. Firstly, it enables us to express the discontinuities and divisions that are part of the process of reality. Secondly, dualistic language allows us to express the mysteries of divine transcendence/immanence and the survival of the soul without collapsing into monism and materialism, both of which are problematic for Christian epistemology.
2002 / 1-84227-044-3 / xii + 282pp

Leslie McCurdy
Attributes and Atonement
The Holy Love of God in the Theology of P.T. Forsyth
Attributes and Atonement is an intriguing full-length study of P.T. Forsyth's doctrine of the cross as it relates particularly to God's holy love. It includes an unparalleled bibliography of both primary and secondary material relating to Forsyth.
1999 / 0-85364-833-6 / xiv + 328pp

Nozomu Miyahira
Towards a Theology of the Concord of God
A Japanese Perspective on the Trinity
This book introduces a new Japanese theology and a unique Trinitarian formula based on the Japanese intellectual climate: three betweennesses and one concord. It also presents a new interpretation of the Trinity, a co-subordinationism, which is in line with orthodox Trinitarianism; each single person of the Trinity is eternally and equally subordinate (or serviceable) to the other persons, so that they retain the mutual dynamic equality.
2000 / 0-85364-863-8 / xiv + 256pp

Eddy José Muskus
The Origins and Early Development of Liberation Theology in Latin America
With Particular Reference to Gustavo Gutiérrez
This work challenges the fundamental premise of Liberation Theology, 'opting for the poor', and its claim that Christ is found in them. It also argues that Liberation Theology emerged as a direct result of the failure of the Roman Catholic Church in Latin America.
2002 / 0-85364-974-X / xiv + 296pp

John G. Kelly
One God, One People
The Differentiated Unity of the People of God in the Theology of Jürgen Moltmann
The author expounds and critiques Moltmann's doctrine of God and highlights the systematic connections between it and Moltmann's influential discussion of Israel. He then proposes a fresh approach to Jewish–Christian relations building on Moltmann's work using insights from Habermas and Rawls.
2005 / 0-85346-969-3 / approx. 350pp

Mark F.W. Lovatt
Confronting the Will-to-Power
A Reconsideration of the Theology of Reinhold Niebuhr
Confronting the Will-to-Power is an analysis of the theology of Reinhold Niebuhr, arguing that his work is an attempt to identify, and provide a practical theological answer to, the existence and nature of human evil.
2001 / 1-84227-054-0 / xviii + 216pp

Neil B. MacDonald
Karl Barth and the Strange New World within the Bible
Barth, Wittgenstein, and the Metadilemmas of the Enlightenment
Barth's discovery of the strange new world within the Bible is examined in the context of Kant, Hume, Overbeck, and, most importantly, Wittgenstein. MacDonald covers some fundamental issues in theology today: epistemology, the final form of the text and biblical truth-claims.
2000 / 0-85364-970-7 / xxvi + 374pp

Keith A. Mascord
Alvin Plantinga and Christian Apologetics
This book draws together the contributions of the philosopher Alvin Plantinga to the major contemporary challenges to Christian belief, highlighting in particular his ground-breaking work in epistemology and the problem of evil. Plantinga's theory that both theistic and Christian belief is warrantedly basic is explored and critiqued, and an assessment offered as to the significance of his work for apologetic theory and practice.
2005 / 1-84227-256-X / approx. 304pp

Keith Ferdinando
The Triumph of Christ in African Perspective
A Study of Demonology and Redemption in the African Context
The book explores the implications of the gospel for traditional African fears of occult aggression. It analyses such traditional approaches to suffering and biblical responses to fears of demonic evil, concluding with an evaluation of African beliefs from the perspective of the gospel.
1999 / 0-85364-830-1 / xviii + 450pp

Andrew Goddard
Living the Word, Resisting the World
The Life and Thought of Jacques Ellul
This work offers a definitive study of both the life and thought of the French Reformed thinker Jacques Ellul (1912-1994). It will prove an indispensable resource for those interested in this influential theologian and sociologist and for Christian ethics and political thought generally.
2002 / 1-84227-053-2 / xxiv + 378pp

David Hilborn
The Words of our Lips
Language-Use in Free Church Worship
Studies of liturgical language have tended to focus on the written canons of Roman Catholic and Anglican communities. By contrast, David Hilborn analyses the more extemporary approach of English Nonconformity. Drawing on recent developments in linguistic pragmatics, he explores similarities and differences between 'fixed' and 'free' worship, and argues for the interdependence of each.
2006 / 0-85364-977-4 / approx. 350pp

Roger Hitching
The Church and Deaf People
A Study of Identity, Communication and Relationships with Special Reference to the Ecclesiology of Jürgen Moltmann
In *The Church and Deaf People* Roger Hitching sensitively examines the history and present experience of deaf people and finds similarities between aspects of sign language and Moltmann's theological method that 'open up' new ways of understanding theological concepts.
2003 / 1-84227-222-5 / xxii + 236pp

Tim Chester
Mission and the Coming of God
Eschatology, the Trinity and Mission in the Theology of Jürgen Moltmann
This book explores the theology and missiology of the influential contemporary theologian, Jürgen Moltmann. It highlights the important contribution Moltmann has made while offering a critique of his thought from an evangelical perspective. In so doing, it touches on pertinent issues for evangelical missiology. The conclusion takes Calvin as a starting point, proposing 'an eschatology of the cross' which offers a critique of the over-realised eschatologies in liberation theology and certain forms of evangelicalism.
2006 / 1-84227-320-5 / approx. 224pp

Sylvia Wilkey Collinson
Making Disciples
The Significance of Jesus' Educational Strategy for Today's Church
This study examines the biblical practice of discipling, formulates a definition, and makes comparisons with modern models of education. A recommendation is made for greater attention to its practice today.
2004 / 1-84227-116-4 / xiv + 278pp

Darrell Cosden
A Theology of Work
Work and the New Creation
Through dialogue with Moltmann, Pope John Paul II and others, this book develops a genitive 'theology of work', presenting a theological definition of work and a model for a theological ethics of work that shows work's nature, value and meaning now and eschatologically. Work is shown to be a transformative activity consisting of three dynamically inter-related dimensions: the instrumental, relational and ontological.
2005 / 1-84227-332-9 / xvi + 208pp

Stephen M. Dunning
The Crisis and the Quest
A Kierkegaardian Reading of Charles Williams
Employing Kierkegaardian categories and analysis, this study investigates both the central crisis in Charles Williams's authorship between hermetism and Christianity (Kierkegaard's Religions A and B), and the quest to resolve this crisis, a quest that ultimately presses the bounds of orthodoxy.
2000 / 0-85364-985-5 / xxiv + 254pp

Paternoster Theological Monographs
(All titles uniform with this volume)
Dates in bold are of projected publication

Emil Bartos
Deification in Eastern Orthodox Theology
An Evaluation and Critique of the Theology of Dumitru Staniloae

Bartos studies a fundamental yet neglected aspect of Orthodox theology: deification. By examining the doctrines of anthropology, christology, soteriology and ecclesiology as they relate to deification, he provides an important contribution to contemporary dialogue between Eastern and Western theologians.

1999 / 0-85364-956-1 / xii + 370pp

Graham Buxton
The Trinity, Creation and Pastoral Ministry
Imaging the Perichoretic God

In this book the author proposes a three-way conversation between theology, science and pastoral ministry. His approach draws on a Trinitarian understanding of God as a relational being of love, whose life 'spills over' into all created reality, human and non-human. By locating human meaning and purpose within God's 'creation-community' this book offers the possibility of a transforming engagement between those in pastoral ministry and the scientific community.

2005 / 1-84227-369-8 / approx. 380 pp

Iain D. Campbell
Fixing the Indemnity
The Life and Work of George Adam Smith

When Old Testament scholar George Adam Smith (1856–1942) delivered the Lyman Beecher lectures at Yale University in 1899, he confidently declared that 'modern criticism has won its war against traditional theories. It only remains to fix the amount of the indemnity.' In this biography, Iain D. Campbell assesses Smith's critical approach to the Old Testament and evaluates its consequences, showing that Smith's life and work still raises questions about the relationship between biblical scholarship and evangelical faith.

2004 / 1-84227-228-4 / xx + 256pp

Stephen I. Wright
The Voice of Jesus
Studies in the Interpretation of Six Gospel Parables
This literary study considers how the 'voice' of Jesus has been heard in different periods of parable interpretation, and how the categories of figure and trope may help us towards a sensitive reading of the parables today.
2000 / 0-85364-975-8 / xiv + 280pp

Paternoster
9 Holdom Avenue,
Bletchley,
Milton Keynes MK1 1QR,
United Kingdom
Web: www.authenticmedia.co.uk/paternoster

July 2005

Kevin Walton
Thou Traveller Unknown
The Presence and Absence of God in the Jacob Narrative
The author offers a fresh reading of the story of Jacob in the book of Genesis through the paradox of divine presence and absence. The work also seeks to make a contribution to Pentateuchal studies by bringing together a close reading of the final text with historical critical insights, doing justice to the text's historical depth, final form and canonical status.
2003 / 1-84227-059-1 / xvi + 238pp

George M. Wieland
The Significance of Salvation
A Study of Salvation Language in the Pastoral Epistles
The language and ideas of salvation pervade the three Pastoral Epistles. This study offers a close examination of their soteriological statements. In all three letters the idea of salvation is found to play a vital paraenetic role, but each also exhibits distinctive soteriological emphases. The results challenge common assumptions about the Pastoral Epistles as a corpus.
2005 / 1-84227-257-8 / approx. 324pp

Alistair Wilson
When Will These Things Happen?
A Study of Jesus as Judge in Matthew 21–25
This study seeks to allow Matthew's carefully constructed presentation of Jesus to be given full weight in the modern evaluation of Jesus' eschatology. Careful analysis of the text of Matthew 21–25 reveals Jesus to be standing firmly in the Jewish prophetic and wisdom traditions as he proclaims and enacts imminent judgement on the Jewish authorities then boldly claims the central role in the final and universal judgement.
2004 / 1-84227-146-6 / xxii + 272pp

Lindsay Wilson
Joseph Wise and Otherwise
The Intersection of Covenant and Wisdom in Genesis 37–50
This book offers a careful literary reading of Genesis 37–50 that argues that the Joseph story contains both strong covenant themes and many wisdom-like elements. The connections between the two helps to explore how covenant and wisdom might intersect in an integrated biblical theology.
2004 / 1-84227-140-7 / xvi + 340pp

David Powys
'Hell': A Hard Look at a Hard Question
The Fate of the Unrighteous in New Testament Thought
This comprehensive treatment seeks to unlock the original meaning of terms and phrases long thought to support the traditional doctrine of hell. It concludes that there is an alternative—one which is more biblical, and which can positively revive the rationale for Christian mission.
1997 / 0-85364-831-X / xxii + 478pp

Sorin Sabou
Between Horror and Hope
Paul's Metaphorical Language of Death in Romans 6.1-11
This book argues that Paul's metaphorical language of death in Romans 6.1-11 conveys two aspects: horror and hope. The 'horror' aspect is conveyed by the 'crucifixion' language, and the 'hope' aspect by 'burial' language. The life of the Christian believer is understood, as relationship with sin is concerned ('death to sin'), between these two realities: horror and hope.
2005 / 1-84227-322-1 / approx. 224pp

Rosalind Selby
The Comical Doctrine
The Epistemology of New Testament Hermeneutics
This book argues that the gospel breaks through postmodernity's critique of truth and the referential possibilities of textuality with its gift of grace. With a rigorous, philosophical challenge to modernist and postmodernist assumptions, Selby offers an alternative epistemology to all who would still read with faith *and* with academic credibility.
2005 / 1-84227-212-8 / approx. 350pp

Kiwoong Son
Zion Symbolism in Hebrews
Hebrews 12.18-24 as a Hermeneutical Key to the Epistle
This book challenges the general tendency of understanding the Epistle to the Hebrews against a Hellenistic background and suggests that the Epistle should be understood in the light of the Jewish apocalyptic tradition. The author especially argues for the importance of the theological symbolism of Sinai and Zion (Heb. 12:18-24) as it provides the Epistle's theological background as well as the rhetorical basis of the superiority motif of Jesus throughout the Epistle.
2005 / 1-84227-368-X / approx. 280pp

Robin Parry
Old Testament Story and Christian Ethics
The Rape of Dinah as a Case Study

What is the role of story in ethics and, more particularly, what is the role of Old Testament story in Christian ethics? This book, drawing on the work of contemporary philosophers, argues that narrative is crucial in the ethical shaping of people and, drawing on the work of contemporary Old Testament scholars, that story plays a key role in Old Testament ethics. Parry then argues that when situated in canonical context Old Testament stories can be reappropriated by Christian readers in their own ethical formation. The shocking story of the rape of Dinah and the massacre of the Shechemites provides a fascinating case study for exploring the parameters within which Christian ethical appropriations of Old Testament stories can live.

2004 / 1-84227-210-1 / xx + 350pp

Ian Paul
Power to See the World Anew
The Value of Paul Ricoeur's Hermeneutic of Metaphor in Interpreting the Symbolism of Revelation 12 and 13

This book is a study of the hermeneutics of metaphor of Paul Ricoeur, one of the most important writers on hermeneutics and metaphor of the last century. It sets out the key points of his theory, important criticisms of his work, and how his approach, modified in the light of these criticisms, offers a methodological framework for reading apocalyptic texts.

2006 / 1-84227-056-7 / approx. 350pp

Robert L. Plummer
Paul's Understanding of the Church's Mission
Did the Apostle Paul Expect the Early Christian Communities to Evangelize?

This book engages in a careful study of Paul's letters to determine if the apostle expected the communities to which he wrote to engage in missionary activity. It helpfully summarizes the discussion on this debated issue, judiciously handling contested texts, and provides a way forward in addressing this critical question. While admitting that Paul rarely explicitly commands the communities he founded to evangelize, Plummer amasses significant incidental data to provide a convincing case that Paul did indeed expect his churches to engage in mission activity. Throughout the study, Plummer progressively builds a theological basis for the church's mission that is both distinctively Pauline and compelling.

2006 / 1-84227-333-7 / approx. 324pp

Scott J. Hafemann
Paul, Moses and the History of Israel
The Letter/Spirit Contrast and the Argument from Scripture in 2 Corinthians 3
An exegetical study of the call of Moses, the second giving of the Law (Exodus 32–34), the new covenant, and the prophetic understanding of the history of Israel in 2 Corinthians 3. Hafemann's work demonstrates Paul's contextual use of the Old Testament and the essential unity between the Law and the Gospel within the context of the distinctive ministries of Moses and Paul.
2005 / 1-84227-317-5 / xii + 498pp

Douglas S. McComiskey
Lukan Theology in the Light of the Gospel's Literary Structure
Luke's Gospel was purposefully written with theology embedded in its patterned literary structure. A critical analysis of this cyclical structure provides new windows into Luke's interpretation of the individual pericopes comprising the Gospel and illuminates several of his theological interests.
2004 / 1-84227-148-2 / xviii + 388pp

Stephen Motyer
Your Father the Devil?
A New Approach to John and 'The Jews'
Who are 'the Jews' in John's Gospel? Defending John against the charge of antisemitism, Motyer argues that, far from demonising the Jews, the Gospel seeks to present Jesus as 'Good News for Jews' in a late first century setting.
1997 / 0-85364-832-8 / xiv + 260pp

Esther Ng
Reconstructing Christian Origins?
The Feminist Theology of Elizabeth Schüssler Fiorenza: An Evaluation
In a detailed evaluation, the author challenges Elizabeth Schüssler Fiorenza's reconstruction of early Christian origins and her underlying presuppositions. The author also presents her own views on women's roles both then and now.
2002 / 1-84227-055-9 / xxiv + 468pp

Andrew D. Clarke
Secular and Christian Leadership in Corinth
A Socio-Historical and Exegetical Study of 1 Corinthians 1–6

This volume is an investigation into the leadership structures and dynamics of first-century Roman Corinth. These are compared with the practice of leadership in the Corinthian Christian community which are reflected in 1 Corinthians 1–6, and contrasted with Paul's own principles of Christian leadership.

2005 / 1-84227-229-2 / 200pp

Stephen Finamore
God, Order and Chaos
René Girard and the Apocalypse

Readers are often disturbed by the images of destruction in the book of Revelation and unsure why they are unleashed after the exaltation of Jesus. This book examines past approaches to these texts and uses René Girard's theories to revive some old ideas and propose some new ones.

2005 / 1-84227-197-0 / approx. 344pp

David G. Firth
Surrendering Retribution in the Psalms
Responses to Violence in the Individual Complaints

In *Surrendering Retribution in the Psalms*, David Firth examines the ways in which the book of Psalms inculcates a model response to violence through the repetition of standard patterns of prayer. Rather than seeking justification for retributive violence, Psalms encourages not only a surrender of the right of retribution to Yahweh, but also sets limits on the retribution that can be sought in imprecations. Arising initially from the author's experience in South Africa, the possibilities of this model to a particular context of violence is then briefly explored.

2005 / 1-84227-337-X / xviii + 154pp

Scott J. Hafemann
Suffering and Ministry in the Spirit
Paul's Defence of His Ministry in II Corinthians 2:14–3:3

Shedding new light on the way Paul defended his apostleship, the author offers a careful, detailed study of 2 Corinthians 2:14–3:3 linked with other key passages throughout 1 and 2 Corinthians. Demonstrating the unity and coherence of Paul's argument in this passage, the author shows that Paul's suffering served as the vehicle for revealing God's power and glory through the Spirit.

2000 / 0-85364-967-7 / xiv + 262pp

Daniel J-S Chae
Paul as Apostle to the Gentiles
His Apostolic Self-awareness and its Influence on the Soteriological Argument in Romans

Opposing 'the post-Holocaust interpretation of Romans', Daniel Chae competently demonstrates that Paul argues for the equality of Jew and Gentile in Romans. Chae's fresh exegetical interpretation is academically outstanding and spiritually encouraging.

1997 / 0-85364-829-8 / xiv + 378pp

Luke L. Cheung
The Genre, Composition and Hermeneutics of the Epistle of James

The present work examines the employment of the wisdom genre with a certain compositional structure and the interpretation of the law through the Jesus tradition of the double love command by the author of the Epistle of James to serve his purpose in promoting perfection and warning against doubleness among the eschatologically renewed people of God in the Diaspora.

2003 / 1-84227-062-1 / xvi + 372pp

Youngmo Cho
Spirit and Kingdom in the Writings of Luke and Paul

The relationship between Spirit and Kingdom is a relatively unexplored area in Lukan and Pauline studies. This book offers a fresh perspective of two biblical writers on the subject. It explores the difference between Luke's and Paul's understanding of the Spirit by examining the specific question of the relationship of the concept of the Spirit to the concept of the Kingdom of God in each writer.

2005 / 1-84227-316-7 / approx. 270pp

Andrew C. Clark
Parallel Lives
The Relation of Paul to the Apostles in the Lucan Perspective

This study of the Peter-Paul parallels in Acts argues that their purpose was to emphasize the themes of continuity in salvation history and the unity of the Jewish and Gentile missions. New light is shed on Luke's literary techniques, partly through a comparison with Plutarch.

2001 / 1-84227-035-4 / xviii + 386pp

Mark Bonnington
The Antioch Episode of Galatians 2:11-14 in Historical and Cultural Context
The Galatians 2 'incident' in Antioch over table-fellowship suggests significant disagreement between the leading apostles. This book analyses the background to the disagreement by locating the incident within the dynamics of social interaction between Jews and Gentiles. It proposes a new way of understanding the relationship between the individuals and issues involved.
2005 / 1-84227-050-8 / approx. 350pp

David Bostock
A Portrayal of Trust
The Theme of Faith in the Hezekiah Narratives
This study provides detailed and sensitive readings of the Hezekiah narratives (2 Kings 18–20 and Isaiah 36–39) from a theological perspective. It concentrates on the theme of faith, using narrative criticism as its methodology. Attention is paid especially to setting, plot, point of view and characterization within the narratives. A largely positive portrayal of Hezekiah emerges that underlines the importance and relevance of scripture.
2005 / 1-84227-314-0 / approx. 300pp

Mark Bredin
Jesus, Revolutionary of Peace
A Non-violent Christology in the Book of Revelation
This book aims to demonstrate that the figure of Jesus in the Book of Revelation can best be understood as an active non-violent revolutionary.
2003 / 1-84227-153-9 / xviii + 262pp

Robinson Butarbutar
Paul and Conflict Resolution
An Exegetical Study of Paul's Apostolic Paradigm in 1 Corinthians 9
The author sees the apostolic paradigm in 1 Corinthians 9 as part of Paul's unified arguments in 1 Corinthians 8–10 in which he seeks to mediate in the dispute over the issue of food offered to idols. The book also sees its relevance for dispute-resolution today, taking the conflict within the author's church as an example.
2006 / 1-84227-315-9 / approx. 280pp

Paternoster Biblical Monographs

(All titles uniform with this volume)
Dates in bold are of projected publication

Joseph Abraham
Eve: Accused or Acquitted?
A Reconsideration of Feminist Readings of the Creation Narrative Texts in Genesis 1–3
Two contrary views dominate contemporary feminist biblical scholarship. One finds in the Bible an unequivocal equality between the sexes from the very creation of humanity, whilst the other sees the biblical text as irredeemably patriarchal and androcentric. Dr Abraham enters into dialogue with both camps as well as introducing his own method of approach. An invaluable tool for any one who is interested in this contemporary debate.
2002 / 0-85364-971-5 / xxiv + 272pp

Octavian D. Baban
Mimesis and Luke's on the Road Encounters in Luke-Acts
Luke's Theology of the Way and its Literary Representation
The book argues on theological and literary (mimetic) grounds that Luke's on-the-road encounters, especially those belonging to the post-Easter period, are part of his complex theology of the Way. Jesus' teaching and that of the apostles is presented by Luke as a challenging answer to the Hellenistic reader's thirst for adventure, good literature, and existential paradigms.
2005 */ 1-84227-253-5 / approx. 374pp*

Paul Barker
The Triumph of Grace in Deuteronomy
This book is a textual and theological analysis of the interaction between the sin and faithlessness of Israel and the grace of Yahweh in response, looking especially at Deuteronomy chapters 1–3, 8–10 and 29–30. The author argues that the grace of Yahweh is determinative for the ongoing relationship between Yahweh and Israel and that Deuteronomy anticipates and fully expects Israel to be faithless.
2004 / 1-84227-226-8 / xxii + 270pp

Jonathan F. Bayes
The Weakness of the Law
God's Law and the Christian in New Testament Perspective
A study of the four New Testament books which refer to the law as weak (Acts, Romans, Galatians, Hebrews) leads to a defence of the third use in the Reformed debate about the law in the life of the believer.
2000 / 0-85364-957-X / xii + 244pp

Index

36, 37, 38, 39, 41, 42, 59, 60, 61, 62, 63, 69, 70, 72, 74, 75, 77, 78, 90, 91, 114, 140, 141, 143
ritual, 7, 22, 23, 24, 25, 72, 73, 105
sacrament, 36
salvation, 2, 20, 22, 27, 34, 41, 42, 43, 62, 64, 68, 75, 77, 78, 79, 97, 121, 133, 135
save, 84, 126, 128
seed, 28, 67
senses, 9, 13, 50, 111
sin, x, 1, 2, 3, 4, 5, 7, 15, 16, 18, 20, 28, 31, 32, 36, 37, 38, 41, 42, 53, 54, 56, 57, 58, 59, 60, 61, 62, 63, 64, 69, 70, 71, 74, 75, 78, 79, 80, 81, 91, 93, 94, 96, 97, 105, 106, 108, 113, 115, 117, 118, 119, 120, 121, 122, 123, 124, 125, 126, 128, 129, 130, 131, 132, 133, 134, 135, 136, 137, 140, 141, 142, 143
slave, 9, 63, 133
slavery, 11, 17, 32, 69, 80, 85, 119, 120, 122, 133, 137, 142
solidarity, 20, 35, 126
soul, 6, 8, 9, 10, 12, 16, 23, 24, 76, 77, 86, 88, 89, 112, 128, 133, 134
spirit, 8, 23, 67, 134
Spirit, 2, 32, 40, 90, 102, 104, 105, 106, 114, 150, 155
submission, 33, 59
suffering, 17, 20, 26, 31, 34, 36, 40, 41, 64
temple, 18
transformation, 30, 74
truth, 9, 10, 16, 30, 49, 50, 67, 83, 90, 97, 111
underworld, 18, 22, 25, 26
vehicle, 16, 18, 29, 41, 52, 55, 56, 57, 79, 82, 93, 94, 139, 141
water, 18, 32, 72, 81, 90, 96, 97, 99, 102, 103, 104, 105, 109
wisdom, 9, 12
worship, 20, 85

28, 33, 47, 53, 54, 61, 76, 78, 79, 83, 88, 92, 101, 105, 110, 111, 112, 114, 115, 118, 119, 125, 126, 129, 130, 133
exile, 11
exodus, 17
experience, 6, 7, 17, 18, 20, 21, 22, 24, 27, 29, 30, 31, 33, 41, 53, 71, 76, 79, 90, 97, 105, 107, 123, 134, 139, 141
fate, 11, 14, 20, 24, 26, 27, 86, 87, 123
Father, 12, 13, 16, 60, 61, 62
freedom, 11, 62, 85, 133
glory, 13, 40, 61, 84, 106, 124, 144
God, xiii, 1, 4, 5, 10, 14, 15, 17, 18, 19, 28, 32, 35, 36, 37, 38, 39, 41, 42, 59, 60, 61, 62, 63, 65, 67, 68, 69, 75, 77, 78, 79, 81, 82, 85, 89, 90, 93, 97, 99, 105, 106, 107, 108, 109, 110, 111, 113, 115, 121, 123, 129, 130, 131, 132, 135, 140, 143, 148, 150, 151, 152, 154, 156
gospel, 31, 75, 77, 78, 107, 141
grace, 1, 2, 4, 5, 36, 38, 42, 80, 97, 106, 108, 132
grave, 14, 22, 90
Hellenism, 7
hellenistic, 6, 139
holy, 21
Horus, 22, 23, 24, 25
inclusive, 33, 34
incorporation, 20, 37
initiation, 17, 19, 21, 22, 25, 26, 27, 79, 105, 107
Isis, 21, 22, 25
king, 23, 24, 28, 32, 35, 36, 37, 42, 65, 66, 68, 69, 86, 92, 93, 130, 140, 143
Kore, 26
life, 1, 2, 3, 5, 6, 7, 8, 10, 11, 12, 13, 14, 15, 16, 19, 20, 21, 22, 25, 26, 27, 28, 29, 30, 32, 34, 36, 37, 40, 42, 46, 47, 53, 56, 57, 60, 61, 62, 69, 70, 71, 75, 77, 78, 80, 87, 88, 90, 91, 93, 97, 99, 102, 103, 106, 108, 109, 113, 115, 116, 118, 120, 123, 130, 131, 132, 133, 136, 137, 138, 140, 142, 143

love, xiii, 9, 76, 89, 106, 135
master, 31, 32, 42, 59, 61, 69, 77, 135, 137, 142
Metamorphoses, 20, 21, 145
Metaneira, 26
metaphor, 7, 12, 13, 14, 15, 16, 18, 29, 31, 33, 41, 42, 44, 45, 46, 47, 48, 49, 50, 51, 52, 53, 54, 55, 56, 57, 58, 79, 82, 89, 90, 93, 94, 95, 96, 97, 98, 99, 102, 105, 107, 108, 109, 110, 114, 115, 116, 124, 133, 137, 139, 140, 141, 143
mind, 11, 12, 30, 51, 56, 76, 77, 80, 89, 115
mystery religions, 18, 19, 20, 21, 139
mystes, 18
nature, 9, 10, 16, 39, 45, 76, 79, 81, 87, 111, 112, 113, 114, 118, 127, 134
old man, 5, 32, 33, 42, 43, 53, 56, 57, 78, 81, 89, 94, 117, 118, 119, 120, 137, 142
Osiris, 19, 20, 22, 23, 24, 25
participation, 5, 17, 19, 20, 37, 38, 40, 41, 79, 90, 98, 134, 137, 142
pattern, 22, 24, 75, 141
peace, 11, 12, 142
Persephone, 25, 26
philosophy, 8, 9, 10, 12, 13, 44, 50
pleasure, 9, 10, 45, 76, 88
power, 11, 14, 16, 20, 22, 23, 27, 32, 38, 42, 51, 59, 61, 62, 63, 67, 74, 75, 77, 81, 105, 107, 110, 123, 130, 134, 135, 142
prayer, 18
providence, 22
qualifiers, 29, 42, 53, 56, 57, 58, 89, 93, 94, 96, 97, 99, 105, 108, 139, 141
reason, 2, 9, 10, 15, 34, 36, 41, 63, 68, 69, 76, 85, 87, 90, 97, 98, 100, 111, 113, 121, 125, 127, 129, 130, 133
rebirth, 22
reign, 24, 42, 82, 133, 142
release, 9, 10, 33, 58, 80, 88, 133
representation, 18, 20, 27, 28, 35, 42, 51, 53, 70, 71, 75, 76, 77, 78, 93, 110, 113, 141
resurrection, 3, 4, 7, 17, 19, 32, 34, 35,

Index

Abraham, 15, 28, 29, 89, 110
Adam, xi, 16, 25, 27, 28, 29, 32, 34, 36, 40, 42, 58, 71, 78, 82, 90, 99, 106, 116, 117, 118, 119, 120, 121, 122, 123, 124, 126, 129, 130, 131, 132, 133, 135, 137, 142, 143, 148, 149, 151, 152, 154, 155
Adonis, 20
age, 11, 12, 19, 25, 32, 42, 46, 47, 61, 62, 71, 92, 117, 118, 123, 136, 142
apocalyptic, 29, 30, 81, 82, 123
Apuleius, 18, 19, 20, 21, 145
Attis, 20, 26
baptism, 3, 4, 5, 7, 17, 18, 19, 20, 30, 31, 32, 36, 37, 38, 41, 42, 53, 57, 70, 72, 73, 75, 79, 81, 89, 90, 94, 95, 96, 97, 98, 99, 100, 101, 104, 105, 106, 107, 108, 109, 118, 141, 143
beauty, 9, 13, 16
blessing, 28, 135
blood, 26, 104
body, 6, 9, 10, 11, 12, 13, 16, 24, 33, 39, 56, 80, 81, 84, 85, 88, 89, 94, 102, 103, 112, 114, 115, 117, 133, 134, 135, 136, 137, 141, 142, 143
Christ, ix, x, 1, 3, 4, 5, 6, 7, 16, 17, 18, 19, 20, 21, 27, 28, 29, 30, 31, 32, 33, 34, 36, 37, 38, 39, 40, 41, 42, 43, 53, 56, 57, 58, 59, 60, 61, 62, 63, 64, 65, 66, 68, 69, 70, 71, 72, 73, 74, 75, 77, 78, 79, 80, 81, 82, 90, 93, 94, 95, 96, 97, 98, 99, 100, 101, 105, 106, 107, 108, 109, 110, 113, 114, 115, 116, 117, 118, 120, 121, 122, 123, 124, 125, 132, 135, 137, 139, 140, 141, 142, 143, 148, 149, 151, 152, 153, 154, 155, 156
commentatio mortis, ix, 6, 7, 13, 16, 139
communion, 10
control, 3, 15, 22, 59, 63, 118, 122, 133, 134, 137
conversion, 8, 31, 32, 79, 107, 118
cross, 17, 30, 31, 34, 39, 61, 63, 64, 79, 80, 81, 83, 84, 85, 87, 89, 105, 119, 142
crucifixion, 31, 33, 42, 43, 53, 56, 58, 74, 78, 79, 80, 81, 82, 83, 85, 88, 89, 93, 98, 119, 142, 143
cult, 18, 20, 21, 22, 26, 73
Cybele, 26
death, x, xiii, 1, 2, 3, 4, 5, 6, 7, 8, 9, 10, 11, 12, 13, 14, 15, 16, 17, 18, 19, 20, 21, 22, 25, 26, 27, 28, 29, 31, 32, 34, 35, 36, 37, 38, 39, 40, 41, 42, 43, 53, 54, 56, 57, 58, 59, 60, 61, 62, 63, 64, 69, 70, 71, 72, 73, 74, 75, 77, 78, 79, 80, 81, 82, 83, 84, 85, 86, 90, 91, 92, 93, 94, 97, 98, 99, 100, 101, 102, 103, 105, 106, 107, 108, 109, 110, 113, 114, 115, 116, 117, 118, 120, 122, 123, 124, 125, 126, 129, 130, 131, 132, 133, 135, 136, 137, 139, 140, 141, 142, 143
deity, 18, 20, 21
Demeter, 25, 26, 146
destiny, 20, 21, 100, 137
discipleship, 17, 36
discipline, 18
divinity, 8, 19, 46
dominion, 3, 4, 5, 16, 32, 34, 36, 37, 42, 56, 59, 62, 63, 71, 75, 81, 99, 119, 120, 131, 132, 137, 140, 141, 142
dying, 5, 6, 7, 8, 10, 17, 18, 19, 20, 21, 27, 28, 29, 30, 31, 33, 34, 36, 37, 38, 39, 40, 41, 42, 57, 59, 64, 90, 93, 139, 140, 141, 143
dynasty, 24, 91, 92, 143
Eleusis, 25, 26, 153
essence, 8, 9, 13, 51
example, 2, 10, 13, 14, 15, 20, 25, 27,

The Expository Times 42 (1930) 562-5.

Witherington, B. III, *Paul's Narrative Thought World: The Tapestry of Tragedy and Triumph* (Louisville, Kentucky: Westminster/John Knox Press, 1994).

Wright, N. T., *The Climax of the Covenant: Christ and the Law in Pauline Theology* (Edinburgh: T. and T. Clark, 1991); 316 pp.

- *The Messiah and the People of God* (unpublished PhD dissertation; Oxford, 1980).

Zeller, D., 'The Life and Death of the Soul in Philo of Alexandria: The Use and Origin of a Metaphor', *The Studia Philonica Annual* 7 (1995) 19-55.

Zerwick, M., *A Grammatical Analysis of the Greek New Testament* (Rome: PBI, 1974), vol 1.

Ziesler, J., *Paul's Letter to the Romans* (London: SCM, 1989).

Strauss, M. L., *The Davidic Messiah in Luke-Acts: The Promise and Its Fulfillment in Lukan Christology* (Sheffield: SAP, 1995).
Stuhlmacher, P., *Biblische Theologie Des Neuen Testaments* (Band I; Gottingen: Vandenhoeck & Ruprecht, 1992, 1997).
- *Paul's Letter to the Romans: A Commentary* (Edinburgh: T&T Clark, 1994).
- *Reconciliation, Law and Righteousness: Essays in Biblical Theology* (Philadelphia: Fortress, 1986).
Tannehill, R. C., *Dying and Rising with Christ: A Study in Pauline Theology* (Berlin: Verlag Alfred Töpelmann, 1967).
Tromp, N. J., *Primitive Conceptions of Death and the Nether World in the Old Testament* (Rome: Pontifical Biblical Institute, 1969).
Turner, M. M. B., 'Spirit Endowment in Luke-Acts: Some Linguistic Considerations', *Vox Evangelica* 12 (1981) 45-63.
- *Power from on High: The Spirit in Israel's Restoration and Witness in Luke-Acts* (Sheffield: SAP, 1996).
Vanhoozer, K. J., *Biblical Narrative in the Philosophy of Paul Ricoeur* (Cambridge: Cambridge University of Press, 1990).
Vanni, U., ''Ομοίωμα in Paolo (Rm 1,23: 5,14: 6,5: 8,3: Fil 2,7): Un'interpretazione Esegetico-Theologica Alla Luce Dell'uso Dei LXX, 1a Parte', *Gregorianum* 58 (1977) 321-45.
- ''Ομοίωμα in Paolo (Rom 1,23; 5,14; 6,5; 8,2; Fil 2,7): Un'interpretazione Esegetico-Theologica Alla Luce Dell'uso Dei LXX, 2a Parte', *Gregorianum* 58 (1977) 431-70.
von Rad, G., ''Righteousness' and 'Life' in the Cultic Language of the Psalms', in *The Problem of Hexateuch and Other Essays* (E. W. Trueman Dicken, trans.; London: SCM Press Ltd, 1984).
Wagner, G., *Pauline Baptism and the Pagan Mysteries: The Problem of the Pauline Doctrine of Baptism in Romans VI.1-11, in the Light of Its Religio-Historical "Parallels"* (London: Oliver and Boyd, 1967).
Watson, F., *Paul, Judaism and the Gentiles: A Sociological Approach* (Cambridge: CUP, 1986).
Wedderburn, A. J. M., 'Adam in Paul's Letter to the Romans', in *Studia Biblica 1978 III* (Sheffield: JSOT, 1980), pp. 413-30.
- *Baptism and Resurrection: Studies in Pauline Theology Against Its Graeco-Roman Background* (Tübingen: Mohr, 1987).
- 'The Theological Structure of Romans V.12', *NTS* 19 (1972-73) 332-54.
- *Adam and Christ: An Investigation Into the Background of 1 Corinthians XV and Romans V 12-21* (PhD Dissertation University of Cambridge, 1970).
Wenham, D., *Paul: Follower of Jesus or Founder of Christianity?* (Grand Rapids, Cambridge: Eerdmans, 1995).
Westerholm, S., *Israel's Law and the Church's Faith: Paul and His Recent Interpreters* (Grand Rapids: Eerdmans, 1988).
Wilckens, U., *Der Brief an die Römer* (1; Zürich: Neukirchener Verlag, 1978).
- *Der Brief an die Römer* (2; Zurich: Neukirchener, Benzinger, 1980).
Wilson, W. E., 'The Development of Paul's Doctrine of Dying and Rising with Christ',

TynB 41 (1990) 3-30.
Reitzenstein, R., *Hellenistic Mystery-Religions: Their Basic Ideas and Significance* (trans. by John E. Steely; Pittsburgh, Pennsylvania: The Pickwick Press, 1978).
Ricoeur, P., 'Biblical Hermeneutics', *Semeia* 4 (1975) 29-148.
Ridderbos, H. N., *Paul: An Outline of His Theology* (Grand Rapids: Eerdmans, 1975).
Röhser, G., *Metaphorik und Personifikation der Sünde* (Tübingen: J C B Mohr (Paul Siebeck), 1987).
Rundle Clark, R. T., *Myth and Symbol in Ancient* (London, 1960).
Sanday, W. and Headlam, A. C., *A Critical and Exegetical Commentary on the Epistle to the Romans* (Edinburgh: T. and T. Clark, 1902).
Schlatter, A., *Romans: The Righteousness of God* (S. S. Schatzmann, trans.; Peabody, Mass.: Hendrickson, 1995).
Schlier, H., *Der Römerbrief* (Freiburg: Herder, 1977).
Schmithals, W., 'θάνατος', *NIDNTT* II 430-41.
Schnackenburg, R., *Ephesians A Commentary* (Helen Heron, tr; Edinburgh: T&T Clark, 1991).
- *Baptism in the Thought of St. Paul: A Study in Pauline Theology* (trans. by G. R. Beasley-Murray; Oxford: Basil Blackwell, 1964).
Schnelle, U., *The History and Theology of the New Testament Writings* (M. Eugene Boring, trans.; London: SCM Press Ltd, 1998).
- *The Human Condition: Anthropology in the Teachings of Jesus, Paul, and John* (Edinburgh: T&T Clark, 1996).
Schreiner, T. R., *Romans* (Grand Rapids, Michigan: Baker Books, 1998).
Schweitzer, A., *Paul and His Interpreter: A Critical History* (London: Black, 1912).
- *The Mysticism of Paul the Apostle* (William Montgomery, trans.; London: Adam & Charles Black, 1953).
Schweizer, E., 'Dying and Rising with Christ', *NTS* 14 (1967-68) 1-14.
Scroggs, R., *The Last Adam* (Oxford: Blackwell, 1966).
Seeley, D., *The Noble Death: Graeco-Roman Martyrology and Paul's Concept of Salvation* (Sheffield: JSOT Press, 1990).
Shaw, I. and Nicholson, P., ed, 'Coffin Texts', in *British Museum, Dictionary of Ancient Egypt* (London: British Museum Press, 1995), p. 69.
- 'Pyramid Texts', in *British Musem, Dictionary of Ancient Egypt* (London: British Musem Press, 1995), pp. 235-6.
Smith, J. Z., 'Dying and Rising Gods', in Mircea Eliade, ed., *The Encyclopedia of Religion* (4; New York: Macmillan, 1987), pp. 521-6.
Soskice, J., *Metaphor and Religious Language* (Oxford: Clarendon, 1985).
Spicq, C. O. P., 'σύμφυτος, συμφύω', in *Theological Lexicon of the New Testament* (3; James D. Ernest, trans.; Peabody, Mass.: Hendrickson, 1994), pp. 321-3.
Stauffer, E., *New Testament Theology* (John Marsh, trans.; London: SCM, 1955).
Stein, R. H., *Difficult Passages in the Epistles* (Leicester: IVP, 1988).
Stiver, D. R., *The Philosophy of Religious Language, Sign, Symbol, and Story* (Cambridge, Massachusetes: Blackwell Publishers, 1996).
Stone, I. F., *The Trial of Socrates* (London: Jonathan Cape, 1988).

Louw, J. P., *A Semantic Discourse Analysis of Romans. Commentary* (2; Pretoria: Dept. of Greek University of Pretoria, 1979).
Louw, J. P. and Nida, E. A., eds, *Greek-English Lexicon of the New Testament Based on Semantic Domains* (New York: United Bible Societies, 1988, 1989).
Lyonnet, S.,and Sabourin, L., *Sin, Redemption, and Sacrifice: A Biblical and Patristic Study* (Rome: Biblical Institute Press, 1970).
MacRae, G. S. J., 'Messiah and Gospel', in Jacob Neusner, William Scot Green and Ernst S. Frerichs, eds, *Judaisms and Their Messiahs at the Turn of the Christian Era* (Cambridge: Cambridge University Press, 1987), pp. 169-185.
Marshall, I. H., 'The Meaning of the Verb "to Baptize"', *EvQ* 45 (1973) 130-40.
Martin, B. L., *Christ and the Law in Paul* (Leiden: Brill, 1989).
Martyn, J. L., *Galatians* (New York: Doubleday, 1997).
Merill, E. H., 'מות', *NIDOTTE* II 886-8.
Merklein, H., 'Paulus und die Sünde', in *Studien zu Jesus und Paulus* (II; Tübingen: Mohr Siebeck, 1998), pp. 316-56.
Minois, G., *Istoria Infernurilor* (Alexandra Cunita, trans.; Bucuresti: Humanitas, 1998).
Moo, D., J., *Romans 1-8* (Chicago: Moody, 1991).
- *The Epistle to the Romans* (Grand Rapids, Michigan / Cambridge: Wm. B. Eerdmans Publishing Co., 1996).
Mooij, J. J. A., 'Metaphor and Truth: A Liberal Approach', in F.R. Ankersmit; J.J.A. Mooij, eds, *Knowledge and Language* (III; Dordrecht, Boston, London: Kluwer Academic Press, 1993).
Moule, C. F. D., 'Death 'to Sin', 'to Law' and 'to the World': A Note on Certain Datives', in *Essays in New Testament Interpretation* (Cambridge: Cambridge University Press, 1982), pp. 149-58.
Moule, C. F. D., *The Origin of Christology* (Cambridge: CUP, 1977).
Mounce, R. F., *Romans* (Nashville: Broadman & Holman, 1995).
Murphy-O'Connor, J., *Paul: A Critical Life* (Oxford: Clarendon Press, 1996).
Murray, J., *The Epistle to the Romans* (London: Marshall, Morgan and Scott, 1967).
Mylonas, C. E., *Eleusis and Eleusinian Mysteries* (Princeton: Princeton University Press, 1961).
Nock, A. D., *Conversion: The Old and the New in Religion from Alexander the Great to Augustine of Hippo* (Oxford: Clarendon Press, 1952).
Nygren, A., *Commentary on Romans* (Philadelphia: Fortress, 1949).
O'Brien, P. T., *Colossians, Philemon* (Waco, Texas: Word, 1982).
O'Collins, G. G., 'Crucifixion', in David Noel Freedman, editor-in-chief, *The Anchor Bible Dictionary. Volume 1: A-C* (New York: Doubleday, 1992), pp. 1207-10.
Pedersen, J., *Israel, Its Life and Culture* (I-II; London, Copenhagen: Oxford University Press, Branner Og Korch, 1926).
Penna, R., *Paul the Apostle: Jew and Greek Alike* (1; O.S.B. trans. by Thomas P. Wahl; Collegeville, Minnesota: The Liturgical Press, 1996).
Pomykala, K. E., *The Davidic Dynasty Tradition in Early Judaism; Its History and Significance for Messianism* (Atlanta: Scholars Press, 1995).
Porter, S. E., 'The Pauline Concept of Original Sin in Light of Rabbinic Background',

University Press, 1990), pp. 73-85.
- *From Adam to Christ: Essays on Paul* (Cambridge: Cambridge University Press, 1990).
- 'A Further Note on Romans 1', in *From Adam to Christ* (Cambridge: Cambridge University Press, 1990), pp. 85-7.
- 'Interchange and Suffering', *From Adam to Christ: Essays on Paul* (1990) 42-56Cambridge: Cambridge University Press.

Horbury, W., *Jewish Messianism and the Cult of Christ* (London: SCM Press Ltd., 1998).

Jervell, J., *Imago Dei* (Göttingen: Vandenhoeck & Ruprecht, 1960).

Jewett, R., *Paul's Anthropological Terms* (Leiden: Brill, 1971).

Johnson, S. L., Jr., 'Romans 5.12 - An Exercise in Exegesis and Theology', in Richard N. Longenecker and Merrill C. Tenney, eds, *New Dimensions in New Testament Study* (Grand Rapids, Michigan: Zondervan, 1974), pp. 298-316.

Jüngel, E., *Theological Essays* (1; J. B. Webster, tr and ed; Edinburgh: T&T Clark, 1989).

Käsemann, E., *Commentary on Romans* (Grand Rapids, Michigan: Eerdmans, 1980).
- 'On Paul's Anthropology', in *Perspectives on Paul* (London: SCM Press Ltd, 1971), pp. 1-31.
- 'The Theological Problem Presented by the Motif of the Body of Christ', in *Perspectives on Paul* (London: SCM Press Ltd, 1971), pp. 102-21.

Kaye, B. N., 'βαπτίζειν εἰς with Special Reference to Romans 6', in Elizabeth A. Livingstone, ed., *Studia Evangelica VI* (Berlin: Akademie Verlag, 1973), pp. 281-6.
- *The Thought Structure of Romans with Special Reference to Chapter 6* (Austin, Texas: Schola Press, 1979).

Keck, L. E., 'Jesus in Romans', *JBL* 108/3 (1989) 443-60.

Kirby, J. T., 'The Syntax of Romans 5.12: A Rhetorical Approach', *NTS* 33 (1987) 283-6.

Klausner, J., *The Messianic Idea in Israel* (W. F. Stinespring, tr; London: George Allen and Unwin Ltd, 1956).

Kramer, W., *Christ, Lord, Son of God* (London: SCM, 1966).

Kümmel, W. G., *Theology of New Testament* (London: SCM Press Ltd, 1973).

Kuss, O., *Der Römerbrief* (1; Regensburg: Verlag Friedrich Pustet, 1963).

Laato, A., *A Star is Rising* (Atlanta, Georgia: Scholars Press, 1997).

Laato, T., *Paul and Palestinian Judaism: An Anthropological Approach* (T. McElwain, trans.; Atalanta: Sholars Press, 1995).

Landman, L., ed, *Messianism in the Talmudic Era* (New York: Ktav Publishing House, Inc., 1979).

Leenhardt, F. J., *The Epistle to the Romans: A Commentary* (London: Lutterworth Press, 1961).

Levison, J. R., *Portraits of Adam in Early Judaism: From Sirach to 2 Baruch* (Sheffield: SAP, 1988).

Lincoln, A., *Ephesians* (Dallas: Word, 1990).

Lohse, E., *The New Testament Environment* (London: SCM Press Ltd, 1976).

Fazekaš, L., 'Taufe Als Tod in Röm. 6.3ff', *Theologische Zeitschrift* 22 (1966) 305-18.
Fee, G. D., *The First Epistle to the Corinthians* (Exeter: Paternoster, 1987).
Ferguson, E., *Backgrounds of Early Christianity* (Grand Rapids, Michigan: Wm. B. Eerdmans, 1993).
Fitzmyer, J. A., 'The Consecutive Meaning of ΕΦ* Ω in Romans 5.12', *NTS* 39 (1993) 321-39.
- 'Crucifixion in Ancient Palestine, Qumran Literature, and the New Testament', in *To Advance the Gospel New Testament Studies* (New York: Crossroad, 1981), pp. 125-46.
- *Romans* (New York: Doubleday, 1993).
Furnish, V. P., *Theology and Ethics in Paul* (Nashville: Abingdon, 1968).
Green, J. B., 'Crucifixion', in Gerald F. Hawthorne and Ralph P. Martin, eds., *Dictionary of Paul and His Letters* (Downers Grove, Illinois; Leicester, England: IVP, 1993), pp. 197-9.
Grundmann, W., 'Χριστός in Paul's Epistles', in Gerhard Friedrich, ed., Geoffrey W. Bromiley, trans. and ed, *TDNT* (9; Grand Rapids, Michigan: W. B. Eerdmans, 1974), pp. 540-80.
Gundry, R. H., *Sōma In Biblical Theology: With Emphasis on Pauline Anthropology* (Cambridge: CUP, 1976).
Gunton, C., *The Actuality of Atonement* (Edinburgh: T&T Clark, 1988).
Hadot, P., *Ce Este Filosofia Antica?* (George Bondor and Claudiu Tipurita, trans.; Iasi: Polirom, 1997).
Hahn, F., 'Χριστός', in *Exegetical Dictionary of the New Testament* (3; Grand Rapids, Michigan: W. B. Eerdmans, 1993), pp. 478-86.
Hartman, L., *'Into the Name of the Lord Jesus': Baptism in the Early Church* (Edinburgh: T&T Clark, 1997).
Hays, R. B., *First Corinthians: A Bible Commentary for Teaching and Preaching* (Louisville: John Knox Press, 1997).
Heiny, S. B., '2 Corinthians 2:14-4:6: Motives for Metaphor', in K.H. Richards, ed., *Society of Biblical Literature 1987 Seminar Papers* (Atlanta: Scholars Press, 1987), pp. 1-22.
Hengel, M., *The Cross of the Son of God* (trans. by John Bowden; London: SCM, 1986).
- *Crucifixion in the Ancient World and the Folly of the Message of the Cross* (John Bowden, trans.; London: SCM Ltd, 1977).
- 'Jesus, the Messiah of Israel', in *Studies in Early Christology* (Edinburgh: T&T Clark, 1995).
Hesse, M. B., 'Models, Metaphors and Truth', in F.R. Ankersmit, J.J.A. Mooij, eds, *Knowledge and Language* (III; Dordrecht, Boston, London: Kluwer Academic Press, 1993).
Hobbes, T., *Leviathan* (New York: Liberal Arts Press, 1958).
Hofius, O., 'Die Adam-Christus-Antithese und das Gesetz: Erwägungen zu Röm 5.12-21', in James D. G. Dunn, ed., *Paul and the Mosaic Law* (Tübingen: Mohr Siebeck, 1996).
Hooker, M. D., 'Adam in Romans 1', in *From Adam to Christ* (Cambridge: Cambridge

Dasenbrock, R. W., 'Redrawing the Lines: An Introduction', in Reed Way Dasenbrock, ed., *Redrawing the Lines: Analytic Philosophy, Deconstruction, and Literary Theory* (Minneapolis: University of Minnesota Press, 1989), pp. 3-25.

Day, J., ed, *King and Messiah in Israel and the Ancient Near East: Proceedings of the Oxford Old Testament Seminar* (Sheffield: Sheffield Academic Press, 1998).

de Boer, M. C., *The Defeat of Death: Apocalyptic Eschatology in 1 Corinthians 15 and Romans 5* (Sheffield: JSOT Press, 1988).

de Jonge, M., 'Christos', in David Noel Freedman, ed., *Anchor Bible Dictionary* (1; New York: Doubleday, 1992), pp. 914-21.

Di Giuseppe, R., *La teoria della morte nel Fedone platonico* (Napoli: Societa Editrice Il Mulino, 1993).

Dilman, I., *Philosophy and the Philosophical Life: A Study in Plato's Phaedo* (London: Macmillan, 1992).

Droge A. J. and Tabor, J. D., *A Noble Death: Suicide and Martyrdom Among Christians and Jews in Antiquity* (New York: HarperSanFrancisco, 1992).

Dunn, J. D. G., 'Paul's Understanding of the Death of Jesus as Sacrifice', in S. W. Sykes, ed., *Sacrifice and Redemption: Durham Essays in Theology* (Cambridge: Cambridge University Press, 1991), pp. 35-52.

- *The Theology of Paul the Apostle* (Edinburgh: T&T Clark Ltd., 1998).
- *Baptism in the Holy Spirit: A Re-Examination of the New Testament Teaching on the Gift of the Spirit in Relation to Pentecostalism Today* (London: SCM, 1970).
- *Jesus and the Spirit* (London: SCM, 1975).
- *Romans* (Waco: Word, 1988).
- *Unity and Diversity in the New Testament: An Enquiry Into the Character of Earliest Christianity* (London: SCM, 1977).
- 'Baptized as Metaphor', in Stanley E. Porter and Anthony R. Cross, eds, *Baptism, the New Testament and the Church: Historical and Contemporary Studies in Honor of R. E. O. White* (Sheffield: Sheffield Academic Press, 1999), pp. 298-310.
- *The Epistles to the Collossians and to Philemon: A Commentary on the Greek Text* (Grand Rapids, Carlisle: W. B. Eerdmans, The Paternoster Press, 1996).

Eco, E., *Limitele Interpretarii* (Constanta: Editura Pontica, 1996).

- *Semiotics and the Philosophy of Language* (London: Macmillan, 1984).

Edwards, J. R., *Romans* (Peabody, Mass.: Hendrickson, 1992).

Eliade, M., *A History of Religious Ideas: From the Stone Age to the Eleusinian Mysteries* (1; Willard R. Trask, tr; London: Collins, 1979).

Elliger, W., 'σύμφυτος', in Horst Balz and Gerhard Schneider, eds, *Exegetical Dictionary of the New Testament* (3; Grand Rapids, Michigan: Wm. B. Eerdmans, 1993), p. 290.

Elliot, N., *Liberating Paul: The Justice of God and the Politics of the Apostle* (Sheffield: Sheffield Academic Press, 1995).

- *The Rhetoric of Romans: Argumentative Constraint and Strategy and Paul's Dialogue with Judaism* (Sheffield: JSOT, 1990).

Englezakis, B., 'Rom. 5.12-21 and the Pauline Teaching on the Lord's Death: Some Observations', *Biblica* 58 (1977) 231-5.

Bibliography

Blass F. and Debrunner, A., *A Grammar of the New Testament and Other Early Christian Literature* (Robert W. Funk, tr; Cambridge; Chicago: Cambrige University Press; The University of Chicago Press, 1961).

Bornkamm, G., 'Baptism and New Life in Paul (Romans 6)', in *Early Christian Experience* (London: SCM, 1969), pp. 71-104.

- *Paul* (trans. by D. M. G. Stalker; London: Hodder and Stoughton, 1971).

Bowker, J., *The Meanings of Death* (Cambridge: Cambridge University Press, 1993).

Brown, A., *Metaphorical Language in Relation to Baptism in the Pauline Literature* (unpublished PhD dissertation, Edinburgh; 1982).

Bruce, F. F., *The Letter of Paul to the Romans* (Leicester: IVP, 1985(2)).

Bultmann, R., *Theology of the New Testament* (1, London: SCM, 1952).

Burkert, W., *Ancient Mystery Cults* (Cambridge, Mass.; London: Harvard University Press, 1987).

- *Greek Religion* (Cambridge, Mass.: Harvard University Press, 1985).

Byrne, B., *Romans* (Collegeville, Minnesota: The Liturgical Press, 1996).

Cambier, J., 'Péchés Des Hommes et Péché d'Adam en Rom. V.12', *NTS* 11 (1964-1965) 217-55.

Campbell, A., 'Dying with Christ: The Origin of a Metaphor?' in Stanley E. Porter and Anthony R. Cross, eds, *Baptism, the New Testament and the Church: Historical and Contemporary Studies in Honour of R.E.O. White* (Sheffield: Sheffield Academic Press, 1999), pp. 273-93.

Charlesworth, J. H., 'From Messianology to Christology: Problems and Prospects', James H. Charlesworth, ed., in *The Messiah* (Minneapolis: Fortress, 1992), pp. 3-35.

- ed., *The Messiah* (Minneapolis: Fortress, 1992).

Collins, R. F., *First Corinthians* (Collegeville, Minnesota: The Liturgical Press, 1999).

Conzelmann, H., *An Outline of the Theology of the New Testament* (London: SCM, 1969).

- *A Commentary on the First Epistle to the Corinthians* (James W. Leitch, trans.; Philadelphia: Fortress Press, 1975).

Cotterell, P. and Turner M., *Linguistics & Biblical Interpretation* (Downers Grove: IVP, 1989).

Cousar, C. B., *A Theology of the Cross: The Death of Jesus in the Pauline Letters* (Minneapolis: Fortress Press, 1990).

Cranfield, C. E. B., *A Critical and Exegetical Commentary of the Epistle to the Romans* (Vols 1 and 2; Edinburgh: T. & T. Clark, 1975 & 1979).

Dahl, N. A., 'Messianic Ideas and the Crucifixion of Jesus', D. H. Juel, rev, in James H. Charlesworth, ed., *Messiah: Developments in Earliest Judaism and Christianity* (Minneapolis: Fortress Press, 1992).

- 'The Messiahship of Jesus in Paul', in *The Crucified Messiah and Other Essays* (Minneapolis: Augsburg Publishing House, 1974).

- *Studies in Paul* (Minneapolis, Minnesota: Augsburg Publishing House, 1977).

Danker, F. W., 'Romans v. 12: Sin Under Law', *NTS* 14 (1967-8) 424-39.

Danto, A. C., 'Metaphor and Cognition', in F.R. Ankersmit, Mooij, eds, *Knowledge and Language* (III; Dordrecht, Boston, London: Kluwer Academic Press, 1993).

Secondary Literature

Aageson, J. W., 'Control' in Pauline Studies and Culture: A Study in Rom 6', *NTS* 42 (1996) 79-81.

Adams, E., *Constructing the World: A Study in Paul's Cosmological Language* (Edinburgh: T&T Clark, 2000).

Ankersmit, F. R.; Mooij, J. J. A., 'Introduction', in F.R. Ankersmit; J.J.A. Mooij, eds, *Knowledge and Language* (III; Dordrecht, Boston, London: Kluwer Academic Press, 1993).

Aune, D. E., 'Religions, Greco-Roman', in Gerald F. Hawthorne, Ralph Martin and Daniel Reid, eds, *Dictionary of Paul and His Letters* (Downers Grove: IVP, 1993), pp. 786-96.

Aune, D. E., 'Human Nature and Ethics in Hellenistic Philosophical Traditions and Paul: Some Issues and Problems', in Troels Engberg-Pedersen, ed., *Paul in His Hellenistic Context* (Studies of The New Testament and Its World; Edinburgh: T&T Clark, 1994), pp. 291-312.

Bailey, L. R., *Biblical Perspectives on Death* (Overtures to Biblical Theology; Philadelphia: Fortress Press, 1979); 159.

Barrett, C. K., *A Commentary on the Epistle to the Romans* (London: A & C Black, 1991).

- *From First Adam to Last: A Study in Pauline Theology* (London: Adam & Charles Black, 1962).

Barth, M. *Ephesians* (New York:: Doubleday, 1974).

Bauer, W., *A Greek-English Lexicon of the New Testament and Other Early Christian Literature* (W. Ardnt; F.W. Gingrich; W. Danker, tr. and rev., Chicago; London: The University of Chicago Press, 1957, 1979).

Beasley-Murray, G. R., 'Dying and Rising with Christ', in Gerald F. Hawthorne, Ralph P. Martin and Daniel G. Reid, eds, *Dictionary of Paul and His Letters* (Downers Grove; Leicester: IVP, 1993), pp. 218-22.

- *Baptism in the New Testament* (London: Macmillan, 1962).

Becker, J., *Paul Apostle to the Gentiles* (Louisville: Westminster/John Knox Press, 1993).

Beker, J. C., 'The Relationship Between Sin and Death in Romans', in Robert T. Fortna and Beverly R. Gaventa, eds, *The Conversation Continues: Studies in Paul and John in Honor of J. Louis Martin* (Nashville: Abingdon, 1990).

- *Paul the Apostle: The Triumph of God in Life and Thought* (Edinburgh: T. & T. Clark, 1980).

Best, E., *A Critical and Exegetical Commentary on Ephesians* (Edinburgh: T&T Clark, 1998).

Betz, H. D., *Galatians* (Philadelphia: Fortress Press, 1979).

- 'Transferring a Ritual: Paul's Interpretation of Baptism in Romans 6', in Troels Engberg-Pedersen, ed., *Paul in His Hellenistic Context* (Edinburgh: T&T Clark, 1994), pp. 84-118.

Black, M., *Romans* (London: Marshall, Morgan and Scott, 1973).

Philo, *On Dreams (De Somnis)* (F. H. Colson and G. H. Whitacker, trans.; Cambridge, Mass.; London: Harvard University Press; William Heinemann Ltd, 1988).
Philo, *On Husbandry (De Agricultura)* (III; F. H. Colson and G. H. Whitaker, trans.; London, Cambridge, Mass.: William Heinemann Ltd, Harvard University Press, 1968).
Philo, *On the Giants (De Gigantibus)* (II; F. H. Colson and G. H. Whitaker, trans.; London, Cambridge, Mass.: William Heinemann Ltd, Harvard University Press, 1968).
Philo, *On the Posterity and Exile of Cain (De Posteritate Caini)* (F. H. Colson and G. H. Whitaker, trans.; Cambridge, Mass.; London: Harvard University Press; William Heinemann Ltd, 1979).
Philo, *Questions and Answers on Genesis (Quaestiones et Solutiones in Genesin)* (Ralph Marcus, trans.; London; Cambridge, Mass.: William Heinemann Ltd; Harvard University Press, 1961).
Plato, *Euthyphro, Apology, Crito, Phaedo, Phaedrus* (I; Harold North Fowler, trans.; Cambridge, Mass., London: Harvard University Press, William Heinemann Ltd, 1982).
Plato, *Laws* (II; R. G. Bury, tr; Cambridge, Mass.; London: Harvard University Press; William Heinemann Ltd, 1984).
Plato, *The Republic* (Paul Shorey, tr; Cambridge, Mass.; London: Harvard University Press; William Heinemann Ltd, 1987).
Plutarch, 'Cimon', in *Lives* (II; Bernadotte Perrin, trans.; Cambridge, Mass.; London: Harvard University Press; William Heinemann Ltd, 1968).
Plutarch, 'De Curiositate', in *Moralia* (VI; W. C. Helmbold, trans.; Cambridge, Mass., London: Harvard University Press, William Heinemann Ltd, 1970).
Ps. Plato, *The Axiochus: On Death and Immortality* (E. H. Blankeney, trans.; London: Frederick Muller Ltd, 1937).
Quintilian, *The Institutio Oratoria* (H.B. Butler, tr; Cambridge, Mass.; London: Harvard University Press; William Heinemann Ltd., 1966).
Seneca, *Ad Lucilium Epistulae Morales* (IV; Richard M. Gummere, trans.; Cambridge, Mass., London: Harvard University Press, William Heinemann Ltd, 1979).
Seneca, 'De Vita Beata', in *Moral Essays* (II; John W. Basore, trans.; Cambridge, Mass.; London: Harvard University Press; William Heinemann Ltd, 1979).
Septuaginta (Alfred Rahlfs, ed.; Stuttgart: Biblia-Druck, 1935, 1979).
Stone, M. E., *Fourth Ezra* (Frank Moore Cross, ed.; Minneapolis: Fortress Press, 1990).
Vermes, G., *The Complete Dead Sea Scrolls in English* (London: Penguin Books Ltd, 1998).
TLG Workplace (Silver Mountain Software, 1993, 1998).
Xenophon, *Memorabilia* (E. C. Marchant, trans.; Cambridge, Mass.; London: Harvard University Press; William Heinemann Ltd, 1979).

(Oxford: Clarendon Press, 1963).

Cicero, *Against Verres: Part Two Books III, IV and V* (London; Cambridge, Mass.: William Heinemann Ltd; Harvard University Press, 1953).

Cicero, *Orator* (H. M. Hubbell, tr; London; Cambridge, Mass.: William Heinemann Ltd.; Harvard University Press, 1952).

Cicero, *Pro Rabirio Perduellionis* (H. Grose Hodge, trans.; London; Cambridge, Mass.: William Heinemann Ltd; Harvard University Press, 1959).

Cicero, *Rhetorica Ad Herennium* (Harry Caplan, tr; London; Cambridge, Mass.: Harvard University Press; William Heinemann Ltd., 1954).

Demetrius, *On Style* (W. Rhys Roberts, tr; Cambridge, Mass.; London: Harvard University Press; William Heinemann Ltd., 1982).

Dio Chrysostom, *Discourses* (XII; J. W. Cohoon, trans.; Cambridge, Mass., London: Harvard University Press, William Heinemann Ltd, 1939).

Faulkner, R. O., *The Ancient Egyptian Coffin Texts* (1 Spells 1-354; Warminster England: Aris & Phillips Ltd, 1973).

Hadas, M., ed and trans, *The Third and Fourth Books of Maccabees* (New York: Ktav Publishing House, Inc., 1953).

Herodotus, *Books V-VII* (A. D. Godley, tr; Cambridge, Mass.; London: Harvard University Press; William Heinemann Ltd, 1971).

Hesiod, 'The Homeric Hymn to Demeter', in *The Homeric Hymns and Homerica* (Hugh G. Evelyn-White, tr; Cambridge, Mass.; London: Harvard University Press; William Heinemann Ltd, 1982).

Josephus, *Jewish Antiquities, Books IX-XI* (Ralph Marcus, trans.; Cambridge, Mass.; London: Harvard University Press; William Heinemann Ltd, 1987).

Josephus, *Jewish Antiquities, Books XII-XIV* (Ralph Marcus, trans.; Cambridge, Mass.; London: Harvard University Press; William Heinemann, 1976).

Josephus, *Jewish Antiquities, Books XV-XVII* (Allen Wickgren, comp. and ed.; Ralph Marcus, trans.; Cambridge, Mass.; London: Harvard University Press; William Heinemann Ltd, 1980).

Josephus, *The Jewish War, Books I-III* (H. St. J. Thackeray, trans.; Cambridge, Mass.; London: Harvard University Press, 1989).

Josephus, *The Jewish War, Books IV-VII* (H. St. J. Thackeray, trans.; Cambridge, Mass.; London: Harvard University Press; William Heinemann Ltd, 1979).

The Works of Josephus, Complete and Unabridged (William Whiston, tr; Peabody, Mass.: Hendrickson, 1987).

Judaic Classics Library (Davka Corporation, version IId, David Kantrowitz, 1991-1998).

Longinus, *On the Sublime* (H. Hamilton Fyfe, tr; Cambridge, Mass.; London: Harvard University Press; William Heinemann Ltd., 1982).

Manetho, *Aegyptiaca* (W. G. Waddell, tr; London; Cambridge, Mass.: William Heinemann Ltd.; Harvard University Press, 1964).

Novum Testamentum Graece, (Nestle-Aland, ed., 26th edition, Stuttgart: Biblia Druck, 1983).

PHI Workplace (version 7.0, Silver Mountain Software, 1993, 1998).

Bibliography

Primary Literature

The Ancient Egyptian Pyramid Texts (R. O. Faulkner, tr; Oxford: Clarendon Press, 1969).

H. Anderson, '4 Maccabees, A New Translation and Introduction', *The Old Testament Pseudepigrapha* (2; James H. Charlesworth, ed.; London: Darton, Longman & Todd, 1985)

Apuleius, *Metamorphoses* (II (Books VII-XI); J. Arthur Hanson, ed and tr; Cambridge, Mass.; London: Harvard University Press, 1989).

Aristotle, *The 'Art' of Rhetoric* (John Henry Freese, tr; Cambridge, Mass.; London: Harvard University Press; William Heinemann Ltd, 1982).

Aristotle, *Historia Animalium* (A. L. Peck, trans.; Cambridge, Mass., London: Harvard University Press, William Heinemann Ltd, 1979).

Aristotle, *The Poetics* (H. Hamilton Fyfe, tr; Cambridge, Mass.; London: Harvard University Press; William Heinemann Ltd., 1982).

Aristotle, *Politics* (Rackham. H., tr; Cambridge, Mass.; London: Harvard University Press, 1944).

The Complete Works of Aristotle (2; Jonathan Barnes, ed.; Princeton, New Jersey: Princeton University Press, 1984).

S. Aurelii Augustini, 'Contra duas epistolas Pelagianorum', in *Sancti Aurelii Augustini, Hipponensis Episcopi, Opera Omnia* (Tomus Decimus; J. P. Migne, accurante; 1865).

S. Aurelii Augustini, 'De peccatorum meritis remissione et de baptesimo parvulorum', in *Sancti Aurelii Augustini, Hipponensis Episcopi, Opera Omnia* (Tomus Decimus; J. P. Migne, accurante; 1865).

Saint Augustine, 'Against Two Letters of the Pelagius', in *The Anti-Pelagian Works* (III; Peter Holmes and Robert Ernest Wallis, trans.; Edinburgh: T & T Clark, 1876).

Saint Augustine, 'De Peccatorum Meritis et Remissione', in *The Anti-Pelagian Works* (1; Peter Holmes, trans.; Edinburgh: T & T Clark, 1872).

Lancelot C. L. Brenton, trans, *The English Translation of the Septuagint Version of the Old Testament* (London: Samuel Bagster and Sons, 1844, 1851).

The Cambridge Annotated Study of Apocrypha New Revised Standard Version (Howard Clark Kee, ed.; Cambridge: Cambridge University Press, 1994)

Charles, R. H., ed.; *The Apocrypha and Pseudepigrapha of the Old Testament in English*

tomb). This fact of being 'a dead member of his family,' 'buried in the family's tomb' has as its result the start of walking in the newness of life, walking which is described as being possible because of Christ's resurrection. In other words, God makes us part of his family and buried us in the family's tomb; that place was the place where his glory raised Christ from the dead and so makes us able to walk in the newness of life.

the believers have to refuse to let sin reign over them again. The construction from the beginning of 6.6 (τοῦτο γινώσκοντες) points to another implied element, namely, that of the fact that a 'crucifixion' was carried out in a known or visible place for being seen/known by many; in other words the kind of 'end' of the previous 'slavery' is seen/known by all.

Thus, this complex network of ideas from Rom. 6:6 has to be integrated in every interpretation of the 'dying' language from Romans 6. The elements are those of the environment inaugurated by the sin of Adam, body, sin, and the metaphor of crucifixion.

The usual stage after a death is a burial (the second moment of the Calvary event), even if in the case of one who was crucified the burial was not allowed. Paul does not speak simply of a burial of someone who died but about somebody who is buried *with* someone else. *We argue*[6] *that this idea of being buried with someone else points to the fact that they are part of the same family or dynasty.* Thus, Paul says that by the 'baptism towards death' the believers who were 'crucified' are 'buried with' Christ. In this way it is shown that they are part of the same family. The reality of death is in place but the point is that by that overwhelming action of God (pictured by the rite of baptism) towards Christ's death, they are 'buried with him,' so that they are considered as *belonging* to him (as his family). The result of this, keeping in view the reality of Christ's resurrection, is starting to walk in the newness of life. Therefore, the role of the 'burying with' language is to show that the believers are part of *his* family/people (the point is not that they are really dead, even if this is part of the meaning), and as a consequence of the fact that they were with him in the 'same' tomb, as he was raised they also have to start to walk in the newness of life. In other words the idea is not that something arrives truly at an end (burial as the seal of death) but that something *starts* because of the reality of *belonging* to the same family. In the examined Jewish texts almost always the reference is to those who were part of the royal families as being buried with their fathers/ancestors. Keeping in view that Paul works with the idea of Χριστός as being 'the Anointed davidic king' the believers are 'buried with' their king. This idea of being part of the same 'family' occurs also in Rom. 8:29 where it is said about Christ that he is 'first born within a large family' (πρωτότοκον ἐν πολλοῖς ἀδελφοῖς). Thus, in his argument for defending his thesis from Rom. 6:2 (ἀπεθάνομεν τῇ ἁμαρτίᾳ) Paul extends his metaphor by pointing to 'burial with' (it is natural to speak about 'burial' after saying about someone that he 'died'), but his point is not that since they are 'buried' they are 'really dead', but to show that this language of 'death' from his argument has in view the fact that they are part of the same family with Christ. When God 'overwhelmed' us he did that by 'pushing' us toward a particular event, namely, Christ's death. This action of God, 'burying the believer with Christ', shows that the believers are part of his family (only so they can be buried in *his*

---

[6] See the argument in Chapter 3.

The Calvary event is discussed specifically at the moments of crucifixion and burial. These two moments are applied metaphorically to the believers as far as the question of sin is concerned.

In his discourse from Romans 6:1-14 Paul integrates the element of *sin* in order to defend his thesis in 6:2. He does it against a complex network of ideas in 6:6. He works with *his* way of speaking about the believers' past, namely 'our old man', which we interpreted[5] as being a way of speaking about our past in the age inaugurated by the sin of Adam. It is *an understanding of human life as this is shaped by the effects of Adam's sin*. The environment created by Adam's sin is hostile and the powers of sin and death subdue 'all men'. The man participates in this world and lives as part of it — these are the implications of using σῶμα in 6:6. This participation involves a 'slavery' to the powers of the 'old age'; the power of sin is in view in the phrase σῶμα τῆς ἁμαρτίας. By juxtaposing ἁμαρτία with δουλεύω (6:6) Paul identifies 'sin' as 'a master of slaves' (its 'dominion' is mentioned also in 6:12, 14, 16, 17, 18, 20, 22). About this network of ideas Paul says that he 'was *crucified* with him [Christ]' in order that his body will be released from sin, in order no longer to be enslaved by sin. In other words there is a 'crucifixion' with the purpose of releasing σῶμα. What are the 'activated' ideas from the set of ideas associated with 'crucifixion'? The fundamental idea behind this form of punishment was that of *terror/horror*. In this way the peace of the empire was maintained. In war time the crucifixion of prisoners could lead to surrender. It was inflicted mainly upon slaves. It was such a horrible death that a Roman citizen should remove the word cross not only from his person, but from his thoughts, his eyes and his ears. Thus, Paul is saying that 'our old man' experienced such a horrible death and as a result the body is released from the reign of sin. How does a 'crucifixion' lead to that liberation? The other major affirmations in which 'sin' is an important element in the argument of Rom. 6:1-14 point to a mental activity/attitude from the part of believers. He says λογίζεσθε ἑαυτοὺς εἶναι νεκροὺς [...] τῇ ἁμαρτίᾳ (6:11); Μὴ οὖν βασιλευέτω ἡ ἁμαρτία (6:12); μηδὲ παριστάνετε τὰ μέλη ὑμῶν ὅπλα ἀδικίας τῇ ἁμαρτίᾳ (6:13); ἁμαρτία γὰρ ὑμῶν οὐ κυριεύσει· (6:14). We argue for the fact that *'releasing' in Rom. 6:6 is a result of 'crucifixion' in the sense that that 'condemnation/punishment' (crucifixion) inflicted upon our past lived in the age inaugurated by the sin of Adam (ὁ παλαιὸς ἄνθρωπος) is such a horrible event that the believers have to stay away from sin, since it is sin that which leads to such a punishment.* They have 'to have that view' about the 'end' of the past in which they were subdued to the dominion of sin. The reasoning is that 'if that "slavery" leads to that kind of "punishment" you do not have to let sin reign over you any longer.' Thus, Paul uses the language of 'crucifixion' as a rhetorical device for pointing to the fact that 'the slavery of sin from the past' has to be seen as having *horrific* consequences. Because of this horrific 'end'

---

[5] See Chapter 4.

The Question of Development/Explanation

In the scholarly debate, as we analysed it in Chapter 1, we identified different elements which were considered important by the scholars in their interpretation of the 'dying' language in Romans 6. These were as follows: 'dying with Christ' as a past and present experience (R. Tannehill), predestination, Messiah and community (A. Schweitzer), 'dying with Christ' as a sacramental experience (R. Schnackenburg; H. Ridderbos), the role of baptism for understanding the experience of 'dying with Christ' (V.P. Furnish), the death of Christ as an event in which the believers can share (W.G. Kümmel), the role of Christology and Anthropology for understanding 'dying with Christ' (J.D.G. Dunn), the need to work with different perspectives in Christology (M.D. Hooker). The approach in the present project is moulded by the mechanism of the metaphor. The interpreter has to explore the 'encyclopaedic' world of the chosen *vehicle* in order to propose an interpretation of the metaphor. In order to do that he also has to understand the role of different qualifiers used by Paul in guiding the understanding of his readers/hearers. That is why we organised the structure of the project as we did: Chapter 3 is an analysis of the *vehicle* — language of 'death', and Chapter 4 is a study of the qualifiers — baptism, σύμφυτος, ὁ παλαιὸς ἄνθρωπος, body of sin.

It should be noted that Paul both for the origin of the metaphor and for its development brings forth the Calvary event. Paul says that this event is 'available' to the people. The way in which this event is an *available* reality is by being proclaimed vividly. To express that Paul uses the term ὁμοίωμα. We argued[4] that ὁμοίωμα means here 'representation' referring to a discourse — the proclamation of death and resurrection of Χριστός. The result of a positive attitude of the hearer/reader towards this proclamation is described metaphorically by the term σύμφυτος. The σύμφυτος metaphor points to the fact that the believers are 'coalesced' with what they heard about Christ's death; this 'coalescence' has to be understood as one in which each 'component' (the believer and the content of the proclamation about Christ's death) preserves its character — they share nothing but coalescence. Each brings forth its own fruit. If one component is removed or the union is broken up, both wither away. Paul's point is that there is a real unity which is *vital* for the believers' lives, and that unity preserves both components as *distinct*. If that unity is broken up both components wither away. At this point the imperatives from Paul's argument (6:11, 12, 13) are important. Remaining free from the dominion of sin depends on the quality of this 'coalescence' with Christ's death *as* it was proclaimed in the gospel. To this 'pattern of teaching' (the gospel) the believers were entrusted and thus they were liberated from sin (Rom. 6:17). The reality of this 'coalescence' (εἰ γάρ) is the basis for another 'coalescence' — that with what was proclaimed in the gospel about the resurrection (6:5).

---

[4] See Chapter 3.

unknown.[1] If the metaphoric invention is a highly original one, the way in which it was generated is almost impossible to trace.[2] When we interpret a metaphor, the metaphor is *already* there. Knowing this difficulty we identified two elements which can guide us towards an understanding of Paul's creativity: 1) the design of Paul's language and 2) the idea(s) which made it possible.

1) *This language of 'death' to sin is taken from his insight about Christ's death as being 'a death to sin'.* Paul transfers this phrase into the area of the Christian life but with a different meaning. Christ 'died to sin'[3] in the sense that by his being raised from the dead death itself was defeated and no longer rules over him and so the 'wage' of sin (which is death) is no longer in place as far as Christ is concerned. Thus, sin was 'ruined/abolished' as far as its effect is concerned — namely, eschatological death. The believer is a mortal being (Rom. 8:10), but eschatological death is no longer in view because Christ died to sin; the believers will be 'coalesced' with what was proclaimed ('likeness') about resurrection, a fact which is based on their 'coalescence' with what was proclaimed ('likeness') about Christ's death. Believers' 'death to sin' is to be defined in the terms given by 6:3-7 and not by 6:10, since by their 'death' sin is not 'abolished' in the sense that their 'death' has salvific effects, but in the sense that 'death' does not help sin to 'increase'. The irony is that what was an ally of sin in exercising its dominion, namely death, is now used (transferred) by Paul to define the kind of relationship which 'restrains' sin from its 'dominion' in the life of Christians.

2) *Christ's 'death to sin' has a 'sharing' reality/possibility of 'dying with' because he died as the Anointed [davidic] king when he won that victory over sin and death by being raised from the dead.* Those who belong to the Anointed king of God share in his victory (if the king is victorious his people is free). Based on this fact (the identity of Χριστός) Paul develops his συν* language ('coalesced with the likeness of his death', 'crucified with', 'buried with'). These are Paul's elements through which he explains/develops the thesis from 6:2 (ἀπεθάνομεν τῇ ἁμαρτίᾳ).

These two elements help us to build a proposal for the 'origin' question. *What we have here is Paul's creativity at work: bold metaphors for which the only (satisfactory) parallel which we found is that from Rom. 6:10. It is his own insight into the meaning of Christ's death (a 'death to sin') and his understanding of the identity of Christ in his death (he died as the Anointed davidic king) which guided him in creating this metaphor of 'dying to sin' as a way of describing the relationship of the believer with sin.* This metaphor is developed/explained, as we argued, in Rom. 6:3-7.

---

[1] Cf. Eco, *Limitele*, 163.
[2] Cf. Eco, *Limitele*, 163.
[3] See the argument in Chapter 3.

Chapter 5

ἀπεθάνομεν τῇ ἁμαρτίᾳ: Interpreting the Metaphorical Language of 'Death' in Romans 6:1-11

This last chapter will offer an interpretation of Paul's metaphorical language of 'death' in Romans 6:1-11. The conclusions of the third and fourth chapter will be interpreted together, each qualifier at its place in Paul's argument.

The present argument of this proposed interpretation is made in relation to the scholarly discussion in Chapter 1. There were two major elements identified in that chapter which are present in the scholarly debate about 'dying' language in Romans 6: 1) the question of the origin of this idea and 2) the way in which it is developed. We will not give again a detailed analysis of those views (that was provided in Chapter 1) but a compact summary of them in order to provide a clearer picture of what we consider to be the contribution of this project.

The Question of Origin

In the scholarly debate we identified six major places proposed by different scholars proposed as the place of origin for Paul's language of 'death'. These are as follows: the *commentatio mortis* tradition from the hellenistic philosophic writings (D. E. Aune), mystery religions (R. Reitzenstein, R. Bultmann, E. Lohse, R. Penna, U. Schnelle), the teaching of Jesus (D. Wenham), Adamic Christology (G. Wagner, A. J. M. Wedderburn), eschatological 'being with Christ' (E. Schweizer), and the personal experience of Paul (W. Wilson and A. Campbell).

As we argued in this project the right method for interpreting a metaphor depends on a right understanding of how a metaphor works. It is that mechanism which has to provide the hermeneutical key for exegesis. That is why we organized the whole project as we did (a study on the metaphor, an investigation of the vehicle of the metaphor and one of the qualifiers of the chosen vehicle, arguing that only then will we be in a position to interpret the metaphors from Romans 6). How can an interpreter investigate the origin of a metaphor? The process of the generation of a metaphor is into a great degree things helps Paul to show a direct connection to Adam's 'heritage' and also that our life does not have anything 'special' being a 'failure' with eschatological consequences as his was. The difference between the meaning of ὁ παλαιὸς ἄνθρωπος and σῶμα τῆς ἁμαρτίας is that the first interprets our life from the perspective of Adam and the 'environment' created by his sin and the second has its focus on the effects of that sin on us as embodied persons in that environment.

The Qualifiers of the Metaphor of 'Death'

By juxtaposing ἁμαρτία with δουλεύω (6:6) Paul identifies 'sin' as 'a master of slaves'. Its 'dominion/control' is mentioned again in 6:12, 14, 16, 17, 18, 20, 22. The end of this dominion/control is called 'liberation' (6:18, 20, 22) and this is also the meaning of καταργέω in 6:6, 'to be released from',[295] or 'to abolish.'[296] Thus 6:6 can be rendered 'we know that our old man was crucified with him so that the body subdued by sin to be released and we might not longer be enslaved to sin.' From this it can be concluded that all of Paul's argument in Rom. 6 is focused on this issue of 'releasing' from the 'control' of sin.[297]

THE INTEGRATION OF THE DATA IN RELATION TO ROMANS 6:6

The relevance of the study in Rom. 5:12-21 for understanding ὁ παλαιὸς ἄνθρωπος in Rom. 6:6 resides in the fact that we have to understand our past in close relationship with what *Adam did*.[298] His action shaped the life of humankind in that that we do not enter a neutral world. Something is already there and, according to Paul, this has the result of 'Adam like' destiny. This is a life in which sin reigns and death is both the physical and eschatological destiny of our lives. The relationship between Adam and the world can be formulated, as Stuhlmacher has, in the manner that 'what is true for Adam is true for all,'[299] or, more specifically, what happened to Adam we experienced too.

The environment created by him is hostile and its powers of sin and death subdue 'all men'. Man 'participates in creation and functions as part of creation'[300] (these are the implications of using σῶμα). The 'participation' in that kind of 'world' is actually a 'slavery'. By using this metaphor of ὁ παλαιὸς ἄνθρωπος Paul shows that we and Adam have many things in common. Adam is used for speaking about our past because this way of putting

---

[295] BAGD, 417; see also Rom. 7:2, 6. See also the discusssion in James W. Aageson, ''Control' in Pauline Language and Culture: A Study in Rom 6', *New Test. Stud.* 42 (1996) 79-81.

[296] Louw and Nida, *Lexicon*, 683.

[297] See also Dunn, *Theology of Paul*, 112.

[298] The debate about the presence or absence of Adam in other places in Romans such as Rom. 1:18-32 and 7:7-13 does not have an implication for our argument. For these discussions, among others, see C. K. Barrett, *From First Adam to Last: A Study in Pauline Theology* (London: Adam & Charles Black, 1962); A.J.M. Wedderburn, 'Adam in Paul's Letter to the Romans', in *Studia Biblica* 1978 III (Sheffield: JSOT, 1980), 413-30; Morna D. Hooker, 'Adam in Romans 1', in *From Adam to Christ* (Cambridge: Cambridge University Press, 1990), 73-85; Morna D. Hooker, 'A Further Note on Romans 1', in *From Adam to Christ* (Cambridge: Cambridge University Press, 1990), 85-7; Dunn, *Theology of Paul*, 91-101.

[299] Stuhlmacher, *Romans*, 85.

[300] Dunn, *Theology of Paul*, 61.

basic anthropological term that seemed especially suited for him for the description of the concrete creatureliness of humans',[283] and also that

> human corporeality is a special expression of human creatureliness, because that means—if we sketch Rom. 5:12-21 a little bit—that in their corporeality human beings are bound into the antithesis of obedience and disobedience, of life and death. [...] Corporeality seems to be the sign of fundamental dependence (1 Cor. 4:7) and therefore of due responding obedience.'[284]

Recently Dunn integrated these positions by putting together the physical/createdness aspect and that existence when he says:

> σῶμα as denoting human body includes the physical body but is more than that. A better word to use, [...] is the term '*embodiment*' — *sōma* as the embodiment of the person. In this sense *sōma* is a relational concept. It denotes the person embodied in a particular environment. It is the means of living in, of experiencing the environment.[285]

Thus, '*sōma* expresses [...] the character of created humankind—that is, as embodied existence.'[286] He understands σῶμα τῆς ἁμαρτίας as denoting 'man as belonging to the age ruled by sin.'[287]

In Romans Paul uses σῶμα for speaking about the physical body[288] (see here Rom 1:24; 4:19; 6:12; 7:24; 8:10, 11, 23; 12:4[289]), but also in Rom. 6:12-14 σῶμα (6:12) is substituted with τὰ μέλη ὑμῶν in 6:13 and with ὑμῶν in 6:14. This discussion in 6:12-14 is the detailed discussion which has its starting point in the phrase τὸ σῶμα τῆς ἁμαρτίας of 6:6.[290] From this interchangeability it can be concluded that Paul understands σῶμα as including the physical body but pointing beyond that (all 'human faculties, capabilities, capacities');[291] we as physical beings/persons,[292] who 'are bound into the antithesis of obedience and disobedience,'[293] or 'being conscious of his dependency on certain forces and powers'.[294]

---

[283] Becker, *Paul,* 384.

[284] Becker, *Paul,* 385.

[285] Dunn, *Theology of Paul,* 56; also Tannehill, 'σῶμα is clearly man in his physicalness, i.e., in his connection to the outside world and interaction with it.' (Tannehill, *Dying,* 72)

[286] Dunn, *Theology of Paul,* 61.

[287] Dunn, *Romans,* 320.

[288] Louw and Nida, *Lexicon,* 93; BAGD,799.

[289] See also 1 Cor. 7:4; 5:3; 2 Cor. 5:6, 8; 12:2-3; Gal. 6:17.

[290] See also Stuhlmacher, *Theologie,* 274.

[291] See the discussions in Barrett, *Romans,* 119; Käsemann, *Romans,* 177; Cranfield, *Romans,* 317; Dunn, Romans, 337; Schreiner, *Romans,* 323.

[292] Louw and Nida, *Lexicon,* 105; MM, 621.

[293] Becker, *Paul,* 385.

[294] Käsemann, 'Body,' 114.

This position is reiterated as follows:

> it [corporeality] is related, not to existence in isolation, but the the world in which forces and persons and things clash violently—a world of love and hate, blessing and curse, service and destruction, in which man is largely determined by sexuality and death and where nobody, fundamentally speaking, belongs to himself alone.[274]

He understands σῶμα τῆς ἁμαρτίας as meaning the same thing as παλαιὸς ἄνθρωπος (Adam individualized and represented in us) but 'from the point of view of fallenness'. These phrases characterise 'existence in sin's power'.[275]

A mixture of these positions (Bultmann/Käsemann) can be found in that of Schnelle: 'Σῶμα is the person him- or herself'[276]; 'Paul uses σῶμα as the comprehensive expression of the human self.'[277] Also

> As the comprehensive definition of the human self, the σῶμα marks the spot where the powers of the transitory world and God's salvific will for humankind come together. [...] In Paul, therefore, σῶμα comprises both one's self-understanding and one's inclusion in God's creative act of salvation.[278]

He understands σῶμα τῆς ἁμαρτίας as having the same meaning as σῶμα τοῦ θανάτου (Rom. 7:24), 'human beings in their totality are subject to sin and death.'[279] Also Bornkamm says that

> the most important thing is that he [Paul] never regards body and corporeality as just one part of man [...]. As used by Paul, 'body' is man as he actually is. Man does not have a body, he is a body. [...] 'body' designates man as the one who never belongs to himself, but always has a master set over him, sin, death, or the Lord. Because of this, man in his corporeality is always asked: To whom do you belong? (1 Cor. 6:13, 15ff).[280]

Against these positions, especially that of Käsemann,[281] J. Becker argues that: 'Paul's concern is not communication in general; rather his theme is the status of the individual person before God'.[282] Becker understands σῶμα as being 'the

---

of Christ', in *Perspectives on Paul* (London: SCM Press Ltd, 1971), 114; see also Stuhlmacher, *Theologie*, 275.

[274] Käsemann, 'On Paul's Anthropology,' 21.
[275] Käsemann, *Romans,* 169.
[276] Schnelle, *Human Condition*, 56.
[277] Schnelle, *Human Condition*, 57.
[278] Schnelle, *Human Condition*, 58.
[279] Schnelle, *Human Condition*, 56.
[280] Gunther Bornkamm, *Paul* (trans. by D. M. G. Stalker; London: Hodder and Stoughton, 1971), 130-1.
[281] See Stuhlmacher, *Theologie*, 275.
[282] Becker, *Paul,* 385.

of σῶμα. We will give the main positions[269] in relation to σῶμα and the way in which they were applied to the understanding of Rom. 6:6.

Bultmann's study on this subject is well known. His conclusions are:

> *Man, his person as a whole,* can be denoted by *sōma.* [...] *Man is called sōma in respect to his being able to make himself the object of his own action or to experience himself as the subject to whom something happens.* He can be called *sōma,* that is, *as having a relationship to himself*—as being able in a certain sense to distinguish himself from himself. Or, more exactly, he is so called as that self from whom he can deal as the object of his own conduct, and also the self whom he can perceive as subjected to an occurrence that springs from a will other than his own. [...] Since it belongs to man's nature to have such a relationship to himself, a double possibility exists: to be at one with himself or at odds (estranged from himself). The possibility of having one's self in hand or of losing this control and being at the mercy of a power not one's own is inherent to human existence itself.[270]

He understands the phrase σῶμα τῆς ἁμαρτίας in Rom. 6:6 as 'sinful self (the self that is under the sway of sin).'[271]

Against this[272] understanding Käsemann says:

> It is generally assumed as a matter of course that 'body' is primarily a term describing the human 'self' as person. I would urge against this that what is meant is man as a non-isolable existence, i.e., in his need and real capacity for communication as friend or foe—man as a being who finds himself in and is aware of an already existing world, and is conscious of his dependency on certain forces and powers. Thus far, this earthly existence of ours is always characterized by membership and participation.[273]

---

[269] See a detailed discussion of the history of research until 1971 in R. Jewett, *Paul's Anthropological Terms* (Leiden: Brill, 1971), 201-50.

[270] R. Bultmann, *Theology of the New Testament* (London: SCM, 1952), 195-6. Conzelmann follows him when he says: 'σῶμα is thus the I as a subject which acts and an object which is acted upon, especially the I as one that acts upon itself.' (H. Conzelmann, *An Outline of the Theology of the New Testament* (London: SCM, 1969), 177)

[271] Bultmann, *Theology,* 197.

[272] See also Gundry who argues that Paul saw man as an anthropological duality, composed of two substances, the body and the soul-spirit, a corporeal part and an incorporeal part, which are designated to function as a harmonious unity but are capable of being separated. σῶμα forms that part of man in and through which he lives and acts in the world. (R.H. Gundry, *Sōma in Biblical Theology: with Emphasis on Pauline Anthropology* (Cambridge: CUP, 1976), 50) According to Gundry the definition 'whole person' does not find convincing support. (79) σῶμα may represent the whole person but does not mean 'whole person'. (80) Gundry understands τὸ σῶμα τῆς ἁμαρτίας as referring to 'the physical body that has been dominated by sin'. (58)

[273] Ernst Käsemann, 'The Theological Problem Presented by the Motif of the Body

are not consonants; 'sin is not to grace as death is to righteousness'.²⁶⁴ This dominion of sin is described here as a result of the 'slipping in'²⁶⁵ of a new element, announced in 5:13 and reintroduced here, namely, the law. Paul says that by the coming of the law sin increased. He does not say here how this happened, but the 'dominion' of sin has to be understood with the 'slipping in' of the law in the background.

In Rom: 6.6 Paul says that this 'reign/slavery' of sin is at the level of the 'body'. Understanding σῶμα in this text is the purpose of the next section.

σῶμα IN ROMANS 6:6

In explaining his thesis from Rom. 6:2 (ἀπεθάνομεν τῇ ἁμαρτίᾳ), the point at which he reintroduces the main qualifier of his metaphor of 'death', namely, ἁμαρτία is here²⁶⁶ in 6:6. When he does this he presupposes, by his phrase ὁ παλαιὸς ἄνθρωπος, the 'Adam side' of the argument from Rom.5:12-21 and specifies the point at which the 'slavery of sin'²⁶⁷ takes place, namely σῶμα, by using the phrase τὸ σῶμα τῆς ἁμαρτίας. This image of slavery, according to Röhser, points to the fact that the slave cannot contribute anything to his release, and his freedom depends entirely on someone else.²⁶⁸ Every discussion about the meaning of ἀπεθάνομεν τῇ ἁμαρτίᾳ has to include, when discussing the idea of 'sin' in this metaphor, this complex network of ideas found in 5:12-21 (see above) and to clarify the 'anthropological' side/element of it by a study

---

²⁶⁴ Cf. Moo, *Romans*, 350.
²⁶⁵ Cf. Käsemann, *Romans*, 158; Moo, *Romans*, 347.
²⁶⁶ See also Dunn, *Romans*, 320.
²⁶⁷ For examples of 'slavery' metaphorically used in Greek and Jewish literature see Günter Röhser, *Metaphorik und Personification der Sünde* (Tübingen: J C B Mohr (Paul Siebeck), 1987), 104-10. Epictetus, *Disc.* IV:1; II:1:23; Here is an example from Xenophon, *Memorabilia*, I:5:5: Should not every man hold self-control to be the foundation of all virtue, and first lay this foundation firmly to his soul? For who without this can learn any good or practice it worthily? Or what man that is the slave of his pleasures is not in an evil plight body and soul alike? From my heart I declare that every free man should pray not to have such a man among his slaves; and every man who is a slave to such pleasures should entreat the gods to give him good masters: thus, and only thus, may find salvation.' (Xenophon, *Memorabilia* (E. C. Marchant, trans.; Cambridge, Mass.; London: Harvard University Press; William Heinemann Ltd, 1979)) See also Philo, Quast. Gen. II:8: '... For there was no other reason for the destruction of man to take place than having become slaves of pleasures and appetites, they did everything and suffered, wherefore they attained a life of the very utmost misery.' (Philo, *Questions and Answers on Genesis (Quaestiones et Solutiones in Genesin)* (Ralph Marcus, trans.; London; Cambridge, Mass.: William Heinemann Ltd; Harvard University Press, 1961)) Also *Quod Omnis*, 21-25; 59-61; 156-159. Also 1QH 1:27; 1QS IV:10; 1QM XIII:5; 1QS IV:9 / Rom. 6:19.
²⁶⁸ Röhser, *Metaphorik*, 110.

text from the NT is Jas. 4:4:[257] μοιχαλίδες, οὐκ οἴδατε ὅτι ἡ φιλία τοῦ κόσμου ἔχθρα τοῦ θεοῦ ἐστιν; ὃς ἐὰν οὖν βουληθῇ φίλος εἶναι τοῦ κόσμου, ἐχθρὸς τοῦ θεοῦ καθίσταται ('whoever wishes to be a friend of the world *becomes* an enemy of God') This meaning of 'to cause to be, to make to be'[258] leads the discussion about 'the sin of Adam and the sin of many' toward a more specific formulation.[259] The ideas from 5:12 are reiterated, focusing not so much on *how* that 'making' of sinners took place but on the *resulting* reality in the life of many: being sinners. The sin of Adam receives a clearer role in attaining this state of being a sinner, namely, that of instrument. Adam's disobedience is a *necessary* action/event which leads to that particular conclusion. But, according to 5:12 and 5:19b (which is to be understood in the light of 5.17 where the 'gift of righteousness' is *received*), this action of Adam is not *sufficient* for attaining that.[260] In 5:12 there is both the action of one man and the action of all. The first has the quality of an instrument which set up a hostile environment and that environment, in turn, has as result the sinning of all. In 5:19b 'many will be made righteous' as a result of the obedience of Christ. The obedience of Christ is the necessary event by which that is made possible, but they also have to receive that 'gift of righteousness' (5:17) in order to be 'made righteous'.[261]

This state is described/summarised[262] in 5:21 where Paul uses the words ἐβασίλευσεν ἡ ἁμαρτία ἐν τῷ θανάτῳ. The 'Adam side of the argument' is summarised in that it is a dominion of sin in [the reality[263] of] death. The phrase ἐν τῷ θανάτῳ is not very clear; we interpreted it as pointing to the 'reality' of death, a formulation which remains vague but which encompasses the ideas of 'sphere or dominion'. ἐν is not instrumental (as a parallel affirmation to that from 5:21b where 'the grace reigns through righteousenss') because the terms

---

[257] See also the texts in which this term means 'to appoint': Acts 6:3; 7:10, 27, 35; Tit. 1:5.

[258] Louw and Nida, *Lexicon*, 150; BAGD, 391.

[259] Against Moo, *Romans*, 346 who argues for preserving the 'forensic flavour of the word'. [...] 'This 'making righteous,' however, must be interpreted in the light of Paul's typical forensic categories. To be 'righteous' does not mean to be morally upright, but to be judged acquitted, cleared of all charges, in the heavenly judgment.' The meaning of καθίστημι here is synonymous to those of ποιέω, τίθημι, ἐργάζομαι, κατεργάζομαι, ἐπάγω, ἐνεργέω, cf. Louw and Nida, *Lexicon*, 150.

[260] See also Scroggs, *Last Adam*, 79; Wedderburn, 'Structure,' 352; Cranfield puts it '...in both cases what one man does affects all other men and is determinative of their existence.' (Cranfield, *Romans*, 291)

[261] See also Wedderburn, 'Structure,' 353. The κατασταθήσονται is understood as a logical future, M. Zerwick, *A Grammatical Analysis of the Greek New Testament* (Rome: PBI, 1974), 471; Fitzmyer, *Romans*, 422.

[262] Also Fitzmyer, *Romans*, 422.

[263] Käsemann understands it as designating 'the sphere' (Käsemann, *Romans*, 158), and Moo as 'dominion' (Moo, *Romans*, 350).

aorist indicative in 5:12d is not a reference to sinning 'in' the sin of Adam but a reference, from the point of view of the writer, to the fact of actual sinning of everyone from that 'environment'. On the one hand Adam's sin 'brings'[250] death and on the other hand sin and death create the particular environment which leads to 'sinning'.

In Rom. 5:13-14 Paul says that even if there was no law until Moses and sin is not counted[251] in that period, sin was in the world and this fact is seen in the reality of the dominion of death[252] even over those who did not sin by transgressing a command of God as Adam did.[253] The law 'effects a change from sin to transgression'.[254] After Adam's sin the world is 'not a neutral place but the field of contending powers that rules it'.[255]

In 5:15 he mentions again the 'result' of Adam's trespass: the death of all. This fact is expressed in different terms in 5:16a: 'for the judgment resulting from one [trespass] leads to condemnation' (see also 5:18a). This verdict refers both to the physical death of all and also to the eschatological death, and is explained again in 5:17a with focus on the 'dominion' of death: ὁ θάνατος ἐβασίλευσεν διὰ τοῦ ἑνός.[256]

In 5:19 the 'deed' of Adam is seen as παρακοή and it is said that it was the instrument of 'making sinners' of many. Here, in order to express the reality of being δίκαιος or ἁμαρτωλός, the same lexeme is used: καθίστημι. The relevant

---

Perpspectives on Paul (London: SCM Press Ltd, 1971), 25; and Schnelle, *Human Condition*, 65; Hofius, 'Adam-Christus-Antithese,' 185; J. Christiaan Beker, 'The Relationship Between Sin and Death in Romans', in Robert T. Fortna and Beverly R. Gaventa, eds, *The Conversation Continues: Studies in Paul and John in Honor of J. Louis Martin* (Nashville: Abingdon, 1990), 58.

[250] This 'causal' aspect of Adam's sin is also present in 5.15a (leads to death of all), 16a (the judgment of his trespass brought condemnation), 17a (leads to the dominion of death), 18a (leads to the condemnation of all), 19a (many were made sinners).

[251] ἐλλογέω 'to keep a record of something', Louw and Nida, *Lexicon*, 394; this term does not refer 'to an absence of guilt or punishment, but to a difference in the way sins are prosecuted.' Westerholm, *Israel's Law,* 181.

[252] For the imagery of death reigning see Hos. 13:14; Wis.1:14.

[253] See also Moo, *Romans*, 332; Helmut Merklein, 'Paulus und die Sünde', in *Studien zu Jesus und Paulus* (II; Tübingen: Mohr Siebeck, 1998), 324; Porter, 'Original sin,' 27; against Nils Alstrup Dahl, *Studies in Paul* (Minneapolis, Minnesota: Augsburg Publishing House, 1977), 91, who says that, 'only in the period before Moses that everybody died as a consequence of Adam's fall which had brought sin and death into the world (5:13-14). Later on, sinners were also accountable for their own transgressions of the Law (5:16);' and 'it was only in the time between Adam and Moses that the relation between one and the many was the same in the order of sin and death as in order of righteousness and life.'

[254] Westerholm, *Israel's Law,* 180.

[255] Käsemann, *Romans,* 150.

[256] Also Porter, 'Original sin,' 28.

Very recently, Fitzmyer's thesis was challenged, in some aspects, by T. Schreiner.[238] Schreiner says that some of Fitzmyer's examples which point to the consecutive meaning could be easily translated 'upon the basis of which'.[239] 'ἐφ' ᾧ forges a logical connection between two propositions, and what that connection is it must be discerned from context.'[240] In this example, 'the *idea* in the ἐφ' ᾧ construction (not the specific word) refers back to death.'[241] Then the whole phrase can be rendered 'On the basis of death entering the world through Adam all people sinned'.[242] The challenge which Schreiner has to answer is how sin is a result of death. He explains this by understanding 'death' as meaning being 'separated from God'[243], and in this sense all human beings enter the world alienated from God, and as a result of this alienation they sin.[244] The position argued for in this section, at this point, goes on the lines traced by Fitzmyer and Schreiner. We understand ἐφ' ᾧ as having a consecutive meaning (based on arguments of Fitzmyer) and the reference of ἐφ' ᾧ including the *reality* of death. The sin of Adam set up a particular kind of environment in which Death entered (see also here another description, τῇ [...] ματαιότητι ἡ κτίσις ὑπετάγη, Rom. 8:19 (21)).[245] Death is seen as a 'king/queen' (ἐβασίλευσεν ὁ θάνατος, 5:14 in describing the period between Adam and Moses). This fact has some implications: all die (5:15) and live there where ἐβασίλευσεν ἡ ἁμαρτία ἐν τῷ θανάτῳ (5:21). So in 5:12c ὁ θάνατος is understood not as the 'end of physical life' but as a power which, in a close relationship with 'sin,' 'embraces' all people who came into the world. Adam's sin started a kind of existence which is characterised by a defective relationship with God (see also the previous discussion on κόσμος).[246] 'As a result' of *this* reality *all* have sinned.[247] Thus, what is true for Adam is true for all.[248] Käsemann puts it 'he [man] is in the grip of the forces which seize his existence and determine his will and responsibility at least to the extent that he cannot choose freely but can only grasp what is already there'.[249] The usage of the

---

[238] Schreiner, *Romans*, 724.

[239] Schreiner, *Romans*, 274.

[240] Schreiner, *Romans*, 274.

[241] Schreiner, *Romans*, 274.

[242] Schreiner, *Romans*, 274; This was the reason for which Byrne rejected Fitzmyer's thesis: it 'makes little sense in the context: the nub of Paul's argument is that sin causes death, not vice versa'. Byrne, *Romans*, 183.

[243] Cambier, 'Péchés,' 235 argues for a similar meaning for death here.

[244] Schreiner, *Romans*, 276-7.

[245] On the 'creation' see especially the discussion in Stuhlmacher, *Theologie*, 269-73.

[246] See also Wedderburn, 'Structure,' 344.

[247] See also Laato, *Paul,* 100, 'Verse 12 expresses therefore at the same time both the universal and catastrophic results of Adam's fall into sin as well as the personal guilt of his physical posterity.'

[248] Cf. Stuhlmacher, *Romans*, 86.

[249] Käsemann, *Romans,* 147; see also 149; Käsemann, 'On Paul's Anthropology', in

examples[233] in which ἐφ' ᾧ, in Greek literature, seems to have a consecutive meaning. We will quote only two examples from his survey, namely those from L. M. Plutarch[234] (perhaps a contemporary with Paul). The first is more important because, as in Romans 5:12d, it contains πάντες with an aorist indicative.

> When silence came (upon all) and I had stopped (lecturing) so that he might read the letter (from the emperor), he was unwilling (to do so) and did not break (the seal) before I had finished the lecture and the audience was dispersed, so that all were amazed (ἐφ' ᾧ πάντες ἐθαύμασαν) at the dignity of the man.[235] (*De curiositate*, 522E 4-6)

And the other example:

> Then with great enthusiasm Cimon, having discovered with difficulty the burial place, placed the bones [of Theseus] and the other things on his own trireme and brought them back to the city with great pomp after almost 400 years with the result (ἐφ' ᾧ) that the citizenry became most kindly disposed toward him.[236] (*Cimon*, 8:6:4)

Fitzmyer says 'that if these examples have any validity [...] we have a solution to Rom. 5:12d'. He translates 5:12 like this:

> Therefore, just as sin entered the world through one man, and death came through sin; so death spread to all human beings, *with the result* that all have sinned. (our italics)

He explains the implications as follows:

> If the consecutive sense of ἐφ' ᾧ is valid, then the connection, expressed by καὶ οὕτως, is confirmed. Paul would thus be attributing the entire perverse corruption of humanity to Adam in the sense that it began with his transgression of the command laid by God upon him but continued as a result in the sinful conduct of those descended from him.[237]

---

[233] These are as follows: Athenaeus of Naucratis, *Deipnosophistae*, 2.49d; Diogenes Laertius, *Vitae philos*, 7:169:4-6; 173:1-5; Plutarch, *Aratus*, 44:4.1; *De curiositate*, 522E, 4-6; Cimon, 8:6:4; Cicero, 36:4:5; Cassius Dio, *Hist. Rom.* 59:19:1-2; 59:20:23; 61:33:8; 63:28:5; 67:4:6; 73:18:2; 78:16:5; Eusebius, *Eccl. Hist.* 9:9:5-6; Libanius, *Or.* 15:43; 18:198. See an analysis of these in Fitzmyer, 'Consecutive Meaning,' 333-8.

[234] Fitzmyer, 'Consecutive Meaning,' 334-5 also Fitzmyer, *Romans*, 416.

[235] Helmbold paraphrases here: 'Because of this incident', Plutarch, 'De Curiositate', in *Moralia* (VI; W. C. Helmbold, trans.; Cambridge, Mass., London: Harvard University Press, William Heinemann Ltd, 1970).

[236] Perrin translates the last part 'This was the chief reason why the people took kindly to him.' (our italics) Plutarch, 'Cimon', in *Lives* (II; Bernadotte Perrin, trans.; Cambridge, Mass.; London: Harvard University Press; William Heinemann Ltd, 1968).

[237] Fitzmyer, 'Consecutive Meaning,' 339.

after mentioning the responsibility of Adam in unleashing sin in the world (and in v. 18-19 it is explained that condemnation is universal because of the sin of Adam).[225] From these two observations Moo asks two questions: (1) Why do all people without exception sin? and (2) How is it that the sin of Adam led to the condemnation of all people? His answers to these difficult questions are given in terms of solidarity of all humanity with Adam in his sin. Paul, says Moo, affirms that but is not able to explain the exact nature of that union. This solidarity can be explained, says Moo, either in terms of sinning in and with Adam or in terms of a corrupt nature inherited from him.[226] Recently this causal understanding of ἐφ' ᾧ as meaning 'because' was challenged by Fitzmyer.[227] He says that if ἐφ' ᾧ means 'since' or 'because' then Paul says something contradictory in 5:12d to what he had said in 5:12a-c. In 5:12a-c sin and death are attributed to Adam and in 5:12d death seems to be owing to human acts.[228] The counter argument of the majority of scholars goes like this: when 5:12 is explained as a whole the focus is on two aspects: first Adam's sin was the cause of the death of all, and human beings did not die simply because of Adam's sin without their own sinning by their own fault.[229] Support for this ambivalence is found in later Jewish writings (2 Syr. Bar. 54:15: 'For though Adam first sinned and brought untimely death upon all, yet of those who were born from him each one of them has prepared for his own soul torment to come'; and 5:19: 'Adam it is therefore not the cause, save only his own soul, but each of us has been the Adam of his own soul'; also 4 Esdra 7:48 [118] and 49[119]), and in Rabbinic literature (*Siphre Deut* 323 (138b) 'you are sons of Adam who brought death upon you and upon all his descendants...' and *Num. R.* 19:18 'all men die because all men sin'.)[230]

But Fitzmyer says that even in this situation it remains to resolve the state that 'there are almost no certain instances in Greek literature where ἐφ' ᾧ is used as the equivalent of causal διότι',[231] and the examples from Pauline literature are 'far from certain'.[232] According to Fitzmyer there are many

---

[225] Moo, *Romans* 1-8, 335.

[226] Moo, *Romans* 1-8, 341.

[227] Fitzmyer, *Romans*, 413-7; Fitzmyer, 'Consecutive Meaning'; Also Mounce adopts this view, Robert H. Mounce, *Romans* (Nashville: Broadman & Holman, 1995), 142.

[228] Fitzmyer, 'Consecutive Meaning,' 327-8.

[229] Cf. Cranfield, *Romans*, 280.

[230] Cf. Cranfield, *Romans*, 280.

[231] Fitzmyer, 'Consecutive Meaning,' 326; Fitzmyer, *Romans*, 415; 'Most of the examples cited by BAGD are invalid' (415). See his analysis of the examples from Diodorus Siculus, Appian, Synesius, A. Aristides (415); contra Porter, 'Original sin,' 24.

[232] Fitzmyer, Romans, 415. He says that in Phil. 3:12, ἐφ' ᾧ means 'that for which'; in Phil. 4:10, 'for whom' or possibly, 'with regard to which'. Not even in 2 Cor. 5:4 does ἐφ' ᾧ certainly mean 'because', [...] there it could easily mean 'because of that which.'

'collective sin'. Adam is seen both as a historical figure and as humankind (he is so because his name means this). So here we have the concept of corporate personality.[212] Because Adam *is* mankind[213] all are said to have sinned in his sin. Thus the theological content of Augustine's interpretation[214] is put together with the grammatical understanding of Cyril and Pelagius concerning ἐφ' ᾧ. Cranfield follows Cyril both in understanding the meaning of the prepositional phrase ἐφ' ᾧ and the meaning of ἥμαρτον, the first being causal and the second being an actual fact caused by weakened human nature as result of man's primal transgression. When he explains 5:12, he gives these two aspects: Adam's sin was the cause of death to all, and human beings did not die simply because of Adam's sin without their own sinning by their own fault.[215] This ambivalence is sustained, according to Cranfield, both by later Jewish writings[216] and by the Rabbinic literature.[217] Dunn discusses this verse only from the point of view of the universality of the effects of Adam's sin. In v.12, he says, we find a continuity with Jewish reflections on the Genesis account of Adam's fall. In this reflection there is a tension between the inevitability of human sin[218] and human responsibility for sinning.[219] In v.12 there is a distinction between 'one' and 'all', a distinction that is matched by the distinction between ἁμαρτία and ἥμαρτον where the latter denotes human responsibility in sinful acts.[220] Dunn argues that because Paul maintains a clear distinction between 'one' and 'all' and because the 'all' are not simply subsumed within 'one' we cannot speak in this text about corporate personality.[221] The last affirmation in 5:12, according to Dunn, is ambiguous, both for us and for the first hearers also, and for this reason we translate it preserving that vagueness: 'in that all sinned'.[222] This statement does not provide an answer concerning the relationship between the primeval act of sin and humankind's act of sin, because Paul simply does not discuss that.[223] Moo, after adopting 'because' as the meaning for ἐφ' ᾧ and following Dunn in his view about Paul's general concern, namely, 'original death',[224] goes beyond that by observing that in this verse Paul affirms the universality of sin (v.12d)

---

[212] F.F. Bruce, *The Letter of Paul to the Romans* (Leicester: IVP, 1985(2)), 126.
[213] Bruce, *Romans*, 130.
[214] Cf. Cranfield, *Romans*, 277.
[215] Cranfield, *Romans*, 280.
[216] 2 Bar. 54:15, 19; 2 Esdr. 7:48 [118] and 49 [119]
[217] Siphre Deut. 323 (138b) and Num R. 19:18.
[218] Philo, Mos. 2:147; 1 QS 3:18-4:1.
[219] 4 Ezra 8:35; 2 Ap. Bar: 54:15,19.
[220] Dunn, *Romans*, 274.
[221] Dunn, *Romans*, 273.
[222] Dunn, *Romans*, 290; Also Wedderburn, 'Structure,' 350 proposes to translate it 'in that'.
[223] Dunn, *Romans*, 290.
[224] Moo, *Romans* 1-8, 334.

mean 'because' (the majority of commentators) or has a consecutive meaning ('with the result that') (Fitzmyer). The understanding of ἐφ' ᾧ as a conjunction is explained in a variety of ways. Here are some of them. Pelagius understood ἐφ' ᾧ as a conjunction meaning 'because' and ἥμαρτον as referring to men's sinning in their own persons quite independently of Adam, though after his example.[210] Cyril of Alexandria understood ἐφ' ᾧ as meaning 'because' but ἥμαρτον to mean actual sinning. This view is in contrast to the Pelagian view in that men's sinning is related to Adam's transgression not merely externally but also internally, as being its natural consequence. 'According to this interpretation, while men does not sin in Adam in Augustine's sense, they do sin in Adam in the sense that they sin in a real solidarity with him, as a result of the entail of his transgression'.[211] F.F. Bruce follows Pelagius and Cyril in understanding of ἐφ' ᾧ as meaning 'because' but ἥμαρτον as a reference to a

---

accurante; 1865)

Thus *quo* is understood either with reference to sin or to Adam. This was in AD 412. Later (AD 420) he chose Adam because he realised that the Greek ἁμαρτία was feminine. He wrote in *Contra duas epistolae Pelagianorum*, fourth book chap. 7:

What, then is the meaning of what follows, 'Wherein all have sinned'? For either the apostle says that in that one man all have sinned of whom he has said, By one man sin entered into the world, or 'in that sin,' or certainly 'in death.' For it need not disturb us that he said not 'in which' [fem.], but 'in whom' [masc.] all have sinned; because death [θάνατος] in the Greek language is of the masculine gender. Let them, then, choose which they will,—for either in that man all have sinned, and it is said because when he sinned all were in him; or in that sin all have sinned, because, in general, it was the doing of all, which all those who were born would have to bear; or it remains for them to say that in that death all sinned. But in what way this can be understood, I do not clearly see. For all die in the sin, they do not sin in the death; for when sin precedes, death follows—not when death precedes, sin follows. Because sin is the sting of death— that is, the sting by whose would death occurs, not the sting with which death strikes. As poison, if it is drunk, is called the cup of death, because by that cup death is caused, not because the cup is caused by the death, or is given by death. But if sin cannot be understood by these words of the apostle as being that in which all have sinned, because in Greek, from which the Epistle is translated, sin is expressed in the feminine gender [ἁμαρτία], it remains that first man, because in him all men were when he sinned (*Quod si propterea non potest illis verbis Apostoli peccatum intelligi, in quo omnes peccaverunt, quia in graeco, unde translata est Epistola, peccatum feminino genere positum est*); whence sin is derived by being born, and is not remitted save by being born again. Saint Augustine, 'Against Two Letters of the Pelagians', in *The Anti-Pelagian Works* (III; Peter Holmes and Robert Ernest Wallis, trans.; Edinburgh: T & T Clark, 1976); the latin text is from S. Aurelii Augustini, *Contra duas epistolas Pelagianorum, in Sancti Aurelii Augustini, Hipponensis Episcopi, Opera Omnia* (Tomus Decimus; J. P. Migne, accurante; 1865).

[209] Cambier, 'Péchés'.

[210] Cf. Cranfield, *Romans*, 274, 277.

[211] Cranfield, *Romans*, 278.

which is very well known[205] but only a summary of it: a) if ᾧ is understood as a relative (masculine) pronoun there are the following proposals for its reference: an implied *nomos* (Danker[206]), death (Stauffer)[207], or ἑνὸς ἀνθρώπου (Augustine,[208] Cambier[209]) and b) if ᾧ is understood as a conjunction it can

---

[205] For surveys of the debate see: Cambier, 'Péchés,' 242-55; Danker, 'Romans V.12,' 435-9; Cranfield, *Romans*, 275-9; Martin, *Christ and the Law*, 73-4; Porter, 'Original sin,' 22-4; Joseph A. Fitzmyer, 'The Consecutive Meaning of ΕΦ' Ω in Romans 5:12', *NTS* 39 (1993) 322-8; Fitzmyer, *Romans,* 413-7; Timo Laato, *Paul and Palestinian Judaism: An Anthropological Approach* (T. McElwain, trans.; Atlanta: Scholars Press, 1995), 97-100; Moo, *Romans,* 320-3.

[206] See his discussion in Danker, 'Romans V.12,' 428-31; he paraphrased the text as follows 'Sin came into the world through one man, and death through sin. And so death passed on to all men, on the legal basis in terms of which all (including the Gentiles) sinned. This must be maintained, for until the law (of Moses) sin was in the world, and one must admit that sin cannot be charged up in the absence of law.' (431)

[207] He says: 'ἐπὶ with its relative pronoun refers back to the preceding θάνατος (ἐφ' ᾧ= ἐπὶ θανάτῳ) and does not mean, as translators mostly suppose, 'on the basis of' but 'in the direction of' [...]; it is also required by the chiasmus of the phrases in Rom. 5:12:

διὰ ἁμαρτίας---------θάνατος
ἐπὶ θανάτῳ-----------ἥμαρτον

[...] So we must accordingly paraphrase: 'death, to which they fell man by man through their sin'. (Ethelbert Stauffer, *New Testament Theology* (John Marsh, trans.; London: SCM, 1955), 270.)

[208] Usually Augustine is quoted very shortly, but his understanding of the phrase was very influential. Here are his main affirmations: (a) Augustine wrote in De peccatorum meritis et remissione, Book 1, chap. 9:10:

so likewise he, in whom all die, besides being an example for imitation to those who wilfully transgress the commandment of the Lord, depraved in his own person all who come of his stock by the hidden corruption on this account, and for no other reason, that the apostle says: 'By one man sin entered into the world, and death by sin, and so death passed upon all men; and in this [sin] all have sinned (*in quo omnes peccaverunt*).

And in Book 1, cap. 10:11 he says

Again, in the clause which follows, 'And in this [sin] all have sinned,' (*In quo omnes peccaverunt*) how cautiously, rightly, and unambiguously is the statement expressed! For if you understand that sin to be meant which by one man entered into the world, and in which all have sinned, it is surely clear enough, that the sins which are peculiar to every man, which they themselves commit and which belong simply to them, mean one thing; and that the one sin, in and by which all have sinned, means another thing, since all were included in that one [primeval] man. If, however, it be not the sin, but this first man that is understood [in this clause, so that it be read] 'in whom' [not, *in which*] 'all have sinned,' what again can be plainer than even this clear statement?' Saint Augustine, 'De Peccatorum Meritis et Remissione', in *The Anti-Pelagian Works* (1; Peter Holmes, trans.; Edinburgh: T & T Clark, 1872); the latin text is from S. Aurelii Augustini, De peccatorum meritis remissione et de baptesimo parvulorum, in *Sancti Aurelii Augustini, Hipponensis Episcopi, Opera Omnia* (Tomus Decimus; J. P. Migne,

near to that in 4 Ezra 3:7: 'And thou didst lay upon him one commandment; but he transgressed it, and immediately thou didst appoint death for him and for his descendants.'[195] The differences between this text and that of Paul are that in Romans 5:12 the presence of God is not mentioned directly as it is in 4 Ezra, and there is still no mention of any commandment as it is implied by παράπτωμα language(5.15 and 5:17). The reference to 'death' in 4 Ezra 3:7 is to physical death[196] but in Romans Paul personifies Death which includes the physical and eschatological aspect.[197] 4 Ezra 7:118 also points in the same direction of connection between Adam's sin and humankind: 'O Adam, what have you done? For though it was you who sinned, the misfortune was not yours alone, but ours also who are your descendants.'[198] And 2 Syr. Bar. 54:15,19:

> For although Adam sinned first and has brought death upon all who were not in his own time, yet each of them who has been born from him has prepared for himself the coming torment. And further, each of them has chosen for himself the coming glory. [...] Adam is, therefore, not the cause, except for himself, but each of us has become our own Adam.[199]

For describing the 'activity' of death Paul uses the metaphor of 'travel around through an area' (διέρχομαι).[200] The image from Acts 13:6 can help here: διελθόντες δὲ ὅλην τὴν νῆσον ἄχρι Πάφου ('when they had travelled throughout the entire island, they came to Paphos')[201] in that it shows the 'thoroughness' of the action in the sense 'to penetrate' (see εἰς πάντας ἀνθρώπους...). The last words of 5:12 come to say that the 'sinning' (Paul never uses ἁμαρτάνω in the sense of 'abstract culpability',[202] but always about personal sins[203]) is universal and also that this is somehow in relationship to Adam's sin.[204] The meaning of the phrase ἐφ' ᾧ is under debate. Here we will not present in detail the debate

---

[195] Michael Edward Stone, *Fourth Ezra* (Frank Moore Cross, ed.; Minneapolis: Fortress Press, 1990), 58.

[196] Also Stone, *Fourth Ezra*, 65; see also Syr. Bar. 17:2-3; 54:14; 56:6.

[197] See also Fitzmyer, *Romans*, 412; Wedderburn, 'Structure,' 347-8.

[198] Stone, *Fourth Ezra*, 253; John R. Levison, *Portraits of Adam in Early Judaism: From Sirach to 2 Baruch* (Sheffield: SAP, 1988), 156. For arguments against a gnostic background see the thesis of Wedderburn, *Adam and Christ*.

[199] See also the discussion in Levison, *Portraits*, 156-7; also for Adam in Jewish literature see Dunn, *Theology of Paul*, 82-90.

[200] Louw and Nida, *Lexicon*, 185, BAGD,194; see also the discussion in Cambier, 'Péchés,' 239.

[201] Cf. Louw and Nida, *Lexicon*, 185.

[202] F. W. Danker, 'Romans v. 12: Sin Under Law', *NTS* 14 (1967-8) 436.

[203] Cf. Cambier, 'Péchés,' 240-1; also Wedderburn, 'Structure,' 351; see discussion in Fitzmyer, *Romans*, 417; Porter, 'Original sin,' 25.

[204] Also Porter, 'Original sin,' 22.

as an apocalyptic power[183] in the present age, and the κατάκριμα language from 5:16a, 18a points to the idea of 'death' as 'eschatological condemnation'. In 5:17, 18, 21 the opposite of θάνατος is not 'physical' life but 'eternal' life.[184] The lexical choice of κόσμος reveals some particularities of the text: Paul does not simply talk about all 'the people who dwell on the earth' (οἰκουμένη or γῆ)[185] but about people who become associated with a world system and estranged from God (κόσμος).[186] Sin is presented as 'someone who enters'; Paul does not explain how 'the deed' of one man was used by sin for 'entering', he says only that sin did that. The 'one man' is identified in 5.14 as Ἀδάμ and thus the Genesis narrative is in the background of this argument.[187] The 'entering' of sin was not only for itself but led to another 'entering', that of 'death'.[188] This 'entering,' of death into the world could be an echo of the affirmation in Wis. 2:24 φθόνῳ δεδιαβόλου θάνατος εἰσῆλθεν εἰς τὸν κόσμον,[189] but the difference is that here the 'entering' is through the Devil's envy whereas in Romans it is through Adam's sin.[190] In 4 Ezra 3:7 the result of sin is death and this was appointed by God.[191] Also in 4 Ezra 3:21, 26 the 'evil heart' is the cause of transgression and it is by this that Adam was overcome and also those who descended from him. Paul does not give these details; his affirmation is a general one: δι' ἑνὸς ἀνθρώπου. καὶ οὕτως in 5:12c points to the connection between Adam's sin and its result which affects 'all men'.[192] Because of the sin of Adam all human beings experience death. As Käsemann puts it: 'the fate of the descendants is settled in the forefather'.[193] It is not very clear whether there is a reference here to 'physical' death or to Death as a power or to the first as an aspect of the 'activity' of the second.[194] This idea is

---

'Structure,' 344-7.

[183] 'Some preparation for this conception of death can be seen in OT and Jewish idea of the angel of death, the destroyer (Exod. 12:23; 1 Chr. 21:12, 15; Job 15:21; Wis. 15:21; 1 Cor. 10:10),' Wedderburn, *Adam and Christ*, 222.

[184] Cf. Hofius, 'Adam-Christus-Antithese,' 182; also Stuhlmacher, *Romans*, 86.

[185] Louw and Nida, *Lexicon*, 106.

[186] Louw and Nida, *Lexicon*, 107; also Cambier, 'Péchés,' 232.

[187] See also Wedderburn, 'Structure,' 340; Käsemann, *Romans*, 142.

[188] Also Cranfield, *Romans*, 274.

[189] See the discussion in Wedderburn, 'Structure,' 340 where he says that 'no other parallel is so close'; also Cambier, 'Péchés,' 231, who maintains that Paul here replaces the word 'death' by 'sin' from Wisd 2:24.

[190] See also Stanislas Lyonnet and Leopold Sabourin, *Sin, Redemption, and Sacrifice: A Biblical and Patristic Study* (Rome: Biblical Institute Press, 1970), 55.

[191] See also the discussion in Peter Stuhlmacher, *Biblische Theologie des Neuen Testaments* (Band I; Gottingen: Vandenhoeck & Ruprecht, 1992, 1997), 279.

[192] See also Fitzmyer, *Romans*, 413, 416; Hofius, 'Adam-Christus-Antithese,' 184.

[193] Käsemann, *Romans*, 143.

[194] See the discussion in Cambier, 'Péchés,' 235, where death is seen as the deprivation of the real relation that all men have with God.

That 'slavery/control of sin' mentioned in Rom. 6:6 has its beginning[173] in 5:12 where Paul says that δι' ἑνὸς ἀνθρώπου ἡ ἁμαρτία εἰς τὸν κόσμον εἰσῆλθεν.[174] The phrase δι' ἑνὸς ἀνθρώπου is a reference to 'the deed' of one man as the 'gate' through which sin entered in the world. The entrance[175] of sin into 'the people of the world' (κόσμος)[176] is bound to the 'sin' of one man.[177] Adam stands at the start of the story of mankind. In a sense here was decided the *direction* which will be followed by the whole 'adamic humankind'.[178] The decision concerning the meaning of κόσμος was taken not only on syntagmatic considerations but on the general idea from 5.12 where the discussion is not about the origin of sin (in what way sin entered 'the universe as an ordered structure' (κόσμος), because 'sin' was already present in the universe but not in the sense of 'ruler')[179] but about the origin of death. This meaning of κόσμος prepares the ground for the idea of 5:12c where death penetrated the whole of *humankind*.[180] In other words 'one man' 'initiated a process of sin and bequeathed mankind a heritage of death'.[181] Also in this way Paul moves from one perspective on death as a consequence and concomitant of sin[182] to another

---

[173] Also J. Cambier, 'Péchés Des Hommes et Péché d'Adam en Rom. V.12', *NTS* 11 (1964-1965) 233; Wedderburn, *Adam and Christ*, 215.

[174] ὥσπερ... begins a comparative clause which is broken off at the end of v.12 and not continued perhaps until v.19. There are suggestions that καί οὕτως (5.12c) completes the construction (Barrett, *Romans*, 109-10; R. Scroggs, *The Last Adam* (Oxford: Blackwell, 1966), 79-80; B. Englezakis, 'Rom. 5:12-21 and the Pauline Teaching on the Lord's Death: Some Observations', *Biblica* 58 (1977) 232; J. T. Kirby, 'The Syntax of Romans 5:12: A Rhetorical Approach', *NTS* 33 (1987) 283-4), but grammatically it is not plausible (Cranfield, *Romans*, 272). If Paul had intended to introduce the conclusion he would have written οὕτως καὶ as he did in 5:18,19; cf. Fitzmyer, *Romans*, 411; Fitzmyer suggests that the conclusion to the comparison is implied in the last clause of v.14, but it is more probable that the very similar wording of 5:19 points to a kind of conclusion of this comparison: ὥσπερ... διὰ τῆς παρακοῆς τοῦ ἑνὸς ἀνθρώπου...

[175] εἰσέρχομαι, 'to go into, to enter,' Louw and Nida, *Lexicon*, 195.

[176] Louw and Nida, *Lexicon*, 107; Ernst Käsemann, *Romans*, 147, 'human world;' Cranfield, *Romans*, 274, 'mankind;' see also Cambier, 'Péchés,' 233.

[177] See also Cambier, 'Péchés,' 233; S. Westerholm, *Israel's Law and the Church's Faith: Paul and His Recent Interpreters* (Grand Rapids: Eerdmans, 1988), 180.

[178] Also Otfried Hofius, 'Die Adam-Christus-Antithese und das Gesetz: Erwägungen zu Röm 5:12-21', in James D. G. Dunn, ed., *Paul and the Mosaic Law* (Tübingen: Mohr Siebeck, 1996), 181.

[179] Louw and Nida, *Lexicon*, 1.

[180] See also discussion in Edward Adams, *Constructing the World: A Study in Paul's Cosmological Language* (Edinburgh: T&T Clark, 2000), 173.

[181] Martin, *Christ and the Law*, 70; see also the discussion in Schnelle, *Human Condition*, 64; Heinrich Schlier, *Der Römerbrief* (Freiburg: Herder, 1977), 180-1.

[182] Also Gen. 2:7; Deut. 30:17f; Rom. 6:23; cf. 6:9; 7:6, 13. For a discussion about different explanations of the origin of death in Jewish literature see Wedderburn,

The Qualifiers of the Metaphor of 'Death' 121

explaining Romans 6:6. Paul's relevant affirmationsarein5:12-14, 15b, 16b, 17a, 18a, 19a, 21a.

The way in which this paragraph of 5:12-21 relates to what was said before is a matter of dispute. The meaning of διὰ τοῦτο from 5:12 is at the heart of this debate. Any solution has to do justice to what was said before, to what is said in the pericope 5:12-21 itself, and to the natural meaning of the phrase 'for this reason'.[161] Scholars agree that διὰ τοῦτο is a marker of an inference drawn from something in the preceding argument, but here the agreement stops, because it is not very clear to what from the preceding argument Paul refers when using διὰ τοῦτο.[162] Do we have here a conclusion drawn from 5:1-11[163] or from 1:16-5:11,[164] or is the phrase merely transitional, introducing a new stage as a conclusion from the preceding argument?[165] It is difficult to differentiate between these because the content of 5:12-21 is a 'development of what precedes,'[166] an 'overview' of the whole situation in the history of salvation where the results of the sin of Adam and of humankind were overthrown by the work of God in Christ. From these, it is natural to include from the previous argument of the letter those points which are on these lines,[167] especially as these are shown in 5:17 (18, 21): the theme of 'righteousness' (see 1:16-17; 3:21-26) and also the 'teaching of assurance of final salvation'[168] in 5:1-11 (2, 9-10).[169]

The contrast which Paul institutes between Adam and Christ in 5:12 is not completed until 5:18-21. In his 'giant anacoluthon'[170] of 5:13-17 (13-14; 15-17) he introduces intermediate thoughts[171] which will be reiterated in relation to the law in 5:20.[172]

---

[161] Also Moo, *Romans*, 318.

[162] See a detailed discussion of the views in Moo, *Romans*, 318.

[163] Cranfield, *Romans*, 271; Käsemann, *Romans*, 146; S. Lewis Johnson, Jr., 'Romans 5.12 - An Excercise in Exegesis and Theology', in Richard N. Longenecker and Merrill C. Tenney, eds, *New Dimensions in New Testament Study* (Grand Rapids, Michigan: Zondervan, 1974), 301; Moo, *Romans*, 318.

[164] Wright, *Climax*, 35; Dunn, *Romans*, 272; Becker, *Paul*, 355 'brings 1:18-4:25 to a conclusion.'

[165] Ulrich Wilckens, *Der Brief an die Römer* (1; Zürich, Neukirchen/Vluyn: Neukirchener, Benziger, 1978), 314.

[166] Käsemann, *Romans*, 141.

[167] See also Sanday and Headlam, *Romans*, 131; S.E. Porter, 'The Pauline Concept of Original Sin in Light of Rabbinic Background', *TynB* 41 (1990) 21; de Boer, *Defeat of Death*, 145, 146.

[168] Moo, *Romans*, 316; also Stuhlmacher, *Romans*, 83; Watson, *Paul, Judaism*, 146.

[169] See also Käsemann, *Romans*, 155.

[170] Käsemann, *Romans*, 146.

[171] See also Cranfield, *Romans*, 270.

[172] Cf. Stuhlmacher, *Romans*, 83.

argument in Rom. 5:12-21 the 'dominion of sin' is the final word of the argument when Paul says: 'ἵνα ὥσπερ ἐβασίλευσεν ἡ ἁμαρτία ἐν τῷ θανάτῳ' (5:21a). This is 'the resulting environment' of the sin of Adam and of all men.

Thus, this subsection will be organised as follows: a) a discussion about the relationship between Rom. 6:1-11 and 5:12-21, b) an analysis of the role of Adam and his sin in relation to humanity in 5:12-21, c) a discussion on the meaning of σῶμα in Rom. 6:6, and d) the integration of the data in relation to Rom. 6:6.

THE RELATIONSHIP BETWEEN ROMANS 6:1-11 AND ROMANS 5:12-21

This section is needed in order to see, at this point in our argument, how 'the Adam side' of the discussion from Rom. 5:12-21 relates to the ideas of 'our old man' and 'slavery of sin' in Rom. 6:1-11. The rhetorical question of Rom. 6:1 (Τί οὖν ἐροῦμεν;) looks back to what precedes it,[155] and it can be seen as pointing to a conclusion that might be drawn from the previous discussion.[156] Here it points to a false conclusion (ἐπιμένωμεν τῇ ἁμαρτίᾳ, ἵνα ἡ χάρις πλεονάσῃ), but what follows in Rom. 6 is mainly an amplification of the 'how much more' argument of 5:12-21[157] opposed to the resulting reality of the 'slavery of sin' (Rom. 6:6, 12, 14, 16, 17, 18, 19, 20, 22) of 'the Adam side' of the argument from there.[158] As Käsemann put it: 'The apostle stands before the task of making intelligible in terms of the reality of everyday life, of the community, and of the individual, the universal realization of eschatological life which he has set forth in ch. 5.'[159] The 'walking in the newness of life' is to be defined in relation to the environment set up by Adam, an environment which is still present. In Rom. 6:1-11 he defines the relationship with sin using the language of 'death'.

ADAM'S SIN AND HUMANKIND'S SIN IN ROMANS 5:12-21

In studying this section, in which Paul 'seems to assume that his readers are well aware of what is he describing',[160] we need to understand the 'Adam side' of the argument in order to be able to build a background of ideas for

---

[155] Elliott, *Rhetoric*, 236.

[156] Cf. Elliott, *Rhetoric*, 238.

[157] Cf. Elliott, *Rhetoric*, 239.

[158] See also Moo, *Romans*, 350; the accent is not so much that 'Paul picks up the contrast of death and life from 5.21 and describes it in further detail', Fitzmyer, *Romans*, 430.

[159] Käsemann, *Romans*, 159.

[160] Alexander John Maclagan Wedderburn, *Adam and Christ: An Investigation Into the Background of 1 Corinthians XV and Romans V 12-21* (PhD Dissertation University of Cambridge, 1970), 212; A.J.M. Wedderburn, 'The Theological Structure of Romans V.12', *NTS* 19 (1972-73) 340.

which Paul again and again speaks of sin)'.¹⁵¹ Tannehill's position is on the same line of 'belonging to' when he says that 'destruction of the "old man" in the cross of Christ meant the death of the believers as men of the old aeon. He is speaking of the destruction of the dominion of sin, of which all believers were a part.'¹⁵² Käsemann understands it as being 'Adam individualized and represented in us' and 'σῶμα τῆς ἁμαρτίας means the same thing from the standpoint of fallenness.'¹⁵³

These positions are not so much 'only conclusions' of some detailed studies provided by these scholars but very much the study of ὁ παλαιὸς ἄνθρωπος phrase itself.

Towards an Understanding of the Meaning of ὁ παλαιὸς ἄνθρωπος

Even if Paul says that the fact of the co-crucifixion of our ὁ παλαιὸς ἄνθρωπος is a *known* idea, we do not have other New Testament examples outside the Pauline corpus in which this phrase is used. It is possible that this teaching of the 'co-crucifixion of our old man' was a part of his λόγος τοῦ σταυροῦ (1 Cor. 1:18). 'The message about the cross,' as this is seen especially in the Corinthian correspondence and Galatians, was a known message (1 Cor. 1:17; Gal. 5:11; 6:12,14). Looking at this phrase from the point of view of the verb ((συ)σταυρόω), there is an example in Pauline corpus, but it is not ὁ παλαιὸς ἄνθρωπος which is used, but 'I': Gal. 2:19: Χριστῷ συνεσταύρωμαι.¹⁵⁴ This example points to the fact that the subject of 'co-crucifixion' can be described from different points of view depending on context. In our text it is the discussion about the Adam from the previous paragraph of 5:12-21 which has a role in the lexical choice in Rom. 6:6.

Also, Rom. 6:6 is the first time when Paul says something about ἁμαρτία after announcing in 6:2 the thesis to be defended in Rom 6:1-11, ἀπεθάνομεν τῇ ἁμαρτίᾳ. The text goes like this: τοῦτο γινώσκοντες ὅτι ὁ παλαιὸς ἡμῶν ἄνθρωπος συνεσταυρώθη, ἵνα καταργηθῇ τὸ σῶμα τῆς ἁμαρτίας, τοῦ μηκέτι δουλεύειν ἡμᾶς τῇ ἁμαρτίᾳ· His mention of ἁμαρτία is in the phrase τὸ σῶμα τῆς ἁμαρτίας. This phrase is important for a good understanding of ὁ παλαιὸς ἄνθρωπος because a particular action in relation to the second (συσταυρόω) leads to a particular result (καταργέω) in relation to the first. Here also will be included a discussion on σῶμα. The whole discussion is developed against the background of 'slavery of sin' (6:6c). Looking at the Adam side of the

---

[151] Ridderbos, *Paul*, 208.
[152] Tannehill, *Dying*, 30.
[153] Käsemann, *Romans*, 170.
[154] Also Gal. 6:14 can be relevant because of its reference to the κόσμος (in Rom. 5:12-21 κόσμος also has a particular role to be discussed): ἐμοὶ δὲ μὴ γένοιτο καυχᾶσθαι εἰ μὴ ἐν τῷ σταυρῷ τοῦ κυρίου ἡμῶν Ἰησοῦ Χριστοῦ, δι' οὗ ἐμοὶ κόσμος ἐσταύρωται κἀγὼ κόσμῳ.

The meaning of the phrase in Colossians is debated along similar lines: either the accent is put upon the fact that this expression is 'a way of indicating a whole way of life, a way of life prior to and characterized by the sort of vices listed in 3:5,8',[140] or the accent is on the fact that the phrase has 'the corporate associations denoting an old... order of existence'.[141]

These two lines of interpretation are present also in the exegesis of Rom. 6:6, even if in many cases they are mixed together, the second being understood in relation to the first. That is why in many cases the distinction is not clear. For example, Nygren understands this phrase as meaning 'the man who belongs to "the old aeon" and is characterised by its nature',[142] but Murray understands it as meaning 'the old self or ego, the unregenerate man in his entirety...'[143] Cranfield says that 'the phrase denotes rather the whole man as controlled by sin [...]. τὸ σῶμα τῆς ἁμαρτίας and ὁ παλαιὸς ἡμῶν ἄνθρωπος are thus identical, the only difference being that the use of σῶμα places more stress on the aspect of the sinful man as an individual, the self as an organized whole.'[144] Ziesler considers that the phrase means 'the whole person, the old man (6:6a), that has been under the control of sin.'[145] Fitzmyer says that 'Paul uses *palaios* to characterize the condition of human life prior to baptism and conversion' and explains it further as meaning 'humanity in its adamic condition'.[146] And Leenhardt says that 'this old man, this decadent being is ourselves considered in our status as sons of Adam; [...] παλαιός [...] qualifies what belongs to the economy of Adam'.[147] Martin says that 'the "old man" (Rom. 6:6), is ourselves in union with Adam';[148] Dunn says that 'παλαιὸς ἄνθρωπος is man belonging to the age of Adam, dominated by sin and death,'[149] and 'the reference is to Christians ("*our* old man") for whom the domination of sin has been broken by their identification with Christ's death'.[150] Ridderbos understands the phrase as being 'intended [...] not as the individual past of believers in their unconverted state, but as the supra-individual sinful mode of existence (entirely in harmony with the manner in

---

Commentary on Ephesians (Edinburgh: T&T Clark, 1998), 436.

[140] James D. G. Dunn, *The Epistles to the Collossians and to Philemon: A Commentary on the Greek Text* (Grand Rapids, Carlisle: W. B. Eerdmans, The Paternoster Press, 1996), 220.

[141] Peter T. O'Brien, *Colossians, Philemon* (Waco, Texax: Word, 1982), 189; see also Tannehill, *Dying,* 51.

[142] Nygren, *Romans,* 234.

[143] Murray, *Romans*, 220.

[144] Cranfield, *Romans*, 309.

[145] Ziesler, *Romans,* 159, 160.

[146] Fitzmyer, *Romans*, 436.

[147] Leenhardt, *Romans*, 161.

[148] Martin, *Christ and the Law,* 196.

[149] Dunn, *Romans,* 318.

[150] Dunn, *Romans*, 318.

relation to the role of Adam in providing an understanding of humanity Paul is near to other Jewish writers. We will study them especially at the point where they discuss the relation between Adam, his sin and humankind. In the literature on Romans 6:6 we did not find a detailed study of this phrase, but only 'affirmations' about its meaning, and the purpose of this section is to provide such a study.

Therefore, this section will be organised in two main subsections: 1) a presentation of the proposed meanings for ὁ παλαιὸς ἄνθρωπος, and 2) an argument toward an understanding of the meaning of the phrase ὁ παλαιὸς ἄνθρωπος.

A Presentation of the Proposed Meanings for ὁ παλαιὸς ἄνθρωπος
This subsection is organised as follows: first, an analysis of other places where this phrase occurs in the ancient writings which we have, and second a presentation of the different positions concerning the meaning of this phrase in Rom. 6:6.

In our search for other places where this phrase was used in existing ancient literature[131] we found only[132] those known examples from the Pauline corpus, namely, Col 3:9 (μὴ ψεύδεσθε εἰς ἀλλήλους, ἀπεκδυσάμενοι τὸν παλαιὸν ἄνθρωπον σὺν ταῖς πράξεσιν αὐτοῦ.) and Eph 4:22 (ἀποθέσθαι ὑμᾶς κατὰ τὴν προτέραν ἀναστροφὴν τὸν παλαιὸν ἄνθρωπον τὸν φθειρόμενον κατὰ τὰν ἐπιθυμίας τῆς ἀπάτης...). There is no similar *metaphorical* usage outside the Pauline corpus for this phrase of 'old man'. In relation to the meaning of it in Ephesians, the most detailed discussion can be found in the commentary of M. Barth[133] where he argues that 'the old man is Adam'[134], namely 'those invested with the characteristics of Adam's fall and death...'.[135] Some authors do not emphasise so much the role of Adam as the 'representative of the human race'[136] without Christ and all humankind as being related to him as the head is related to the body,[137] but they emphasise the idea of 'old personality'[138] as this lives 'under the present evil age and its powers'.[139]

---

[131] We searched TLG database, Judaic Classics Library and Dead Sea Scrolls databases.

[132] See also Jacob Jervell, *Imago Dei* (Göttingen: Vandenhoeck & Ruprecht, 1960), 240ff.

[133] See his discussion 'From the Old Man to the New', M. Barth, *Ephesians* (New York:: Doubleday, 1974), 536-45.

[134] Barth, *Ephesians,* 539.

[135] Barth, *Ephesians,* 539.

[136] Barth, *Ephesians,* 538.

[137] Barth, *Ephesians,* 538.

[138] R. Schnackenburg, *Ephesians* (Helen Heron, tr; Edinburgh: T&T Clark, 1991), 200; A. Lincoln, *Ephesians* (Dallas: Word, 1990), 283.

[139] Lincoln, *Ephesians,* 285; see also Ernest Best, *A Critical and Exegetical*

be left out'.¹²¹ The proposal of these two scholars is important but it is not complete.

The position expressed by Käsemann that 'σύμφυτος, originally an organic term, gradually weakened in sense to "connected" and finally came to indicate only the hyphen between things which does not even presuppose a personal relation'¹²² is unjustified based on the examples given above in which the meanings of σύμφυτος are not 'weakened' but point to a particular kind of 'union'.

The suggestions of Sanday and Headlam that 'we are become one with Christ as the graft becomes one with the tree into which it grows,'¹²³ and that 'the word exactly expresses the process by which a graft becomes united with the life of a tree'¹²⁴ are criticised by Cranfield who says that 'the quite numerous occurrences of the word do not provide the evidence of its having had special associations with grafting.' He proposes the translation 'united' or 'assimilated'.¹²⁵ His observation in relation to Sanday and Headlam's position is correct but his proposal is too general keeping in view the rich imagery of σύμφυτος and the complexity of the argument in Rom. 6:1-11. Schnackenburg,¹²⁶ Fitzmyer,¹²⁷ BAGD,¹²⁸ and Elliger,¹²⁹ among others, understand the term as 'grown together'.

Thus, in the light of our argument from above the metaphor of σύμφυτος from Romans 6:5 describes a *coalescence* which results in a *unity* in which each component/partner preserves its character. If one of these 'partners' is removed or union broken up both wither away.

ὁ παλαιὸς ἄνθρωπος Metaphor (Romans 6:6)

In Romans 6:1-11 the subject who experiences 'death' is ὁ παλαιὸς ἡμῶν ἄνθρωπος. This phrase will be studied as a metaphor in which the pericope of 5:12-21 has an important role since it presents the way in which Paul understood who we 'once' were.¹³⁰ Adam has a particular role in this. In

---

¹²¹ Spicq, 'σύμφυτος, συμφύω,' 323.

¹²² Käsemann, *Romans*, 167.

¹²³ William Sanday and Arthur C. Headlam, *A Critical and Exegetical Commentary on the Epistle to the Romans* (Edinburgh: T. and T. Clark, 1902), 154.

¹²⁴ Sanday and Headlam, *Romans*, 157.

¹²⁵ Cranfield, *Romans*, 307.

¹²⁶ Schnackenburg, *Baptism*, 48.

¹²⁷ Fitzmyer, *Romans*, 435.

¹²⁸ BAGD, 780,

¹²⁹ W. Elliger, 'σύμφυτος', in Horst Balz and Gerhard Schneider, eds, *Exegetical Dictionary of the New Testament* (3; Grand Rapids, Michigan: Wm. B. Eerdmans, 1993), 290.

¹³⁰ Käsemann says that 'παλαιὸς ἄνθρωπος, [...] comes from Adam-Christ typology'; Käsemann, *Romans*, 170.

more detailed, this will be analysed here. Dunn says that it 'is more probable that Paul has in mind the more general biological imagery of the physical and natural growth which, for example, unites in unbroken wholeness the broken edges of a wound or a bone.'[116] He quotes in support of this position only the examples from Liddell and Scott.[117] He says that

> our union with Christ, [...], was like the grafting of a branch on to the main stem so that they become one, or like the healing of wound so that the body is whole; more precisely, it was the coming together of us and the ὁμοίωμα of Christ's death, so that henceforth we were indivisibly united with it in continuing growth and development.[118]

Dunn analyses this metaphor of σύμφυτος as being a depiction of the spiritual reality of death to sin (and life to God).[119]

From the analysis provided above it is clear that the imagery of σύμφυτος is rich, but because the verb usage points mainly to those physical aspects such as healing of a bone or wound, it would be better to give priority to the adjectival usage in relation to the domain of ideas. This is why the present discussion will follow the ideas related to σύμφυτος mainly in a botanical/zoological context. The most relevant examples from Theophrastus and Aristotle also point in that direction. The verb usage is integrated at the aspect of 'union', an aspect which is also retained/communicated by the σύμφυτος. The rich and exact content of σύμφυτος is not fully exploited by Dunn. He restricts his position to the physical aspect, but this 'restriction' is not justified either by the complexity of ideas present in Rom. 6:1-11 or by the rich image of σύμφυτος.

Leenhardt says that

> it is true to say of the baptized Christian that he is as closely associated with the crucified Christ as the young branch is with the trunk to which it is grafted. The image is a very strong one; it brings out the communication of vitality from the trunk to the new branch, [...] The image of the vine and the branches (John 15) has the same point. [...] We have become one single plant.[120]

Spicq argues for the fact that the ideas present in the text of Plutarch *Lyc.* 25:2 ('Lycurgus [...] trained the citizens 'always to form one body with the community like bees, clustered around their leader') form the backround for a good understanding of Rom. 6:5. He also says that the idea of 'growth must not

---

[116] Dunn, *Baptism*, 141; cf. Dunn, *Romans*, 316.

[117] In his commentary the focus is especially on Hippocrates, *Aph.* 6:24; *Art.* 14; Soranus, 2:57.

[118] Dunn, *Baptism*, 141, 142.

[119] Dunn, *Baptism*, 140.

[120] Franz J. Leenhardt, *The Epistle to the Romans: A Commentary* (London: Lutterworth Press, 1961), 160.

his lexical choice of σύμφυτος is moulded by those charges (if we are of God and we are unfaithful will our faithlessness nullify the faithfulness of God?). The metaphor of σύμφυτος describes the following facts relevant for our text: two twigs are split and the halves of each put together and bound... for the halves *to coalesce*. It results in *a unity, but each component preserves its character*, drawing and concocting its food separately and sharing with the other nothing but coalescence. It results *a single nature* and this is why *if one of the partners is removed or union broken up both wither away*.

In line with the last aspect there is an example from Aristotle, *Historia Animalium*, 5:32:557b too

> There is also a small larva which is known as the faggot-bearer, as queer a creature as any of them: its head, which is mottled, projects outside its integument: its feet are at the tip, as in other larvae, but the remainder of its body is enclosed in a cobweb-like tunic, and round it are dry twigs, which look as though they had stuck on to it as it walked along. In fact, however, *they are integral part of its tunic* (ταῦτα δὲ σύμφυτα τῷ χιτῶνί ἐστιν) — just as the shell is an integral part of the snail, so is the whole integument with this larva — they do not drop off, but have to be torn off, as though they were organically attached to it; and if anyone removes the tunic the creature begins to die and becomes as helpless as a snail once its shell has been removed.[113]

Against this understanding of the σύμφυτος metaphor there are other positions which will be analysed.

The most drastic one, that of T. Schreiner,[114] says that in this passage 'the metaphor [of σύμφυτος] is a dead one'; he argues that it is so because there is no conception that believers are gradually growing into the likeness of Christ's death. The perfect tense of γεγόναμεν demonstrates this, as does the focus on the once-for-all nature of the death and resurrection of Christ. Thus the word σύμφυτοι means simply 'united''.[115]

This understanding of σύμφυτος 'mutilates' the multitude of images brought by this word. It is true that the context has to help the interpreter in selecting the relevant ones for understanding the role of the term in the argument, but the way in which Schreiner does this is not, we think, in line with the argument of the pericope as it was shown above. Moreover, Schreiner does not offer any analysis of the meaning of σύμφυτος but only tries to limit Dunn's position as this is expressed in his commentary (316).

One of the best known explanations of σύμφυτος in Romans is that of J. D. G. Dunn (as he expressed it both in *Baptism in the Holy Spirit*, and in *Romans 1-8*). Because in his commentary he reiterates the earlier position which is also

---

[113] Aristotle, *Historia Animalium* (A. L. Peck, trans.; Cambridge, Mass., London: Harvard University Press, William Heinemann Ltd, 1979).

[114] See also Wilckens, *Römer*, 13.

[115] Schreiner, *Romans*, 313.

[3] The same or much the same occurs also when the same tree bears pomegranates or apples of all sorts. For growers first soften up (so to speak) the twigs with the mallet *so that they may coalesce* (ἵνα συμφυῶσιν) because of the bruising, and then bind them together and plant them. The resulting tree is to be sure *a unity by reason of the coalescence* (ἐν τῇ συμφύσει), but each component preserves its character, drawing and concocting its food separately, *and sharing with the others nothing but coalescence* (οὐδὲ δὲ ἄλλω ἢ τῆς συμφύσεως κοινωνοῦν).

Much the same (one might say) occurs also in larger trees and especially those of a fluid nature: *thus the fig will entwine about another tree of this character and then coalesce with it and make a single trunk* (περιπλακεῖσα γὰρ συκῆ καιεῖ τι ἄλλο τοιοῦτόν ἐστι συμφύεταί τε καιἐν ποιεῖ τὸ στέλεχος).

Some such unions are produced by design, *but in others the trees come to coalesce in this way of their own accord* (ἔνια δὲ καὶ αὐτομάτως λαμβάνει τοιύτην σύμφυσιν), when they are friendly and not harmful to one another. For once they entwine and accept one another there results (as it were) a single nature. (καθάπερ φύσις τις αὕτη μία γίνεται). This is why if one of the partners is removed or the union broken up, both wither away, as also happens with trees that are not of the same kind when they sprout together and have been reared with one another, as we said of the tree-climbing vine and the fig. (But such plants as injure a tree by growing round it and into it, like the ivy, give rise to no single nature, since the tree withers away.)

And so we must suppose that these are the causes that make the sort of tree we are discussing bear several sorts of fruit. For the case is in a way similar to that of grafting a single tree with buds from several trees of different kinds. For this last procedure takes a single entity and produces a plurality of starting-points and of natures from it, whereas the former takes several starting-points and produces from them an entity that is unitary in its nature.

Such an extensive discussion as this provides us with some important connotations attached to σύμφυτος. The relevant elements will be selected keeping in view the place which this term has in the argument of Rom. 6:1-11 — Paul's answer to the charge of 6:1 in 6:2. In favor of his answer, in 6:5 he speaks about Christians' relationship with the 'representation' of Christ's death. His way of saying *that* has to keep in view the fact that sin is 'an impossible possibility',[112] that the union is real and brings life, and that the presence of sin does not say anything about the character of God and of Christ. This last aspect is very much in view in Rom. 3:2-8 (see also the charge in Gal. 2:17: 'but if in our effort to be justified in Christ, we ourselves have been found to be sinners, is Christ then a servant of sin?'). In Rom. 6:1-11 Paul answers that charge and

---

[112] J.C. Beker, *Paul the Apostle: The Triumph of God in Life and Thought* (Edinburgh: T. & T. Clark, 1980), 215.

designate everything perceived, thus easily acquiring memories and concepts of innumerable things. [29] How, then, could they have remained ignorant and conceived no inkling of him who had sowed and planted and was now preserving and nourishing them, when on every side they were filled with the divine nature through both sight and hearing, and in fact through every sense? They dwelt upon earth, they beheld the light of heaven, they had nourishment in abundance, for god, their ancestor, had lavishly provided and prepared it to their hand.[109]

And Plato, *Phaedrus* 246d:

> the whole, compounded of soul and body, is called a living being, and is further designated as mortal. It is not immortal by any reasonable supposition, but we have, though we have never seen or rightly conceived a god, imagined an immortal being which has both a soul and a body which are *united* for all time (ἀθάνατόν τι ζῷον, ἔχον μεψυχήν, ἔχον δεσῶμα, τὸν ἀειδεχρόνον ταῦτα συμπεφυκόντα).

In both these texts the idea conveyed by συμφύω is that of a 'very close relationship', 'a union'. At this point there are some more relevant examples, namely those which refer to the healing of fractured bones, Hippocrates, *Artic.* 14: 'The clavicle mends quickly, as do all the other spongy bones' (also Soranus (*Gyn.* 4:5:1)), and severed intestines, Hippocrates, *Aphorisms*, 6:24 'If one of the smaller intestines be severed it does not unite (οὐ συμφύεται).'

However, the example which brings the most detailed image concerning the range of ideas behind the usage of σύμφυτος is found in Theophrastus, *De Causis Plantarum*, 5:5:1,2[110] (c. 371 - c. 287 BC)

[...]

> Grape clusters without pits are grown by removing the core, from which the pit is produced. The vine is made to bear from the same twig both white and black clusters, or the cluster itself both white and black grapes, when two twigs are split and the halves of each (except for the lower part) put together and bound and the whole is then set in the ground, *for the halves to coalesce* (συμφύεται γὰρ ἀλλήλοις). *For anything alive can coalesce with what is alive* (σύμφυτον μεγὰρ ἅπαν τὸ ζῶν τῷ ζῶντι) (and especially if the source is a plant of the same kind) when a wound has been made, and the result is (in a sense) a single nature.[111] But each of the two component shoots also transmits its food separately (and since this is not intermingled, each brings forth its own fruit), which is what rivers do when they meet, like the Cephisus and Melas in Boeotia: each flows in a separate current. In the vine however the two currents do not even meet, but the food for each part flows in a separate and parallel channel.

---

[109] Dio Chrysostom, *Discourses* (XII; J. W. Cohoon, trans.; Cambridge, Mass., London: Harvard University Press, William Heinemann Ltd, 1939).

[110] These examples were found through search in the TLG database.

[111] μία τι φύσις

in 104 BC, *P.Lips* 1:5 (contract for a sale of real estate): ἀμπελῶνα συμφύτου means not a vineyard where (fruit) trees have been planted but one that is fully cultivated (cf. ἀσύμφυτος = not worked, abandoned, *P.Lond.* 1296,18) which, beginning with the third century BC, use this term for cultivated land, no matter what sort of crop it is sown with, *P.Mich.* 311, 13 (AD 34), εἰς χόρτου σπορὰν σύνφυται καὶ κωπὴν ξηρασίας; 562,18 (AD 119): 'Sabinus, son of Socrates, shall return two fully cultivated *arourai* of olive trees' (ἀρούρας δύο ἐλαιῶνος συμφύτους).[108]

This idea of 'unity' is also present in the example from Plutarch, *Lycurgus* 25:3.

In a word, he trained his fellow-citizens to have neither the wish nor the ability to live for themselves; but like bees they were to make themselves always *integral parts* of the whole community (ἀλλ' ὥσπερ τὰς μελίττας τῷ κοινῷ συμφυεῖς ὄντας ἀεί), clustering together about their leader, almost beside themselves with enthusiasm and noble ambition, and to belong wholly to their country.

From the verb usage the following text from Dio Chrysostom, *The Twelfth, or Olympic, Discourse: On Man's First Conception of God*, 27-29 is relevant for our discussion.

[27] Now concerning the nature of the gods in general, and especially that of the ruler of the universe, first and foremost an idea regarding him and a conception of him common to the whole human race, to the Greeks and to the barbarians alike, a conception that is inevitable and innate in every creature endowed with reason, arising in the course of nature without the aid of human teacher and free from the deceit of any expounding priest, has made its way, and it rendered manifest God's kinship with man and furnished many evidences of the truth, which did not suffer the earliest and most ancient men to doze and grow indifferent to them; for inasmuch as these earlier men were not living dispersed far away from the divine being or beyond his borders apart by themselves, [28] but *had grown up* (πεφυκότες) in the very centre of things, or *rather had grown up in his company and had remained close to him in every way* (μᾶλλον δὲ συμπεφυκότες ἐκείνῳ καὶ προσεχόμενοι πάντα τρόπον), they could not for any length of time continue to be unintelligent beings, especially since they had received from him intelligence and the capacity for reason, illuminated as they were on every side by the the divine and magnificent glories of heaven and the stars of sun and, moon, by night and by day encountering varied and dissimilar experiences, seeing wondrous sights and hearing manifold voices of winds and forest and rivers and sea, of animals tame and wild; while they themselves uttered a most pleasing and clear sound, and taking delight in the proud and intelligent quality of the human voice, attached symbols to the objects that reached their senses, so as to be able to name and

---

[107] Cf. Spicq, 'σύμφυτος, συμφύω,' 321.

[108] Spicq, 'σύμφυτος, συμφύω,' 321-2.

The meaning of σύμφυτος is difficult[103] to discern because a) here it is used metaphorically and b) is a *hapax legomenon* in the N.T. The usage is metaphorical because this term, used usually in an agricultural/biological context, is used here to describe a relation between Christians and the 'representation' of[104] Christ's death. This section will explore the input brought by this metaphor for understanding that *relationship/union*.

This word is used in the LXX with the meanings 'innate' or 'inborn' (3 Macc. 3:22)[105] 'cultivated/planted' (Amos 9:13)[106] and 'thickly grown' (Zech. 11:2):

> Let the pine howl, because the cedar has fallen; for the mighty men have been greatly afflicted: howl, ye oaks of the land of Basan; for the thickly planted [grown (?)] forest has been torn down (ὅτι κατεσπάσθη ὁ δρυμὸς ὁ σύμφυτος).

Here this word describes the united power of the cedars as a result of growing together as a forest. The usage in papyri is in 'accord'[107] with this 'agricultural' setting. For example

---

88; against *Fitzmyer, Romans,* 435: 'the expression is probably elliptical, and the dat. is better taken as a dat. of instrument, referring to baptismal washing as the means of growing together;' He argues on these lines because he asks: 'can one grow together with a likeness?' (435) He fails to put together the whole phrase because the meaning of σύμφυτος is not 'grow together' but 'be one with' and also the whole 'image' conveyed by ὁμοίωμα is not explored.

[103] About this difficulty see also Käsemann, *Romans,* 167.

[104] See discussion on ὁμοίωμα in the previous chapter.

[105] 'But they received this in a sense opposite to that intended, and in their inborn malice (τῇ συμφύτῳ κακοηθείᾳ) rejected the good, inclining, as they constantly do, to the base'. Moses Hadas, ed and trans, *The Third and Fourth Books of Maccabees* (New York: Ktav Publishing House, Inc., 1953), RSV translates 'innate malice'.
Other examples in Greek literature are: 'Hippocrates, Vict. 42:2 'innate heat'; 87:1: 'surplus of fullness or of evacuation of natural substances'; Genit. 3:1: 'Man possesses in himself a number of congenital humors' (συμφυέας); 3 Macc. 3:22 - τῇ συμφύτῳ κακοηθείᾳ τὸ καλὸν ἀπωσάμενοι;Philo, Creation 18: the memory that is innate in the architect; Heir. 272, the evils that are congenital to our race; Abraham 160, epithymia is a beast that lives in us (τὸ σύμφυτον ἡμῖν θρέμμα); Moses 1:198, ἐπιείκεια and φιλανθρωπία are connatural to God, hence are divine attributes; Josephus, *Ag. Apion* 1:42: 'It is natural to the Jews (σύμφυτόν ἐστιν), from their birth, to regard these as divine decrees'; Antiphon the Sophist: τῇ φύσει ξυμφύτων (P.Oxy. 1364,44)'. (cf. Ceslas O.P. Spicq, 'σύμφυτος, συμφύω', in *Theological Lexicon of the New Testament* (3; James D. Ernest, trans.; Peabody, Mass.: Hendrickson, 1994), 321)

[106] 'Behold the days come, saith the Lord, when the harvest shall overtake the vintage, and the grapes shall ripen at seedtime; and the mountains shall drop sweet wine, and all the hills shall be planted [cultivated ?] (καὶ πάντες οἱ βουνοὶ σύμφυτοι ἔσονται·). 14 And I will turn the captivity of my people Israel, and they shall rebuild the ruined cities, and shall inhabit them; and they shall plant vineyards (καὶ φυτεύσουσιν ἀμπελῶνας), and shall drink wine from them'; (Brenton's translation).

person is discussed or has to be understood specifically in relation to[94] a particular event from the life of that person (his death).[95] Apparently this aspect is not evident to his addressees.[96] The discussion is expanded according to his purpose[97] in this passage, that is, of sustaining his thesis (ἀπεθάνομεν τῇ ἁμαρτίᾳ) against the charge in 6:1.

With the exception of the συνετάφημεν metaphor, Paul, in his argument so far, does not say anything specific about the *relationship* with Christ in his death. He has not yet defined that particular type of relationship. This is the role of Rom. 6:5, where in speaking about this, Paul (again) uses a metaphor (σύμφυτος) and also a particular understanding of Christ's death.[98] Understanding of this other metaphor is the purpose of the following section.

σύμφυτος Metaphor (Romans 6:5)

There are explanations in Rom. 6:5[99] which develop and clarify[100] what was said in 6:2-4.[101] We treat τῷ ὁμοιώματι together with σύμφυτοι as being a natural reading (a dative following a συν- word).[102]

---

second is 'involved' in the first.

[94] Wedderburn says here that 'it is by no means clear that 'into his death' is a figurative extension of being dipped into water rather than an extension of the idea of being united with a person, an extension of it to a being caught up in the events of that person's life', Wedderburn, *Baptism,* 59. It can be seen that he is still on the same line with others in understanding 'baptism' as a 'killing' or 'destroying' image, but we showed that the cotext of the letter leads the interpretation in a different direction, namely, that of being 'overwhelmed by'. See the argument above.

[95] It is not very clear that 'the apostle was correcting the tradition of the community here,' (Käsemann, *Romans,* 161). Schlatter says that 'it is possible that the believer did not at the time of baptism yet to recognise certain conduct as reprehensible, but later it is understood as sinful.' Schlatter, *Romans,* 137; and Fitzmyer that 'Roman Christians, instructed in apostolic catechesis, should be aquainted with the sublime effects of baptism' Fitzmyer, *Romans,* 433; Wedderburn says that 'at the basis of Christian baptism is our involvement in a death of Christ that occurred 'once and for all time' (Rom. 6:10)', this is true but it is not so much 'our involvement' as us 'being involved' there because this 'overwhelming action of God' which leads us toward that Christ in his death.' Wedderburn, *Baptism,* 390.

[96] Cf. Hartman, *Into the Name,* 70.

[97] Also Kaye, *Structure,* 60.

[98] For the discussion of τῷ ὁμοιώματι τοῦ θανάτου αὐτοῦ see the previous chapter.

[99] For a detailed discussion about the syntactical problems of this verse see Cranfield, *Romans,* 305-8.

[100] See also Moo, *Romans,* 368; Cranfield understands it as a confirmation of the preceding affirmation. Cranfield, *Romans,* 306.

[101] See also Dunn, *Romans,* 330.

[102] Also Cranfield, *Romans,* 307; Dunn, *Romans,* 316; Schnackenburg, *Baptism,* 46; Wilckens, *Römer,* 13; M. Black, *Romans* (London: Marshall, Morgan and Scott, 1973),

βάπτισμα its proper, normal role, namely, that of showing that here it is a metaphor, as it was in 6:3. The verb συνθάπτω is too far for interpreting εἰς τὸν θάνατον with it[88]; also the almost similar phrase from 6:3 (εἰς τὸν θάνατον αὐτοῦ ἐβαπτίσθημεν) is in favour of interpreting βάπτισμα with εἰς τὸν θάνατον.

Moreover this point of contact ('overwhelmed by') points in another direction, that of 'conquest', namely, the victorious result of a previous continuous action.[89] The affirmation in Rom. 2:4 helps us to see the continuing action of God toward humanity for receiving 'the abundance of grace' (cf. 5:19). There Paul says: 'Do you despise the riches of his kindness and forbearence and patience? Do you not realize that God's kindness is meant to lead you to repentance?' God's kindness is meant *to lead* people to repentance. The 'victory' of this action means the beginning of the Christian life as it is shown in baptism. The *specific* point of Rom. 6:3 is that this 'overwhelming by' God is toward *Christ's death*.

Christ's death, as we saw,[90] is mainly depicted as that event in which the effects of sin were 'ruined' (Rom. 6:9-10). He died as the Anointed King in order to gain the liberation of his people from the bondage of sin. This is a 'liberating deed' of the King for his people. What he did he did for the benefit of his people. In other words it is an event from which someone else can gain benefits. Towards this 'liberating' event accomplished by the representative of the people of God, God overwhelms us for sharing in its benefits. The qualifiers εἰς Χριστὸν Ἰησοῦν and εἰς τὸν θάνατον αὐτοῦ are used for showing us the *direction* and *destination*[91] of this overwhelming action of God. Paul starts from something known[92] (ἢ ἀγνοεῖτε ὅτι, ὅσοι ἐβαπτίσθημεν εἰς Χριστὸν Ἰησοῦν) which is detailed and focused on a particular (eschatological) event (εἰς τὸν θάνατον αὐτοῦ ἐβαπτίσθημεν).[93] That event (baptism) in relation to a

---

[88] See also Cranfield, *Romans,* 304; Kasemann, *Romans,* 166; Moo, *Romans,* 361; Against Dunn, *Romans,* 314.

[89] See also Dunn, *Baptism,* 145-6: 'he surrenders himself to God.'

[90] See the previous chapter for a detailed discussion of this.

[91] Schlatter uses language of 'goal', but in relation to renunciation to sin. (Schlatter, *Romans,* 139). This is an integration of mention to 'baptism' in relation to the subject of the pericope.

[92] See G. R. Beasley-Murray, 'Dying and Rising with Christ', in Gerald F. Hawthorne, Ralph P. Martin and Daniel G. Reid, eds, *Dictionary of Paul and His Letters* (Downers Grove; Leicester: IVP, 1993), 219; Moo, *Romans,* 359; 'introduce traditional material', Ziesler, *Romans,* 156; 'apostolic catechesis' Fitzmyer, *Romans,* 433; also Wilckens, *Römer,* 8, 11; see the inference of this known fact in Cranfield, *Romans,* 300.

[93] See also Bruce Norman Kaye, *The Thought Structure of Romans with Special Reference to Chapter 6* (Austin, Texas: Schola Press, 1979), 60; Charles B. Cousar, *A Theology of the Cross: The Death of Jesus in the Pauline Letters* (Minneapolis: Fortress Press, 1990), 71; Kaye, 'Special Reference,' 284; Cranfield, *Romans,* 300, says that the

σωτηρίαν παντὶ τῷ πιστεύοντι... What God did in Christ's death is the manifestation of his saving power (δικαιοσύνη θεοῦ) toward every one who believes.[79]

If this interpretation is right, then Rom. 6:4a (συνετάφημεν οὖν αὐτῷ διὰ τοῦ βαπτίσματος εἰς τὸν θάνατον) is understood on the same lines, namely, this action of God toward us is the *means* of 'burial with Christ'. 'By baptism into death' is understood as a parallel affirmation to that in 6:3b. It is the same 'image' of 'overwhelming toward' Christ's death. Of course here, as in 6:3, there is, by this image of overwhelming, an *allusion* to the event of baptism (being covered by waters, either by immersion or by pouring from above), from which a metaphor is drawn. The reference of this metaphor is the reality of being 'encompassed by' God. In a sense 6:4a 'sharpens 6.3b'[80] showing the 'definitive character'[81] of this overwhelming action of God toward Christ's death. οὖν can be understood either as 'a marker of a conclusion of a process of reasoning', ('therefore'),[82] or as 'a marker of somewhat greater emphasis', ('surely', 'then')[83]. It is not clear whether 6:4a is a 'conclusion' in Paul's argument. Rather, 6:4a gives the argument a particular direction[84] (that of being buried with Christ) of the action of God previously mentioned and reiterated[85] here (διὰ τοῦ βαπτίσματος εἰς τὸν θάνατον); so, οὖν will be interpreted as a marker of emphasis: 'then, we were buried with.'

This metaphorical interpretation of 6:4b does not require entering that complex discussion in which 'reaching at' or 'sharing in' Christ's death is mediated by the rite of baptism (and not by faith) if the reference for διὰ τοῦ βαπτίσματος is the event of baptism per se, or that the answer of a person to the Gospel is baptismal and not in faith.[86] Sometimes 'baptism' was understood here as a 'shorthand' for the whole experience of conversion-initiation as a whole in which baptism is a part,[87] as a way of 'resolving' this dilemma, but there is no clear allusion to this 'comprehensive' way of speaking about this complex experience. It is better to give to the qualifier (εἰς τὸν θάνατον) of

---

[79] See also the language of 'being given over' to the binding doctrine of the gospel, which was revealed by God (6.17).

[80] Käsemann, *Romans*, 166.

[81] Käsemann, *Romans*, 166; also 'draws the conclusion' (idem 188).

[82] Cf. Louw and Nida, *Lexicon*, 783; so Hartman, *Into the Name*, 71.

[83] Cf. Louw and Nida, *Lexicon*, 812.

[84] It is not so much a clarification of the last clause of v.3 (Cranfield, *Romans*, 304), or an illustration of it (Schnackenburg, *Baptism*, 34), or a 'conclusion of the preceding statement' (Hartman, *Into the Name*, 71), but an emphasis on a particular fact from this event of death, namely 'burial'.

[85] Also Hartman, *Into the Name*, 71.

[86] See the discussion in Fitzmyer, *Romans*, 431.

[87] See e.g. R. H. Stein, *Difficult Passages in the Epistles* (Leicester: IVP, 1988), 119; Dunn, *Baptism*, 140; Douglas Moo, *Romans 1-8* (Chicago: Moody, 1991), 379-83; Moo, *Romans*, 366.

This point of comparison is sustained by one of the major lines of argumentation until here in the letter. In the previous pericope the πολλῷ μᾶλλον type of argument points in the same direction. The argument of 5:12-21 ends[75] like this: οὗ δὲ ἐπλεόνασεν ἡ ἁμαρτία **ὑπερεπερίσσευσεν** ἡ χάρις; that is, the manifestation of the overwhelming[76] powerful action of God [in the Coming One] to overthrow the effects of Adam's sin in the human race. In fact Paul's answer (formulated as a rhetorical question[77]) to the perversion of this insight is the main question discussed in Rom 6:1-11: Τί οὖν ἐροῦμεν; ἐπιμένωμεν τῇ ἁμαρτίᾳ, ἵνα ἡ χάρις **πλεονάσῃ**; His instant answer is μὴ γένοιτο. After this he explains why: οἵτινες ἀπεθάνομεν τῇ ἁμαρτίᾳ, πῶς ἔτι ζήσομεν ἐν αὐτῇ; (6:2b). The meaning of this 'death' is explained carefully in the following verses (3-11). We were overwhelmed by God toward (εἰς) Christ's death. God's grace does not 'overflow' if we sin, because God's grace already 'overflowed' when 'the Coming One'/Χριστός died. An 'overflowing' of grace towards us is not realised if we sin more but when we are 'overwhelmed by' God toward that event from the life of Χριστός, namely his death, where God's grace was given in abundance. Also, ὑπὸ χάριν from 6.14 says the same thing, that the believers are 'overwhelmed by God's grace'.

What can be said against this interpretation is that here Christ's death is the place of 'overflowing' of grace and that this is not so much directly 'toward' us, but the relation between this 'overwhelming' action of God in Christ's death and 'us' as being 'overwhelmed by' God toward Christ is explained in some aspects in Rom. 5:5-6. Our hope of sharing the glory of God (5:3) does not disappoint us, because God's love has been *poured* into our hearts through the Holy Spirit that has been given to us. This *pouring* of God's love toward us is explained as being manifested when Christ died for the ungodly; 'God proves his love for us that while we were sinners Christ died for us' (5:8). Paul uses the language of 'baptism' in Rom. 6:3-4 to point to the beginning of the Christian life when the rite of baptism was administered. He considers the event of baptism not as pointing to the fact that when the believer was 'covered by' waters (either by immersion or by outpouring from above[78]) he was 'buried' with Christ, but as an image of being 'overwhelmed by' God toward (εἰς) Christ's death, the place where God's grace was given in abundance.

This point of comparison is also sustained by the major idea announced in 1:16: οὐ γὰρ ἐπαισχύνομαι τὸ εὐαγγέλιον, **δύναμις γὰρ θεοῦ ἐστιν εἰς**

---

consequences'. Marshall, 'Baptize,' 131.

[75] See also Hartman, *Into the Name*, 69.

[76] ὑπερπερισσεύω: 'an extraordinary degree, involving a considerable excess over what would be expected'. Louw and Nida, *Lexicon*, 689; 'be present in greater abundance', BAGD, 841.

[77] Hartman rewrites it: 'No, we who died to sin cannot live in it any more'. Hartman, *Into the Name*, 70.

[78] See a discussion on the 'modes of baptism' in Marshall, 'Baptize,' 130-40.

envisaging the experience of judgment and tribulation that he [John the Baptist] expected the Coming One to introduce',[70] but according to Turner the point of contact is 'with the purpose for which the rite is performed. John baptised using water to wash and so to *cleanse* the repentant Israel of the contagion of sin; *mutatis mutandis*, the messiah will "cleanse it" in the fuller sense, that is, restore it as Utopian Zion.'[71] It is not the purpose of this section to enter into this debate here in Luke but this example was used to show that βαπτίζω has a metaphorical meaning whose *tenor* has to be discerned by a close analysis of the qualifiers used by the author to elucidate his metaphor.

Keeping in view these occurrences in Jewish writings (Isa. 21:4; *Ant.* 10:168-169; *War* 4:135-137) in which the figurative extension of the meaning of βαπτίζω as 'to be overwhelmed by' is found, we argue, as the point of comparison is concerned, that it is *an overwhelming* powerful action of God (*pictured* by the event of baptism).[72] It is generally accepted that the agent of the verb βαπτίζω here is God.[73] The preposition εἰς is 'a marker of an involved experiencer', being translated 'to, toward'. This point of comparison points in the same direction of meaning as the definition provided by Louw and Nida in their *Lexicon*: 'to cause someone to have a highly significant religious experience involving special manifestation of God's power and presence'.[74]

---

to all sides of the world.
In all their channels
a consuming fire shall destroy
every tree, green and barren, on their banks;'
Geza Vermes, *The Complete Dead Sea Scrolls in English* (London: Penguin Books Ltd, 1998).

[70] Dunn, 'Baptized as Metaphor,' 304; see also the discussion in Turner, *Power*, 171-5.

[71] Turner, *Power*, 183. Turner's earlier conclusion is different than this one, when he said: 'The point is not that the Holy Spirit is like a large expanse of water (nor indeed that baptizing with Spirit must be some kind of initiation, by analogy with Christian water baptism!), but that the future encounter with God's Holy Spirit-and-fire will be like an angry sea engulfing and sinking a boat, or like a massive surge of flood water suddenly sweeping down on a man as he attempts to cross the river, and overwhelming him.' Turner, 'Spirit Endowment,' 51. In this earlier understanding the accent is much on the 'sinking', 'sweeping down', 'overwhelming', and in the recent one the cotext receives a more important role focusing on 'purpose of the ritual', namely 'to cleanse the repentant Israel'.

[72] Either by immersion or by pouring from above; see Marshall, 'Baptize,' 130-40.

[73] See Cranfield, *Romans*, 303; Dunn, *Romans*, 314.

[74] Louw and Nida, *Lexicon*, 539. Marshall's understanding is on similar lines: '...not that we have been dipped in Christ or in his death, on the analogy of dipping into water, but rather that the fact of Christian baptism with water and its accompanying acts of faith and repentance brings us into a particular relationship with Jesus and his death. Here, therefore, the verb has lost its literal sense, although overtones of it still persist, and it refers more to the carrying out of a Christian initiation rite with spiritual

stole into poor Jerusalem— [136] a city under no commanding officer and one which, according to hereditary custom, unguardedly admitted all of Jewish blood, and the more readily at that moment when it was universally believed that all who were pouring into it came out goodwill as its allies. [137] Yet it was just this circumstance which, irrespectively of the sedition, eventually *wrecked* the city;[62] (ὃ δὴ καὶ δίχα τῆς στάσεως ὕστερον ἐβάπτισεν τὴν πόλιν·) for supplies which might have sufficed for the combatants were squandered upon a useless and idle mob, who brought upon themselves, in addition to the war, the miseries of sedition and famine.[63]

This image of 'overwhelming' (and 'devastation') communicated by βαπτίζω is used by Josephus in describing the suicide of Simon in *War* 2:476

After slaying every member of his family, he [Simon] stood conspicuous on the corpses, and with right hand uplifted to attract all eyes, *plunged* the sword up to the hilt into his own throat (ὅλον εἰς τὴν ἑαυτοῦ σφαγὴν ἐβάπτισεν τὸ ξίφος).[64]

This literal and metaphorical usage of βαπτίζω[65] is also found in the New Testament writings. In texts like Lk 3:16 both usages are present: 'I baptize you with water; but one who is more powerful than I is coming, (…). He will baptize you with the Holy Spirit and fire'.[66] The point of comparison of this metaphorical usage is under debate.[67] According to Dunn, the imagery of 'the baptism in the Spirit' here has to be understood on the similar lines as those expressed in Isa. 35:27-28[68] and 1QH 11 (formerly 3):29,[69] as being a way 'of

---

[62] Whiston translates here: 'although these very men, besides the seditions they raised, were otherwise the direct cause of the city's destruction also;' (our italics); Josephus.

[63] (Our italics); Josephus, *The Jewish War*, Books IV-VII (H. St. J. Thackeray, trans.; Cambridge, Mass.; London: Harvard University Press; William Heinemann Ltd, 1979).

[64] (Our italics); Josephus, *The Jewish War*, Books I-III.

[65] See discussion in Marshall, 'Baptize,' 130-40.

[66] For recent discussions of this passage and the meaning of 'baptised in the Spirit' see Dunn, 'Baptised as Metaphor,' 304; Turner, *Power*, 171-175; also Marshall, 'Baptise,' 131-2.

[67] See an analysis of it in Turner, *Power*, 180-3.

[68] 'See, the name of the LORD comes from far away,
burning with his anger, and in thick rising smoke;
his lips are full of indignation,
and his tongue is like a devouring fire;
[28]his breath is like an overflowing stream
that reaches up to the neck—
to sift the nations with the sieve of destruction,
and to place on the jaws of the
peoples a bridle that leads them astray.' (NRSV)
In LXX the beginning of verse 28 goes like this:
καὶ τὸ πνεῦμα αὐτοῦ ὡς ὕδωρ ἐν φάραγγι σῦρον ἥξει ἕως τοῦ τραχήλου.

[69] 'The torrents of Satan shall reach

This meaning of 'going under the water', 'immersion' is also used by Josephus when he speaks about the 'sinking' of the ship with which Jonah intended to flee, in *Ant.* 9:213-213

> At first they did not dare to do so, regarding it as an impious act to take a man who was a stranger and had entrusted his life to them, and cast him out to so certain death; but finally, as their distress pressed more heavily upon them and the vessel was on the point of *sinking*, (τελευταῖον δ' ὑπερβιαζομένου τοῦ κακοῦ καὶ ὅσον οὔπω μέλλοντος **βαπτίζεσθαι** τοῦ σκάφους) and since they were driven to it both by the prophet himself and by fear for their own lives, they cast him into the sea. And so the storm was stilled; as for Jonah, the story has it that he was swallowed by a whale and after three days and as many nights was cast up on the shore of the Euxine sea, still living and unharmed in body.[59]

This action of 'going under the water' is also used metaphorically by Josephus with the meaning of 'being overwhelmed by' alcohol or by a mob in the following examples: *Ant.* 10:168-169:

> And so Jōannēs and those of the leaders who were with him went away without being able to convince Gadalias. But, when a period of thirty days had elapsed, Ismaēlos came with ten men to Gadalias at the city of Masphatha, where he entertained them with a splendid banquet and presents and, in his cordial reception of Ismaēlos and those with him, went so far as to become drunk. [169] Seeing him in this condition, *sunken* into unconsciousness[60] and a drunken sleep, (θεασάμενος δ' αὐτὸν οὕτως ἔχοντα καὶ **βεβαπτισμένον** εἰς ἀναισθησίαν καὶ ὕπνον ὑπὸ τῆς μέθης) Ismaēlos sprang up with his ten friends and slaughtered Gadalias and those reclining with him at the banquet table;[61]

and *War* 4:135-137:

> ...In the end, satiated with their pillage of the country, the brigand chiefs of all these scattered bands joined forces and, now merged into one pack of villainy,

---

Heinemann Ltd, 1980).

[59] Josephus, *Jewish Antiquities*, Books IX-XI (Ralph Marcus, trans.; Cambridge, Mass.; London: Harvard University Press; William Heinemann Ltd, 1987); see also 'After this catastrophe of Cestius many distinguished Jews abandoned the city as swimmers desert a sinking ship' Μετὰ δὲ τὴν Κεστίου συμφορὰν πολλοὶ τῶν ἐπιφανῶν Ἰουδαίων ὥσπερ **βαπτιζομένης** νεὼς ἀπενήχοντο τῆς πόλεως)' (*War,* II.556)

'It is noble to destroy oneself,' another will say. Not so, I retort, but most ignoble; in my opinion there could be no more arrogant coward than the pilot who, for fear of a tempest, deliberately sinks his ship before the storm (ὅστις χειμῶνα δεδοικὼς πρὸ τῆς θυέλλης **ἐβάπτισεν** ἑκὼν τὸ σκάφος.)' (*War,* III.368-369)

Josephus, *The Jewish War*, Books I-III (H. St. J. Thackeray, trans.; Cambridge, Mass.; London: Harvard University Press, 1989).

[60] Whiston translates here: '...when Ishmael saw him in that case, and that he was drowned in his cups to the degree of insensibility,...' (Our italics); Josephus.

[61] (Our italics); Josephus, *Jewish Antiquities*, Books IX-XI.

action described by βαπτίζω is into *a person* and into *an event* from the life of that person, his death. Thus we have a lexeme used in an *unexpected* area of thought.

This kind of metaphorical transfer of the literal meaning of βαπτίζω is also met in the Jewish writings.[54] In Sirach 34:25 it is used with the meaning of 'ceremonial washing': **βαπτιζόμενος** ἀπὸ νεκροῦ καὶ πάλιν ἁπτόμενος αὐτοῦ, τί ὠφέλησεν ἐν τῷ λουτρῷ αὐτοῦ;[55] and in 2 Kings 5:14 (LXX) it means 'immersion': καὶ κατέβη Ναιμαν καὶ **ἐβαπτίσατο** ἐν τῷ Ἰορδάνῃ ἑπτάκι κατὰ τὸ ῥῆμα Ελισαιε. This image of 'immersion' is transferred to the moral life in Isa. 21:4 (LXX): ἡ καρδία μου πλανᾶται, καὶ ἡ ἀνομία με **βαπτίζει**, ἡ ψυχή μου ἐφέστηκεν εἰς φόβον. A literal translation of 21:4b is 'the lawlessness baptises me', but the qualifier ἡ ἀνομία helps us to see the metaphor. Here the lawlessness 'overwhelms'[56] the subject.

In Josephus we find a similar situation (literal meaning and metaphorical transfer). The killing of Aristobulus is described in *Ant.* 15:53-55. It was a killing by drowning and βαπτίζω is used to describe this.

> When the festival was over and they were being entertained at Jericho as the guest of Alexandra, he showed great friendliness to the youth and led him on to drink without fear, and he was ready to join in his play and to act like a young man in order to please him. But as the place was naturally hot, they soon went out in a group for a stroll, and stood beside the swimming-pools, of which there were several large ones around the palace, and cooled themselves off from the excessive heat of the noon. [55] At first they watched some of the friends (of Herod) as they swam, and then, at Herod's urging, the youth was induced (to join them). But with darkness coming on while he swam, some of the friends, who had been given orders to do so, kept pressing him down and *holding him under the water*[57] as if in sport, and they did not let up until they had quite suffocated him (τῶν φίλων οἷς ταῦ α ἐπιτέτακτο, σκότους ἐπέχοντος, βαροῦντες ἀεὶ καὶ **βαπτίζοντες** ὡς ἐν παιδιᾷ νηχόμενον οὐκ ἀνῆκαν ἕως καὶ παντάσιν ἀποπνῖξαι). In this manner was Aristobulus done away with when he was at most eighteen years old and had held the high priesthood for a year.[58]

---

[54] See also Dunn, 'Baptized as Metaphor,' 302-3; M.M.B. Turner, 'Spirit Endowment in Luke-Acts: Some Linguistic Considerations', *Vox Evangelica* 12 (1981) 50-3; Max Turner, *Power from on High: The Spirit in Israel's Restoration and Witness in Luke-Acts* (Sheffield: SAP, 1996), 182-4.

[55] 'He that washeth himself after the touching of a dead body, if he touch it again, what availeth his washing?' (Brenton's translation)

[56] Brenton; Dunn, 'Baptized as Metaphor,' 303.

[57] Whiston translates 'dipped him as he was swimming, and plunged him under the water'. *The Works of Josephus, Complete and Unabridged* (William Whiston, tr; Peabody, Mass.: Hendrickson, 1987).

[58] Josephus, *Jewish Antiquities*, Books XV-XVII (Allen Wikgren, comp. and ed.; Ralph Marcus, trans.; Cambridge, Mass.; London: Harvard University Press; William

(Mk. 1:4) things are easier; the texts say something about the significance or results of the act of baptism. Also when ὄνομα is used after this prepositional phrase the meaning is pursued on bookkeeping/property lines, but when εἰς following βαπτίζειν is followed by a person[48] the meaning is not clear because it is difficult to defend the fact that Paul says here that 'we were baptised' and this shows/signifies something about 'Christ' and 'his death'.[49]

Another observation is that the traditional meaning (the formula of 6:3 as a short form of a longer one) always implies the description of a person but in 6:3b there is the death of Christ. The implication can be that, as Wilckens put it: 'εἰς τὸν θάνατον αὐτοῦ kann darum nur verstanden werden, wenn in ἐβαπτίσθημεν die konkrete Bedeutung 'eintauchen' mitgehört wird.'[50] There is also *no* other example in which the longer formula is parallelled by the phrase εἰς τὸν θάνατον αὐτοῦ ἐβαπτίσθημεν for supporting the suggestion that the phrase in 6:3a is a shorter form of a longer one.

Even so all these observations are not enough for a definitive argument for one of these two paths of interpretation. We will follow the metaphorical path because it needs only to take the context and *design* of Paul's discourse as this is related to the context of this pericope. We treat these two formulas ('baptism into the name of Jesus' and 'baptism into Christ') not as synonyms but as distinct ones, but the longer one as being rewritten/abbreviated metaphorically by Paul.[51] If Paul had said ἢ ἀγνοεῖτε ὅτι, ὅσοι ἐβαπτίσθημεν and after that had continued to explain the relevance of baptism, the literal approach would have been the better path for interpretation, namely a discussion of the rite of baptism as such,[52] but Paul says more than that using that 'image'. The natural qualifier for a literal interpretation of βαπτίζω is ὕδωρ[53] but in our text the

---

[48] The expression from 1 Cor 10:2 (καὶ πάντες εἰς τὸν Μωυσῆν ἐβαπτίσθησαν ἐν τῇ νεφέλῃ καὶ ἐν τῇ θαλάσσῃ) cannot be used to explain our text because, as many commentators say, this εἰς τὸν Μωυσῆν ἐβαπτίσθησαν is 'nowhere found in Jewish sources' (cf. Richard B. Hays, *First Corinthians: A Bible Commentary for Teaching and Preaching* (Louisville: John Knox Press, 1997), 160; Raymond F. Collins, *First Corinthians* (Collegeville, Minnesota: The Liturgical Press, 1999), 368) and it is very probable that this type of language was coined by Paul on the basis of Christian language about baptism (Hays, *First Corinthians,* 160; G.D. Fee, *The First Epistle to the Corinthians* (Exeter: Paternoster, 1987), 445; Hans Conzelmann, *A Commentary on the First Epistle to the Corinthians* (James W. Leitch, trans.; Philadelphia: Fortress Press, 1975), 166). Against B.L. Martin, *Christ and the Law in Paul* (Leiden: Brill, 1989), 137 who says that Rom. 6:3 has 'to be understood in the light of 1 Cor. 10:2.'
[49] See also Dunn's analysis of this, Dunn, *Romans,* 311.
[50] Cf. Wilckens, *Römer,* 11.
[51] See also Wedderburn, *Baptism,* 60.
[52] See also Brown, *Baptism,* 125.
[53] See Mat. 3:11: Ἐγώ με ὑμᾶς βαπτίζω ἐν ὕδατι; Mk. 1:8: ἐβάπτισα ὑμᾶς ὕδατι; Lk 3:16: Ἐγὼ με ὕδατι βαπτίζω ὑμᾶς· John 1:31: ἐγὼ ἐν ὕδατι βαπτίζων John 1:33: ὁ πέμψας με βαπτίζειν ἐν ὕδατι; also Brown, Baptism, 125.

βαπτίζω lead the process of interpretation in that direction. It is difficult to make a choice between this approach and that which argues that here there is a short form of a longer formula. The arguments on both sides are not definitive. The closest parallel to 6:3a is Gal. 3:27 (εἰς Χριστὸν ἐβαπτίσθητε, Χριστὸν ἐνεδύσασθε) where the metaphorical reading is also a valid option. Also, Paul was familiar with the longer formula as 1 Cor. 1:13,15 attest.[41] This is the only place in Pauline literature where Paul uses this formula. The reason for this is clear as the context shows: the act of baptism was administrated 'in the name of Jesus' and that means that now they belong to Jesus not to a particular apostle who administered the baptism.

Kaye says that 'in the New Testament εἰς is used following βαπτίζειν to indicate the substance into which the baptisand was dipped or immersed only at Mark 1.9[42] in reference to Jesus' baptism by John. [...] the preposition εἰς is used to indicate the significance of the baptism, e.g. Mat. 3:11 'with reference to, or with the significance of, repentance'.[43]

> In the Pauline letters βαπτίζειν is followed by εἰς at Rom. 6:3; 1 Cor. 1:13, 15; 10:2; 12:13 and Gal. 3:27. In 1 Cor. 1:13 [...] the real point he is using in the argument, is not the formula but the significance which was attached to it, namely allegiance to Christ and not to Paul. Hence the prepositional phrase introduced by εἰς following βαπτίζειν gives the significance or reference of the baptism, not the material or substance of it.[44]

Kaye says that in Rom. 6:3 also εἰς following βαπτίζειν has to be understood as having the meaning 'with reference to'.[45] In this case the argument goes like this: 'Do you not know that as many of us as were baptised with reference to Christ Jesus, were baptised with reference to his death. Therefore we were buried with him, through (that) baptism with reference to (his) death.'[46] Thus, says Kaye, the argument of the passage is 'working out of an implication (not necessarily the only possible implication) of the *significance* of the baptism of the readers.'[47]

Kaye's observation that εἰς following βαπτίζειν shows the significance attached to the baptism leads him to a very technical conclusion: 'baptised with reference to Christ'. This is difficult to understand. When εἰς following βαπτίζειν is followed by μετάνοια (Matt. 3:11) or the phrase ἄφεσιν ἁμαρτιῶν

---

emphasize only the basic motifs, in this case the fellowship of our destiny with that of Christ' (Käsemann, *Romans*, 164-65).

[41] See here Cranfield, *Romans*, 301.
[42] Mk.1:9: Καὶ ἐγένετο ἐν ἐκείναις ταῖς ἡμέραις ἦλθεν Ἰησοῦς ἀπὸ Ναζαρετῆς Γαλιλαίας καὶ ἐβαπτίσθη εἰς τὸν Ἰορδάνην ὑπὸ Ἰωάννου.
[43] Kaye, 'Special Reference,' 282.
[44] Kaye, 'Special Reference,' 283.
[45] Kaye, 'Special Reference,' 285.
[46] Kaye, 'Special Reference,' 285.
[47] Kaye, 'Special Reference,' 286.

of the Christian life in terms which are known as *words*, but as *metaphorical phrases* they are complex. In his discussion in 6:3-4 he draws metaphors from the act of baptism. In 6:4 the prepositional phrase διὰ τοῦ βαπτίσματος, which is understood by many commentators as a reference to the *act* of baptism,[33] is qualified by εἰς τὸν θάνατον. This fact also points to a metaphorical interpretation,[34] but the lexical choice of βαπτίζω and βάπτισμα *alludes* to the initiatory rite of baptism.[35] The element of 'plunging' under water can be used to describe something about the beginning of the Christians' *relationship* with Christ. Dunn puts it as follows: 'Only if baptism continued to provide focus and occasion for the divine-human encounter would it serve as metaphor for the divine initiative.'[36] It is not that 'immersing' under water is a death by 'drowning' as a sharing in Christ's death,[37] because Christ did not die by drowning, but, we will argue, an *'overwhelming' toward* (ἐβαπτίσθημεν εἰς) Christ when he died. He speaks about an 'encompassing' event.[38] He explains in this pericope the way in which this thesis is valid.[39]

The language of 'baptism'[40] in Rom. 6.3-4 will be analysed as a metaphor because the qualifiers (εἰς Χριστὸν Ἰησοῦν and εἰς τὸν θάνατον αὐτοῦ) of

---

[33] E.g. Nygren, *Romans,* 239; Moo, *Romans,* 364, 365; Fitzmyer, *Romans,* 434; Byrne, *Romans,* 190; Edwards, *Romans,* 160.

[34] Contra Brown, *Baptism,* 126; Dunn, *Baptism,* 140; and others, see previous note.

[35] See also I.H. Marshall, 'The Meaning of the Verb "to Baptize"', *EvQ* 45 (1973) 131.

[36] Dunn, *Romans,* 312.

[37] Contra Dunn, 'Baptized as Metaphor,' 307; Dunn, *Baptism*, 140; Fitzmyer, *Romans,* 434.

[38] At this point in the argument it is not so much a question of 'transfer' (Moo, *Romans*, 355; Bornkamm, 'Baptism,' 74) or 'a change of dominion' (Jürgen Becker, *Paul Apostle to the Gentiles* (Louisville: Westminster/John Knox Press, 1993), 391), or a 'tearing... from one's native condition 'in Adam'' (Fitzmyer, *Romans, 430*), even if these are resulting realities of this action of God (see Rom. 6:18), as one of 'being overwhelmed by' God. It is interesting that Cranfield was 'forced' to arrive at a similar conclusion, in some aspects, without accepting openly the 'metaphor' of βαπτίζω; he says: 'Baptism, according to Paul, [...] [is] a decisive event by which a man's life is powerfully and unequivocally claimed by God' (our italics) (Cranfield, *Romans, 304*).

[39] See also Bornkamm: 'In v.2 Paul demonstrates the validity of his proposition by recalling baptism.' Bornkamm, 'Baptism,' 74.

[40] At the beginning of this discussion it is good to quote what Käsemann says in relation to Paul's discussion of baptism here in Romans 6: '...it must be stressed that the text tells us nothing about the prior history of baptism. We learn nothing about its relation to Jewish practices of washing, especially the much cited baptism of proselytes, whose practice at this time is highly problematic, not about the institution of baptism by Jesus and the probable connection with John's baptism, nor about the Jewish-Christian understanding of the eschatological sealing and transferal of the baptised to the risen Lord. [...] Paul never gave a comprehensive account of it [baptism]. This implies that the rite and its meaning were not disputed in his circles. Hence it was necessary to

provided by the Jesus tradition, and probably Jesus' own usage. For in Jesus' tradition there is the well-established recollection that Jesus spoke of his own death as a 'baptism I am to be baptized with' (Mk 10:38; cf Lk. 12:50).[26] In its turn, the origin of such language is hardly difficult to trace, for it is a natural application of the imagery of 'immersion', such as we have already noted (death as being overwhelmed and smothered by a force under which or into which one sinks), and it is a natural extension of the Baptist's imagery of a destructive immersion (drowning).'[27]

Thus, in the usage of the Jesus tradition, death is seen metaphorically as a kind of baptism. Dunn says that if the Jesus tradition is the place of origin for Paul's usage, his usage also is metaphorical. When Paul speaks about a participation in Christ's death he 'uses the imagery of immersion as a drowning to reinforce the point: their death by drowning was a sharing in Christ's death—as Jesus himself has hinted (Mk 10:38).'[28]

Dunn takes the 'imagery' of drowning (which is well attested for βαπτίζω) and applies it to Paul's metaphor. We identify one problem in relation to this interpretation. It is not clear that the metaphor of baptism has the role of 'death' in Rom. 6. We do not have here a death *as* a baptism (as in Jesus' tradition), neither a baptism *as* a death, but 'baptism' as a metaphor for *relating* us to Christ's death. Paul describes our 'death' not by using the image of 'drowning', because this would not fit the way in which Christ died, but that of 'crucifixion'. In other words someone cannot use about someone an image of drowning for relating him to an image of crucifixion.

Our position is close to these two in that it argues for a metaphorical understanding of the baptism phrases, but is different as the meaning conveyed by the metaphor is concerned.

Against the charge of 6:1,[29] which is not new (see 3:8),[30] Paul introduces the subject which will be developed in Rom. 6:1-11 (ἀπεθάνομεν τῇ ἁμαρτίᾳ, 6:2).[31] In doing this he uses metaphorical language.[32] He refers to the beginning

---

310.

[26] Dunn, 'Baptized as Metaphor,' 306.

[27] Dunn, 'Baptized as Metaphor,' 307.

[28] Dunn, 'Baptized as Metaphor,' 307.

[29] This is the 'starting point' of Paul's argument here in Romans, cf. Schnelle, *Human Condition*, 74; this 'question' is the reason of the argument below, Nygren, *Romans*, 239; 'the point of departure for ch.6', Schnackenburg, *Baptism*, 31; also Günther Bornkamm, 'Baptism and New Life in Paul (Romans 6)', in *Early Christian Experience* (London: SCM, 1969), 79; Wilckens, *Römer*, 7; Stuhlmacher, *Romans*, 100.

[30] See also Käsemann, *Romans*, 165; Fitzmyer, *Romans*, 430; Elliott, *Rhetoric*, 237; Watson, *Paul*, 147.

[31] See also Dunn, *Baptism*, 140; Käsemann, *Romans*, 165; Fitzmyer, *Romans*, 430; Kuss, *Der Römerbrief*, 296; Cranfield, *Romans*, 298; Kaye, 'Special Reference,' 284.

[32] Also Dunn, *Baptism*, 141; Wedderburn, *Baptism*, 59.

implies that when he says '... as a ship *sinks* beneath the waves, or a *drowning* man goes under the water, so the baptisant has been immersed into Christ' (our italics).[20] Moreover from these 'images' he selects one which speaks about '*completeness* of immersion'.[21] It is true that in the pericope of Rom. 6:1-11 the 'death' language is central, but 'baptism' is not used as a 'destroying' image, and from this 'image' he points to the aspect of '*completeness* of immersion'. In 6:3 the idea is not so much about the 'depth' of immersion, but rather about what God has done at the beginning of our Christian life.[22] Brown does not relate his reading of the metaphor to the major ideas of the letter as they appear in 1:16; 5:20. The discussion in ch. 6 is about the relation between sin and grace. If the first is abundant the second is more abundant. The charge can be worded: let's do something about the first and the second will increase. The metaphor of βαπτίζω understood along the lines of '*completeness* of immersion' does not fit this line of argument.

Second, his distinction between these two qualifiers of the metaphor is too sharp. Paul argues starting from something known and then advances the argument toward a particular event (perhaps not very known as far as the implications are concerned) from the life of Christ. The first qualifier (εἰς Χριστὸν Ἰησοῦν) has to be understood as a 'general' known truth from which this particular event of his death has to be pointed. It is not so much that in the first we 'entered in the state of being-in-Christ' and that the second is mentioned because the context requires it. The idea is that the beginning of our Christian life has to be equated with an experience of the overwhelming action of God by which we are 'directed' toward what Christ did for our salvation (see our argument below). This is the reason why, we argue that it is not necessary[23] to work with a sharp distinction in meaning between the first and the second qualifier here as also others argue.[24]

J. D. G. Dunn's position as it is argued in his last contribution on the subject[25] is: the origin of Paul's language is

---

[20] Brown, *Baptism*, 127.

[21] Brown, *Baptism*, 128.

[22] See Cranfield here: 'On God's side it [the baptism into Christ's death] is the sign and pledge that the benefits of Christ's death for all men really do apply to this individual in particular, while on man's side, it is the outward ratification of the human decision of faith, of the response already begun to what God has done in Christ.' Cranfield, *Romans*, 303.

[23] See also Wilckens, *Römer*, 11; Dunn, *Romans*, 312; Otto Kuss, *Der Römerbrief* (1; Regensburg: Verlag Friedrich Pustet, 1963), 296.

[24] See Ziesler, *Romans*, 157: '''into his death' cannot have the same connotations of possession that 'into Christ Jesus' has'; see also the distinction made by Wilckens, *Römer*, 11.

[25] James D. G. Dunn, 'Baptized as Metaphor', in Stanley E. Porter and Anthony R. Cross, eds, *Baptism, the New Testament and the Church: Historical and Contemporary Studies in Honor of R. E. O. White* (Sheffield: Sheffield Academic Press, 1999), 298-

J. A. Brown's unpublished PhD thesis[13] is a contribution to the understanding of the metaphorical language in relation to baptism in Pauline literature. He says that

> because Paul wrote ἐβαπτίσθημεν εἰς Χριστὸν Ἰησοῦν [...] the effect of the fuller phrase, is to reveal a metaphorical meaning for ἐβαπτίσθημεν. The word can exist on a literal basis but be restored to a metaphorical sense by being joined to εἰς Χριστὸν Ἰησοῦν (a word being shown to be metaphorical because of the oddness of the context in which is used).[14]

He also says that

> while ἐβαπτίσθημεν is metaphor, it is not that alone, for it does not exclude the thought of the act of baptism. [...] a physical object or event could be spoken of in such a way as to imbue it with significance. This is what Paul does here. βαπτίζω refers to the physical event of baptism, but its mixture with other language, at the same time imparts meaning by metaphor to that event. Only that context can tell us for sure that this double reference is intended. [...] Paul does not employ βαπτίζω as Jesus did (Mk. 10:38; Lk.12:50) as metaphor and metaphor alone. Rather he intends both metaphorical and literal meaning to be understood.[15]

'(...) Put crudely, as a ship sinks beneath the waves, or a drowning man goes under the water, so the baptisant has been immersed into Christ.'[16] '(...) The particular force of the word which seems to be intended is the *completeness* of the immersion into Christ. As the water completely covers a ship or a drowned man, so the baptisand is completely immersed into Christ.'[17]

He discusses the qualifiers of the metaphor of 'baptism' as being distinct (Χριστὸν Ἰησοῦν and τὸν θάνατον αὐτου). The first (ἐβαπτίσθημεν εἰς Χριστὸν Ἰησοῦν) 'describes the manner of entering upon the state of being-in-Christ. Those who are baptised *into* Christ are those who afterwards *are in* Christ.'[18] The second qualifier is called 'a contextual qualifier, for its purpose is to direct our thought to the relevant meaning of the metaphor for *this* context. That metaphor immersed the believers into Christ, (...) v.2 [is] the 'heading' verse of this section and what followed [is] an attempt by Paul to demonstrate that the Christian is dead to sin. This is where the secondary qualifier is needed.'[19]

In relation to Brown's position there are two observations: First, it is not clear that βαπτίζω here is intended as an image of 'killing' or 'destroying'. He

---

[13] A. Brown, *Metaphorical Language in Relation to Baptism in the Pauline Literature* (unpublished PhD dissertation, Edinburgh; 1982).

[14] Brown, *Baptism*, 125.

[15] Brown, *Baptism*, 126.

[16] Brown, *Baptism*, 127.

[17] Brown, *Baptism*, 128.

[18] Brown, *Baptism*, 138.

[19] Brown, *Baptism*, 139.

The Metaphor of 'Baptism' (Romans 6:3)

The meaning of the baptism phrases of Romans 6:3 is under debate. The phrase itself is not very clear. It can be interpreted either as a reference to the *act* of baptism or as a *metaphor* drawn from that act.[4] This dual possibility is seen in the two main lines of interpretation among the scholars: 1) ἐβαπτίσθημεν εἰς Χριστὸν Ἰησοῦν is a reference to the act of baptism being a short form of a longer phrase ἐβαπτίσθημεν εἰς τὸ ὄνομα Χριστοῦ Ἰησοῦ (Tannehill, Beasley-Murray, Barrett, Cranfield, Kaye, Hartmann, Moo). 2) ἐβαπτίσθημεν εἰς Χριστὸν Ἰησοῦν is a metaphor drawn from the rite of baptism (Brown, Dunn).

1) The first position is the most known. This compact Pauline phrase (ἐβαπτίσθημεν εἰς Χριστὸν Ἰησοῦν) in Rom. 6:3 is understood as a short form of a longer formula of ἐβαπτίσθημεν εἰς τὸ ὄνομα Χριστοῦ Ἰησοῦ. Tannehill says that '...baptism εἰς Χριστὸν [is] an abbreviated form of εἰς τὸ ὄνομα,[5] and so as a formula for transfer of ownership'.[6] This reference to the act of baptism and the implications of 'ownership' are also sustained by Fitzmyer who says that 'εἰς Χριστὸν may reflect an image drawn from bookkeeping, being an abbreviation of a fuller expression εἰς τὸ ὄνομα Χριστοῦ Ἰησοῦ'.[7] Barrett argues on similar lines saying that the phrase is an abbreviated form of the longer phrase 'into the name of' and this means 'to become the property of,' and those 'who are baptised into the name of Christ become Christ's men (cf. 1 Cor. 10:2; 1:13)'.[8] In this case Paul speaks about the 'proprietary rights[9] of Christ over the baptised person, and the name of the baptised person would be booked in the ledger to the account of Christ.'[10]

Cranfield says that

> the context requires a purely factual statement and this is immediately followed by a further statement which goes beyond it and offers an interpretation of the objective fact. We take it then that βαπτίζεσθαι εἰς Χριστὸν Ἰησοῦν here is synonymous with βαπτίζεσθαι εἰς τὸ ὄνομα Χριστοῦ Ἰησοῦ.[11]

Paul wants to convey 'the simple fact that the persons concerned have received Christian baptism.'[12]

2) ἐβαπτίσθημεν εἰς Χριστὸν Ἰησοῦν as a metaphor drawn from the rite of baptism.

---

[4] See also Dunn, *Romans*, 311.

[5] Also Wilckens, *Römer*, 11; L. Hartman, *'Into the Name of the Lord Jesus': Baptism in the Early Church* (Edinburgh: T&T Clark, 1997), 70, 77; Edwards, *Romans*, 160.

[6] Tannehill, *Dying*, 22.

[7] Fitzmyer, *Romans*, 433.

[8] Barrett, *Romans*, 114.

[9] See also Ziesler, *Romans*, 156; see also the discussion in Wedderburn, *Baptism*, 57.

[10] Fitzmyer, *Romans*, 433.

[11] Cranfield, *Romans*, 301; see also the discussion in G.R. Beasley-Murray, *Baptism in the New Testament* (London: Macmillan, 1962), 128-9.

[12] Cranfield, *Romans*, 301.

Chapter 4

The Qualifiers of the Metaphor of 'Death' in Romans 6:1-11

Introduction

After studying the *vehicle* of 'death' which is used by Paul in Romans 6:1-11, the next step will be to study the qualifiers of that metaphor, namely those elements used in the argument[1] for guiding the readers toward a good understanding of his language. These qualifiers are also metaphors in themselves. They are: 1) 'we have been baptized into Christ Jesus, were bapitzed into his death' (6:3),2) 'Therefore we have been buried with him by baptism into death' (6:4),3) 'For if we have been united with the likeness of his death'(6:5),4) 'We know that our old man was crucified with him (6:6), 5) 'But if we have died with Christ' (6:8). 2, 3, 4, and 5 are elaborations from particular angles of the first,[2] and 5 is also a summary of all.[3] In order to understand ἀπεθάνομεν τῇ ἁμαρτίᾳ (the subject of the section 6:1-11), a complex set of ideas related to baptism, Christ's death, agriculture/biology, and anthroplogy should be discussed. The unpacking of this set of ideas is the purpose of this chapter. First, the 'βαπτίζω' language will be studied, then the language from agriculture/horticulture/biology (σύμφυτος), and finally that from anthropology (ὁ παλαιὸς ἄνθρωπος). Due to the fact that in this paragraph (6:1-11) ἁμαρτία is personified as 'a Master' which subdues the σῶμα (6:6) these elements (sin and body) will be discussed in 'the anthropology' section. The language of 'death' from 2, 3 and 5 was discussed in the previous chapter on the *vehicle* of 'death'. A final analysis of the metaphor of death here in Romans 6:1-11 will be done after this study of its qualifiers, in the next chapter, which is in fact the conclusion of the whole project.

---

[1] For a discussion of the argument of Romans 6:1-11 see Chapter 1.

[2] See also Dunn, *Baptism,* 140; B. N. Kaye, 'βαπτίζειν εἰς with Special Reference to Romans 6', in Elizabeth A. Livingstone, ed., *Studia Evangelica* VI (Berlin: Akademie Verlag, 1973), 284.

[3] See also Udo Schnelle, *The Human Condition: Anthropology in the Teachings of Jesus, Paul, and John* (Edinburgh: T&T Clark, 1996), 75.

he/she is buried. Against this set of ideas Romans 6:4 will be interpreted in chapter 5.

Thus, the findings of this chapter can be summarised here. As we discussed in chapter 2 a metaphor works in a particular way. The interpreter needs to identify why the author of a metaphor chose that vehicle (the unexpected element used for explication) for that tenor (the thing which is explained). He has to describe the content brought by the vehicle (both rhetorical and semantic—this is done both in this chapter and the next), in our case, the vehicle of 'death' in order to identify the point(s) of the metaphor. Our exegesis of Romans 6 is moulded by the way in which a metaphor works (this is seen in the way in which the whole project is structured).

In Romans 6:1-11 the language of 'death' to sin is taken by Paul from his insight about Christ's death as being 'a death to sin'. This language is 'transferred' by Paul into the area of Christian life with a different meaning.

Christ's 'death to sin' has a 'sharing' reality of 'dying with' because he died as the Anointed [davidic] king when he won that victory over sin and death by being raised from the dead. Those who belong to the Anointed king of God share in his victory.

The believers were and are 'united' with what was proclaimed about Christ's death. The meaning of ὁμοίωμα which was argued for is that of 'representation' referring to a discourse, a melody or drama.

The 'crucifixion' language points to a horrible death. The fundamental idea behind this form of punishment is that of horror/terror.

All these findings will be integrated when we will interpret the metaphorical language of death from Romans 6 in chapter 5. In order to do that a study of the qualifiers of the vehicle is needed. This will be done in the next chapter.

αὐτοῦ·)[159]

In Josephus the idea of being 'buried with' appears in the same context of being buried with someone from the same family or dynasty. Josephus, *Jewish Antiquities* 10:48

> This king imitated those deeds of his father which he had recklessly commited in his youth, and, after a plot was formed against him by his own servants, was put to death in his house at the age of twenty-four years, of which he had reigned for two. But the people punished his murderers and *buried* Ammon *with* his father (τῷ πατρὶ συνθάπτουσι τὸν Ἀμμῶνα); then they gave the kingship to his son Josiah, a boy of eight years, whose mother, named Jedis, came from the city of Bosketh.[160]

Josephus, *Jewish War*, 1.551

> Herod summoned a public assembly, formally accused the officers concerned and Tiro, and enlisted the aid of the populace to dispach them; they and the barber were beaten to death on the spot with cudgels and stones. He then sent his sons to Sebaste, a town not far from Caesarea, and ordered them to be strangled. The order was promptly executed, and direction was given to convey the bodies to the fortress of Alexandrion, for *burial* there *with* Alexander, their maternal grandfather (συνταφησομένους Ἀλεξάνδρῳ τῷ μητροπάτορι). Such was the end of Alexander and Aristobulus.[161]

A relevant example from extra biblical-Greek is that from Herodotus, in *Histories* 5:5 where the same idea of being buried with someone from your family is present:

> Those who dwell above the Crestonaeans have a custom of their own: each man having many wifes, at his death there is a great rivalry among his wives, and eager contention on their friends' part, to prove which wife was best loved by her husband; and she to whom the honour is adjudged is praised by men and women, and slain over the tomb by her nearest of kin, and after the slaying she is buried with the husband (συνθάπτεται τῷ ἀνδρί). The rest of the wives take this sorely to heart, deeming themselves deeply dishonoured.[162]

In these examples the point is not that that person is *truly* dead (that is so) but that that person *belongs* to a particular family and as a result of that he is buried with his fathers/ancestors. The idea is that of *belonging* to those with whom

---

[159] The other texts are: 2 Kgs. 8:24; 9.28; 12:21; 13:13; 14:16,20; 15:7,38; 16:20; 2 Chr. 21:1; 24:16.

[160] Josephus, *Jewish Antiquities,* Books IX-XI (Ralph Marcus, trans.; Cambridge, Mass.; London: Harvard University Press; William Heinemann Ltd, 1987).

[161] Josephus, *The Jewish War,* Books I-III (H. St. J. Thackeray, trans.; Cambridge, Mass.; London: Harvard University Press, 1989).

[162] Herodotus, *Books V-VII* (A. D. Godley, tr; Cambridge, Mass.; London: Harvard University Press; William Heinemann Ltd, 1971).

The Language of 'Death' 91

since burial marks a death that has already taken place.'[154] Moo argues that 'this burial not only marks the end of the old life but is also part of the transition to a new life, in which the believer is now called to 'walk'.[155] 'Burial both sets the seal on death and prepares for that which is to follow: living a new life patterned after the resurrection of Christ.'[156] So, the majority of scholars point to the fact that a burial is the seal of death; when someone is buried it is shown that he is dead. Thus, by saying that the believers died and are buried as far as sin is concerned, Paul emphasizes the definitive character of their death.

It is not clear in the above positions why Paul chose *this* langauge of 'being buried with' or why *this* particular point of contact of 'seal of death' is in view.[157] It is true that usually it is spoken about 'burial' of someone if that person is already dead or his death is expected and others make preparations for burial, but the basic observation, as Paul's text is concerned, is not that by affirming that somebody is 'buried' it means that that one is really dead, but that that person was 'buried *with*' someone else. So, the path to be followed in interpreting this kind of language is by identifying the associated ideas with the idea of burying somebody with someone else. We did not find any scholar to investigate this in relation to Romans 6:4.

The available Jewish texts point in a single direction, namely, that somebody is buried with someone else if they are from the same family or dynasty. συνθάπτω is not used in the LXX but there is used θάπτω + μετά or + παρά[158] for speaking about being 'buried with'. Here are some of the texts:

Rehoboam slept with his ancestors and was *buried with* his ancestors (וַיִּקָּבֵר עִם אֲבֹתָיו) in the city of David. His mother's name was Naamah the Ammonite. His son Abijam succeeded him. (1 Kgs. 14.31) (LXX βασιλειων γ 14:31 καὶ ἐκοιμήθη Ροβοαμ μετὰ τῶν πατέρων αὐτοῦ καὶ **θάπτεται μετὰ** τῶν πατέρων αὐτοῦ ἐν πόλει Δαυιδ, [...])

Then Asa slept with his ancestors, and was *buried with* his ancestors in the city of his father David; his son Jehoshaphat succeeded him. (1 Kgs. 15:24) (LXX βασιλειων γ 15:24 καὶ ἐκοιμήθη Ασα καὶ **θάπτεται μετὰ** τῶν πατέρων αὐτοῦ ἐν πόλει Δαυιδ, [...])

Jehoshaphat slept with his ancestors and was *buried with* his ancestors (וַיִּקָּבֵר עִם אֲבֹתָיו) in the city of his father David; his son Jehoram succeeded him. (1 Kgs. 22:50) (LXX, βασιλειων γ 22:51) καὶ ἐκοιμήθη Ιωσαφατ μετὰ τῶν πατέρων αὐτοῦ καὶ **ἐτάφη παρὰ** τοῖς πατράσιν αὐτοῦ ἐν πόλει Δαυιδ τοῦ πατρὸς

---

[154] Wedderburn, *Baptism*, 370.
[155] Moo, *Romans*, 361.
[156] Moo, *Romans*, 355.
[157] Moo tried to keep both this one and to add the fact that burial starts the transition to a new life.
[158] Only two times: 2 Chr 21:1; 1 Kgs 22:50.

The 'Burial' Language (Romans 6:4)

The role of 'burial' language in Paul's argument is an intriguing element. This metaphor is complex because it is difficult to find aspects of 'similarity' with the new context in which it is used.

The proposed suggestions are as follows: M. Hooker understands 'baptism as a burial into the death of Christ — if we are united with his death, we shall be united with his resurrection.'[147] Fitzmyer argues on similar lines when he says that 'the baptismal rite symbolically represents the death, burial, and resurrection of Christ; the person descends into the baptismal bath, is covered with its waters, and emerges to a new life.'[148] Cranfield has a similar understanding that 'by stating that we have been buried with Christ (cf. Col. 2:12) Paul expresses in the most decisive and emphatic way the truth of our having died with Christ; for burial is the seal[149] set to the fact of death [...] the death which we died in baptism was a death ratified and sealed by burial.'[150] Schlatter accentuates the same aspect: 'Just as his [Jesus] death led to a conclusive result, namely, his being dead in the grave, so the one baptised does not experience an initial death, but a conclusive separation from everything pursued by the wrath of God and destroyed by his judgment.'[151] Dunn says that

> of the completeness of this death the rite of baptism is an excellent symbol: the disappearance, however brief, below the surface of the water represents a burial rather well—and in this case, participation in the completeness and finality of Christ' death.[152]

The reason for which Paul speaks about burial with Christ, according to Tannehill, is 'to emphasize the reality and finality of the believer's death.'[153] Wedderburn says also that 'reference to burial with Christ is appropriate here

---

[147] Morna D. Hooker, *From Adam to Christ: Essays on Paul* (Cambridge: Cambridge University Press, 1990), 34.

[148] Fitzmyer, *Romans*, 434; also Nygren, when he says: 'when he who is baptized is immersed in the water, the act signifies burial 'with Christ'; and when he comes up out of the water, that signifies resurrection with Christ', Nygren, *Romans*, 233; Ziesler argues similarly: 'the picture is that of going down into the water in baptism and of being covered by it, thus representing and conveying death and burial. The old is left behind as finally as the world is left behind by someone who has been buried' Ziesler, *Romans*, 157.

[149] Also Bornkamm uses the same image: 'so 'to be buried with him' is a seal of the believer's dying with him.' Bornkamm, 'Baptism,' 74.

[150] Cranfield, *Romans*, 304.

[151] Schlatter, *Romans*, 138.

[152] J.D.G. Dunn, *Baptism in the Holy Spirit: A Re-Examination of the New Testament Teaching on the Gift of the Spirit in Relation to Penticostalism Today* (London: SCM, 1970), 141.

[153] Tannehill, *Dying*, 34; also 41. For the definitive character of burial see also L. Fazekaš, 'Taufe als Tod in Röm. 6:3ff', *Theologische Zeitschrift* 22 (1966) 308.

posteritate Caini, 61;[144] *De somnis*, 2:213.[145] For a discussion of those texts which speak about the legend of Regulus 'who conquered the cross', see Hengel's interpretation.[146]

These ideas associated with the act of crucifixion (punishment, surrender, revenge, horror) were available to the ancient reader. In this sense there is a common ground between Plato, Seneca, Philo and Paul. All of these authors work in their own way with these ideas associated with crucifixion. The interpreter of Paul has to discern among these and to 'construct' the most probable network of ideas present in an affirmation like that of Romans 6:6. First he has to define the meaning of the qualifier of this metaphor, namely the metaphor of 'our old man' which is a metaphor attested only in the Pauline Corpus amongst the entire ancient literature; this is a task which will be pursued in the fourth chapter where the other qualifiers from Rom. 6 will be analysed ('baptism', being 'one with'). Second, those ideas have to be interpreted according to the lines of Paul's argument here in Romans (that is the final task of this project which will be done in the fifth chapter were we will argue that the idea of *horror* is the point of 'crucifixion' language).

---

that they were free to do so, did not some of them spit upon spectators from their own cross! Seneca, 'De Vita Beata', in *Moral Essays* (II; John W. Basore, trans.; Cambridge, Mass.; London: Harvard University Press; William Heinemann Ltd, 1979).

[144] The soul, then, that submits to bodily couplings has as its inhabitants those mentioned just now. 'Ahiman' meanst 'my brother'; 'Sheshai' 'outside me'; 'Talmai' 'one hanging': for it is a necessity to souls that love the body that the body should be looked upon as a brother, and that external good things should be valued pre-eminently: and all souls in this condition depend on and hang from lifeless things, for, like men crucified and nailed to a tree, they are affixed to perishable materials till they die. But the soul wedded to goodness obtained inhabitants excelling in the virtues, whom the double cave (Gen. xxiii.9) received in pairs, Abraham and Sarah, Isaac and Rebecca, Leah and Jacob, these being virtues and their possessors. Philo, *On the Posterity and Exile of Cain (De Posteritate Caini)* (F. H. Colson and G. H. Whitaker, trans.; Cambridge, Mass.; London: Harvard University Press; William Heinemann Ltd, 1979).

[145] But thanks be to victorious God who, however perfect in workmanship are the aims and efforts of the passionlover, makes them to be of none effect by sending invisibly against them winged beings to undo and destroy them. Thus the mind stripped of the creations of its art will be found as it were a headless corpse, with severed neck nailed like the crucified to the tree of helpless and poverty-stricken indiscipline. Philo, *On Dreams (De Somnis)* (F. H. Colson and G. H. Whitacker, trans.; Cambridge, Mass.; London: Harvard University Press; William Heinemann Ltd, 1988).

[146] Hengel, *Crucifixion*, 64-6.

This element of 'conquering' by nailing is transferred metaphorically in some texts, as for example: Plato, *Phaedo* 83cd:

> Now the soul of true philosopher believes that it must not resist this deliverance, and therefore it stands aloof from pleasures and lusts and griefs and fears, so far as it can, considering that when anyone has violent pleasures or fears or griefs or lusts he suffers from them not merely what one might think—for example, illness or loss of money spent for his lusts—but he suffers the greatest and most extreme evil and does not take it into account.'
>
> 'What is this evil, Socrates?' said Cebes.
>
> 'The evil is that the soul of every man, when it is greatly pleased or pained by anything, is compelled to believe that the object which caused the emotion is very distinct and very true; but it is not. These objects are mostly the visible ones, are they not?'
>
> 'Certainly.'
>
> 'And when this occurs, is not the soul most completely put in bondage by the body?'
>
> 'How so?'
>
> 'Because each pleasure or pain nails it as with a nail to the body (Ὅτι ἑκάστη ἡδονὴ καὶ λύπη ὥσπερ ἧλον ἔχουσα προσηλοῖ αὐτὴν πρὸς τὸ σῶμα) and rivets it on and makes it corporeal, so that it fancies the things are true which the body says are true. For because it has the same beliefs and pleasures as the body it is compelled to adopt also the same habits and mode of life, and can never depart in purity to the other world, but must always go away contaminated with the body;[141]

The victory of the body over the soul is described by using the language of 'nailing/crucifixion'. In that way the soul is put into the bondage by the body and the true philosopher is not able to perceive true realities.[142] Other texts in the same tradition are those from Seneca, *De vita beata*, 7:3;[143] Philo, *De*

---

[141] Plato, *Euthyphro, Apology, Crito, Phaedo, Phaedrus* (I; Harold North Fowler, trans.; Cambridge, Mass., London: Harvard University Press, William Heinemann Ltd, 1982).

[142] See the detailed discussion on the texts in Phaedo in chapter 1.

[143] You say that no one of them practices what he preaches, or models his life upon his own words. But what wonder, since their words are heroic, mighty, and survive all the storms of human life? Though they strive to release themselves from their crosses—those crosses to which each one of you nails himself with his own hand—yet they, when brought to punishment, hang each upon a single gibbet; but these others who bring upon themselves their own punishment are stretched upon as many crosses as they had desires. Yet they are slanderous and witty in heaping insult on others. I might believe

hardly to justify. [201] Observing this, Bassus proceeded to practice a ruse upon the enemy, desiring to intensify their distress as to compel them to purchase the man's life by the surrender of the fort; and in this hope he was not disappointed. [202] For he ordered a cross to be erected, as though intending to have Eleazar instantly suspended; at which sight those in the fortress were seized with deeper dismay and with piercing shrieks exclaimed that the tragedy was intolerable. [203] At this juncture, moreover, Eleazar besought them not to leave him to undergo the most pitiable of deaths, but to consult their own safety by yielding to the might and fortune of the Romans, now that all others had been subdued. [204] Overcome by his appeals, which were backed by many interceders within—for he came of a distinguished and extremely numerous family—[205] they yielded to a compassion contrary to their nature and hastily dispatched a deputation to discuss the surrender of the fortress, stipulating for permission to depart in safety, taking Eleazar with them.[138]

And *Jewish War*, V:449-451

Famine, however, emboldened them to undertake these excursions, and it but remained for them if they escaped unobserved from the town to be taken if they escaped unobserved from the town to be taken prisoners by the enemy. When caught, they were driven to resist, and after a conflict it seemed too late to sue for mercy. They were accordingly scourged and subjected to torture of every description, before being killed, and then crucified opposite the walls. Titus indeed commiserated their fate, five hundred or sometimes more being captured daily; on the other hand, he recognized the risk of dismissing prisoners of war, and that the custody of such numbers would amount to the imprisonment of their custodians; but his main reason for not stopping the crucifixions was the hope that the spectacle might perhaps induce the Jews to surrender, for fear that continued resistance would involve them in a similar fate. The soldiers out of rage and hatred amused themselves by nailing their prisoners in different postures; and so great was their number, that space could not be found for the crosses nor crosses for the bodies.[139]

These examples show the influence which this kind of punishment had in those circumstances: 'a spectacle [which] might induce to surrender.' The element horror is very much in view;[140] the public aspect of such executions was intended for the same purpose.

---

[138] Josephus, *The Jewish War*, Books IV-VII (H. St. J. Thackeray, trans.; Cambridge, Mass.; London: Harvard University Press; William Heinemann Ltd, 1979).

[139] Josephus, *The Jewish War*, Books IV-VII.

[140] See also the story about Alexander Janneus in *Jewish Antiquities* XIII, 379-383 and J*ewish War* I, 97-98 when he ordered 'some eight hundred of Jews to be crucified, and slaughtered their children and wives before their eyes' as an act of revenge for 'the injuries he has suffered.' See also the discussion of this incident in Fitzmyer, 'Crucifixion,' 131, 136, 137, as this is reflected in texts from Qumran.

to sacrifice swine daily. [254] He also ordered them not to circumcise their children, threatening to punish anyone who might be found acting contrary to these orders. He also appointed overseers who should assist in compelling them to carry out his instructions. [255] And so, many of the Jews, some willingly, others through fear of the punishment which had been prescribed, followed the practices ordained by the king, but the worthiest people and those of noble soul disregarded him, and held their country's customs of greater account maltreated daily, and enduring bitter torments, they met their death. [256] Indeed, they were whipped, their bodies were mutilated, and while still alive and breathing, they were crucified, (ζῶντες ἔτι καὶ ἐμπνέοντες ἀνεσταυροῦντο) while their wives and the sons whom they had circumcised in despise of the king's wishes were strangled, the children being made to hang from the necks of their crucified (τῶν ἀνεσταυρωμένων) parents. And wherever a sacred book or copy of the Law was found, it was destroyed; as far those in whose possession it was found, they too, poor wretches, wretchedly perished.[137]

And *Jewish War*, VII:194-205

[Siege of Machaerus] ...

It was, however, invariably the opportunity which, in the main decided the victory in favour of either side: of the Jews if they fell upon their enemy when off his usual guard, of those on the mounds if they foresaw and met their sally in a posture of defence. [195] It was not, however, these encounters which were destined to end the siege, but a casual and surprising incident constrained the Jews to surrender the fortress. [196] Among the besieged was a youth of daring enterprise and strenuous energy named Eleazar. [197] He had distinguished himself in the sallies by stimulating most of his comrades to come out and check the progress of the earthworks, and in the engagements by frequently making fearful havoc of the Romans; besides easing the attack for all who ventured out with him and covering their retreat by being the last to withdraw. [198] Now on one occasion, when the battle was over and both parties had retired, he, disdainfully assuming that none of the enemy would resume the fight, remained outside the gates conversing with his comrades on the wall and devoting his whole attention to them. [199] Thereupon, spying his opportunity, a soldier in the Roman ranks named Rufus, a native of Egypt, made a sudden dash upon him, such as none could have expected, lifted him up, armour and all, while the spectators on the wall were paralysed with astonishment, and succeeded in transporting the fellow to the Roman camp. [200] The general having ordered him to be stripped and carried to the spot most exposed to the view of the onlookers in the city and there severely scourged, the Jews were profoundly affected by the lad's fate, and the whole town burst into such wailing and lamentation as the misfortune of a mere individual seemed

---

[137] Josephus, *Jewish Antiquities*, Books XII-XIV (Ralph Marcus, trans.; Cambridge, Mass.; London: Harvard University Press; William Heinemann, 1976).

history; and you now see why. This place with its view of Italy was deliberately picked out by Verres, that his victim, as he died in pain and agony, might feel how yonder narrow channel marked the frontier between the land of slavery and the land of freedom, and that Italy might see her son, as he hung there, suffer the worst extreme of the tortures inflicted upon slaves (*Italia autem alumnum suum servitutis extremo summoque supplicio affixum videret*). [170] To bind a Roman citizen is a crime, to flog him is an abomination, to slay him is almost an act of murder: to crucify him is—what? There is no fitting word that can possibly describe so horrible a deed. Not satisfied with all the cruelty I have told you of, 'Let him be in sight of his native land,' he cries, 'let him die with justice and freedom before his eyes.' It was not Gavius, not one obscure man, whom you nailed upon that cross of agony: it was the universal principle that Romans are free men (*Non tu hoc loco Gavium, non unum hominem nescio quem, sed communem libertatis et civitatis causam in illum cruciatum et crucem egisti.*).— Nay, do but mark the villain's shamelessness! One can imagine how it vexed him to be unable to set up that cross to crucify us Roman citizens in our Forum, in our place of public assembly and public speech: for he picked out the corner of his province that should be most like Rome in its populousness, and nearest to Rome in its position; he would have this memorial of his abandoned wickedness stand in sight of Italy, at the entrance-gate of Sicily, in a place where all who came and went that way by sea must pass close by it.[136]

This text argues that the Roman citizenship of the person accused of some act is a fact which has to be taken in consideration when the kind of punishment for that particular act is decided. Crucifixion must be eliminated from these. It is 'a cruel and disgusting penalty' and 'there is no fitting word that can possibly describe so horrible deed'. This text also points to the reason for which Verres crucified Gavius. That crucifixion of a Roman citizen was intended as a declaration of 'war upon the whole principle of the rights of the Roman citizen body;' as a 'view of Italy and a prospect of [...] home country.' 'The universal principle that Romans are free men' was nailed on that cross. The intention was that the province of Verres should be 'most like Rome in its populousness, and nearest to Rome in its position.' The text also says that this kind of death was usually 'inflicted upon slaves', and was executed 'in a place where all who came and went that way by sea must pass close by it.'

The element of subduing by terror was the main reason for crucifixion, especially in war times. Here are some relevant examples from Josephus. *Jewish Antiquities,* 12:253-256

[253] And he [Antiochus] compelled them to give up the worship of their own God, and to do reverence to the gods in whom he believed; he then commanded them to build sacred places in every city and village, and to set up altars on which

---

[136] Cicero, *Against Verres*: Part Two Books III, IV and V (London; Cambridge, Mass.: William Heinemann Ltd; Harvard University Press, 1953).

dragged off to execution, what cry would you be uttering, save that you were a Roman citizen? You, a stranger among strangers, among savages, among a people inhabiting the farthest and remotest regions of the earth, would have been well served by your claim to that citizenship whose glory is known throughout the world: what, then, of this man whom you were hurrying to execution? whoever he was, he was unknown to you, and he declared himself a Roman citizen: could not that statement, that claim of citizenship, secure from you on your judgment-seat if not remission yet at least postponement of the sentence of death? [167] Poor men of humble birth sail across the seas to shores they have never seen before, where they find themselves among strangers, and cannot always have with them the acquaintances to vouch for them. Yet such trust have they in the single fact of their citizenship that they count on being safe, not only where they find our magistrates, who are restrained by the fear of law and public opinion, and not only among their own countrymen, to whom they are bound by the ties of a common language and civic rights and much else beside: no, wherever they find themselves, they feel confident that this one fact will be their defence. Take away this confidence, take away this defence from Roman citizens; lay it down that to cry 'I am a Roman citizen' shall help no man at all; make it possible for governors and other persons to inflict upon a man who declares himself a Roman citizen any cruel penalty they choose, on the plea that they do not know who the man is; do this, accept that plea, and forthwith you exclude Roman citizens from all our provinces, from all foreign kingdoms and republics, from every region of that great world to which Romans, above all other men, have always had free access until now. And then again, when Gavius named the Roman knight Lucius Raecius, who was in Sicily at the time—might you not at least have written to him at Panhormus? Your Messanian friends would have kept your man in safe custody, you would have had him chained and locked up, till Raecius arrived from Panhormus. Should he identify the man, you would no doubt lessen the extreme severity (*summo supplicio*) of the sentence: should he fail to do so, then you would be free to set up this precedent, if you chose, that a man who was not known to yourself, and could not produce some person of substance to vouch for him, might be put to death on the cross, even if he were a Roman citizen.

[169] But I need say no more about Gavius. It was not Gavius against whom your hate was then displayed: you declared war upon the whole principle of the rights of the Roman citizen body. You were the enemy, I say again, not of that individual man, but of the common liberties of us all. What else was the meaning of your order to the Messanians, who had followed their regular custom by setting up the cross on the Pompeian Road behind the town, to set it up in the part of the town that looks over the Straits? and why did you add words that you cannot possibly deny having used, words that you said openly in the hearing of all—that you purposely chose this spot to give this man, since he claimed to be a Roman citizen, a view of Italy and a prospect of his home country as he hung on his cross? That is the only cross, gentlemen, ever set up in this spot in all Messana's

we may die free men. But the executioner, the veiling of the head, and the very word 'cross' should be far removed not only from the person of a Roman citizen but from his thoughts, his eyes and his ears. For it is not only the actual occurrence of these things or the endurance of them, but liability to them, the expectation, nay, the mere mention of them, that is unworthy of a Roman citizen and a free man.[135]

The ideas of liberty and dignity were at stake when crucifixion was in view. The discourse from Cicero, *Against Verres* 2:5:165-170 gives the important associated ideas with crucifixion and also provides an example of figurative usage of this kind of death. We decided to quote a longer section (see also the three long quotations from Josephus below) from this because it is the most important text which we found in ancient literature where many relevant ideas associated to crucifixion are present; in this way we can 'hear' more about such a death.

> [165] Now when I have given your friends and supporters ample proof of all these facts that I undertake to prove, I intended to lay hold of the very point which you yourself concede me, and proclaim myself content with that. What did you say yourself the other day, when you leapt up terrified by the shouts and angry gestures of your coutrymen—what did you tell us plainly then? That the man kept calling out that he was a Roman citizen simply in order to delay his execution, but was in fact a mere spy. Very well then, my witnesses are telling the truth. It is precisely this that we are told by Gaius Numitorius, by those two well-known gentlemen Marcus and Publius Cottius who come from Tauromenium district, by Quintus Lucceius who has been an important banker in Regium, and by all the rest. For until now the witnesses I have called have been chosen not from among those who were to state that they knew Gavius personally, but from those who were to state that they saw him when he was being dragged off to be crucified in spite of his proclaiming himself a Roman citizen. (*Adhuc enim testes ex eo genere a me sunt dati, non qui novisse Gavium, sed se vidisse dicerent, cum is, qui se civem Romanum esse clamaret, in crucem ageretur.*) This is exactly what you, Verres, say, that is what you admit, that he kept proclaiming himself a Roman citizen, that this mention of his citizenship had not even so much effect upon you as to produce a little hesitation, or to delay, even for a little, the infliction of that cruel and disgusting penalty. (*crudelissimi taeterrimique supplicii*)—[166] Of this admission, gentlemen, I lay hold, I stand by this, I am content with this one thing, all the rest may pass unheeded: his own admission must inevitably ensnare him and put the knife to his throat.—You did not know who he was, you had reasons for believing him a spy? I do not ask you what those reasons were. Out of your own mouth I accuse you: the man claimed to be a Roman citizen. If you Verres, had been made prisoner in Persia or the remotest part of the India, and were being

---

[135] Cicero, *Pro Rabirio Perduellionis* (H. Grose Hodge, trans.; London; Cambridge, Mass.: William Heinemann Ltd; Harvard University Press, 1959).

foreground'.[131] In Cranfield's discourse it is not clear what element from the 'image' of baptism shows that, in God's sight, we were crucified with Christ on Golgotha.

The view of M. de Boer is valuable when he says that 'crucifixion of the old Adam with Christ constitutes Paul's soteriological adaptation and application of the cosmological-apocalyptic motif of God's eschatological destruction of the cosmic powers that have come to reign over the world.'[132] He does not develop that because his main concern was not a study of Romans 6 but of Rom. 5:12-21.

To discern the meaning of the language of 'crucifixion' the interpreter has to be able to 'hear' as much as possible from the associated ideas of this chosen vehicle of the metaphor of death (see below). Then he has to bring that information in this particular context where the qualifier ὁ παλαιὸς ἄνθρωπος (see chapter 4) and the argument of the passage will suggest the elements which are relevant for understanding this language from the whole presupposition pool which he is able to reconstruct.

The references to the crucifixion in the available ancient literature are few and the information provided is limited.[133] The text from Cicero, *Pro Rabirio*, 16, provides an explanation for this small number of references and lack of detail:[134]

> How grievous a thing it is to be disgraced by a public court; how grievous to suffer a fine, how grievous to suffer banishment; and yet in the midst of any such disaster some trace of liberty is left to us. Even if we are threatened with death,

---

[131] Schnackenburg, *Baptism*, 54.

[132] de Boer, *Defeat of Death*, 177.

[133] See the detailed studies of Martin Hengel, Crucifixion in the Ancient World and the Folly of the Message of the Cross (John Bowden, trans.; London: SCM Ltd, 1977); J. B. Green, 'Crucifixion', in Gerald F. Hawthorne and Ralph P. Martin, eds., *Dictionary of Paul and His Letters* (Downers Grove, Illinois; Leicester, England: IVP, 1993), 197-9; Gerald G. O'Collins, 'Crucifixion', in David Noel Freedman, editor-in-chief, *The Anchor Bible Dictionary*. Volume 1: A-C (New York: Doubleday, 1992), 1207-10; Joseph A. Fitzmyer, 'Crucifixion in Ancient Palestine, Qumran Literature, and the New Testament', in *To Advance the Gospel. New Testament Studies* (New York: Crossroad, 1981), 125-46, for the analysis of the archeological evidences.

[134] In the examples from Herodotus in his *Histories* the references (1:128; 3:125; 3:132; 3:159; 9:120) are without detailed additional comments. The reference from 9:120 is

So they carried Artayctes away to the headland where Xerxes had bridged the strait (or by another story, to the hill above the town Madytus), and there nailed him to the boards and hanged him aloft (πρὸς σανίδας προσπασσαλεύσαντες ἀνεκρέμασαν·); and as for his son, they stoned him to death before the father's eyes.'

This crucifixion was executed at the orders of the general Xanthippus because Artayctes wronged Protesilaus of Elaeus. The implied elements are that it was a form of punishment which was executed at a known place to be seen by many.

and makes its crucifixion God's gracious act, is expressed by the genitive that characterises the body: 'the body of sin'.). It is not clear how this underlined aspect of 'grace' contributes to Paul's point here. The argument is not that this 'crucifixion with' is an act of 'grace' but that this form of 'condemnation' ('crucifixion') is a way in which the power of sin is subdued. Also, we will argue that the 'horror' aspect is implied (see below).

Another position is that defended by N. Elliott. He argues for the fact that the cross has to be seen as a 'brutal fact', 'as an instrument of imperial terror.'[120] He follows Hengel in his conclusion that the cross had a 'supreme efficacy as a deterrent'[121] and that in the system of the Roman Empire the cross was an important key for maintaining security.[122] But after saying this, when he discusses the meaning of the affirmations from Romans 6 he highlights only the aspect of the 'apocalyptic scheme of fields of power.'[123] 'The significance of Jesus' death is that through baptism it causes Christians to die to the dominion of sin, just as Christ died to the dominion of sin (6:2, 6-7, 11-14).'[124] In Romans 6 baptism is not a means of killing[125] and Christ's death to sin is not the same as that of believers.[126] It is not clear why Elliott does not work with the ideas associated with crucifixion in the ancient world which he presented in his argument for an understanding of cross in Paul,[127] especially here where the language of 'crucifixion' is present.

Cranfield explains the meaning of crucifixion with Christ by saying that 'in baptism we received the divinely-appointed sign and seal that by God's gracious decision it [our fallen human nature] was, in His sight, crucified with Christ on Golgotha. It is not implied that the old man no longer exists.'[128] This element of 'decision' is highlighted by Stuhlmacher when he says: 'Their old body, given over to and yielding sin, has experienced the death sentence on the cross of Christ'.[129]

Every position which argues from the side of 'baptism'[130] has to face the fact that it is difficult to put together a rite in which water is used and a brutal action by which someone is killed. Schnackenburg is right when he says that this expression 'by no stretch of imagination can it be said to have been determined by the rite. The rite and its symbolic content certainly do not stand in the

---

[120] Elliott, *Liberating*, 93.
[121] Elliott, *Liberating*, 96.
[122] Elliott, *Liberating*, 99.
[123] Elliott, *Liberating*, 129.
[124] Elliott, *Liberating*, 129.
[125] See the argument in chapter 4.
[126] See the argument above.
[127] Elliott, *Liberating*, 93-107.
[128] Cranfield, *Romans*, 309.
[129] Stuhlmacher, *Romans*, 92.
[130] See also Barrett, *Romans*, 117.

Paul chooses this language of 'crucifixion', says Moo, because Christ's death 'took the form of crucifixion.'[114] The way in which this 'crucifixion' leads to a 'release' is explained by Moo as follows: 'Just as Christ's crucifixion meant his release from the realm of sin (6:10) [...], so our crucifixion with Christ means our release from the realm of sin (6:1)'.[115]

Bornkamm points out that

> Paul, [...] with his mind on the present state of baptised believers, speaks only of their being crucified, dead, and buried with Christ. Rising with him, life, is an object of hope (Rom. 6:2-8). Thus their present state is under the auspices of the cross. As crucified with him, believers still wear a 'body of humiliation' (Phil. 3:21; cf. 3:10; Rom. 8:17).[116]

In a position like this there is no reference to the type of language used by Paul in trying to interpret it.

Byrne states that 'for believers "con-crucifixion" involved in the baptismal union with Christ has radically severed their "attachment" to that world (cf. later 7:4). It has put an end once and for all to their slavery of sin, the tyrant overlord of the old era.'[117] Byrne only affirms that 'con-crucifixion [...] has radically severed their attachment to that world' but does not explain how that happens, and why the 'crucifixion' aspect is in view. Also, his affirmation that 'it has put an end once and for all to their slavery of sin' is an extreme affirmation; if that is so what is the place of the imperatives in the same chapter in the letter?

In Schlatter's explanation there is a place for some of the associated ideas of 'crucifixion' that can be present in Paul's argument. He points out that

> here Paul characterises the death of Jesus by a cross; it is the distinguishing mark for the forensic intent of his death. The one who had to end up on the cross has been stripped of all his rights and honour. The believer finds himself totally condemned because he arises from and belongs to present humanity. [...] Yet this radical renunciation of right and life which the individual surrenders in full is altogether free of despair and contempt for human life.[118]

In this context Schlatter understands the meaning of σύν as pointing to the fact that 'the judgment executed upon Jesus was also carried out for us.'[119] Schlatter does not explain why these associated ideas of judgment and of losing all rights are present and not others. When he develops the idea of 'judgment' he accentuates the aspect of 'grace' ('What renders the body worthy of death

---

[114] Moo, *Romans*, 373.

[115] Moo, *Romans*, 373.

[116] Gunther Bornkamm, *Paul* (trans. by D. M. G. Stalker; London: Hodder and Stoughton, 1971), 190; see also Bornkamm, 'Baptism,' 78.

[117] Byrne, *Romans*, 191.

[118] Schlatter, *Romans*, 141.

[119] Schlatter, *Romans*, 141.

The 'Crucifixion' Language (Romans 6:6)

A quotation from Dunn is a good starting point for this section because it points out the nature of Paul's language here in Romans 6.

> In conversion-initiation there was no literal death, no actual burial, no bones fused, no believer nailed on the cross. Nevertheless, something happened that could be described as a death, as a burial, as a fusing (like that of broken bones), as a crucifixion, all terms linked back to and informed by the actual death of Christ. The metaphors expressed a reality/(realities) that could not be expressed in an objectifiable description, 'reality depicting without pretending to be directly descriptive', a word used 'in such a way that it meant something different from the literal referent, but connected through some similarity'.[109]

The discussion among scholars at this point is focused mainly on the question of 'participation', namely, *when* and *how* this 'crucifixion with' Christ took place. Here are the main positions.

J.D.G. Dunn interprets the meaning of the metaphorical language of 'crucifixion' but he does not take into account the ideas associated with the *vehicle* used by Paul; these can offer some ideas about the 'point(s)' of the metaphor. He says that

> the aorist denotes the decisive salvation-history event of the Christ's death whose effect in ending the rule of sin and death enters the experience of those who are identified and identify themselves with that event in the commitment of baptism and thereafter.[110]

Also he does not explain why it is maintained by Paul that 'the cross [...] is the only means by which the rule of sin and death could be broken'.[111] This example from Dunn illustrates the way in which the 'crucifixion' language is interpreted by scholars.[112]

D. Moo argues for a forensic character of Paul's language. He states that

> 'crucified with Christ' refers not to our own burial and death but to our participation in Christ's crucifixion. What is meant is not the believer's duty to put away sin, but the act of God whereby, in response to our faith, he considers us to have died the same death Christ died.[113]

---

[109] James D. G. Dunn, 'Baptized as Metaphor', in Stanley E. Porter and Anthony R. Cross, eds, *Baptism, the New Testament and the Church: Historical and Contemporary Studies in Honor of R. E. O. White* (Sheffield: Sheffield Academic Press, 1999), 300.

[110] Dunn, *Romans,* 319.

[111] Dunn, *Romans,* 319.

[112] See also A. Nygren, *Commentary on Romans* (Philadelphia: Fortress, 1949), 235; Murray, *Romans,* 220; J. Ziesler, *Paul's Letter to the Romans* (London: SCM, 1989), 154, 159.

[113] Moo, *Romans,* 372.

But if ὁμοίωμα means 'representation' and refers to the proclamation of the death and resurrection of Christ, then that event is believed, that is, they are 'coalesced' with it and as Christ was raised from the dead they can walk in the newness of life.[106]

Thus, even if the other possibilities[107] for a different meaning and reference to the ὁμοίωμα are available[108] (see the above positions), the last one is preferred because it is able to explain the way in which someone knows something about the matter in discussion — Christ's death and it was a part of the proclamation of the gospel; this event/action of proclamation stands at the start of the Christian life. According to the text which offers the 'theme' of the letter (Rom. 1:16-17), the 'gospel' has a fundamental role in bringing salvation for every one who believes what is proclaimed about what God did in Christ's death and resurrection for salvation. The 'unity' with this 'representation' of Christ's death and resurrection, says Paul, is a continuous reality in the life of the believers.

The last important reference to the language of 'death' is in Rom. 6:6 where Paul speaks about the 'co-crucifixion of our old man'. Distinguishing the associated ideas of 'crucifixion' language and their relevance for this text is the task of the next section.

---

[106] See also Fitzmyer who says that 'esometha has to be understood as gnomic, expressing a logical sequel to the first part of the verse'. Fitzmyer, *Romans,* 435.

[107] From all the occurrences in the LXX (Exod. 20:4; Deut. 4:12,15,16,17,18,23,25; 5:8; Josh. 22:28; Jud. 8:18; 1 Kgs. 6:5,5;; 4 Kgs. 16:10; 2 Chr. 4:3; Ps. 105 (106):20; 143 (144):12; Cant. 1:11; Sir. 31 (34):3; 38:28; Isa. 40:18,19; Ez. 1:4,5,16,22,26; 2:1 (1:28); 8:2,3; 10:1,8,10,21,22; 23:15; Dan. LXX 3:25 (92); 1 Macc. 3:48), the example from Deut. 4:11-25 is representative.

From the extrabiblical Greek see also Plato, *Parm.* 132d, 133d; *Soph.* 266d; *Crat.* 434a; Aristotle, *Metaph.* 985b, 986a; *Rhet.* I.2. 1356a, 31. The occurrences from inscriptions (Egypt: Hibis II 52; OGIS 52; Prose 52) and papyri (*ChrWick* 1,21; *OMich* 32; *PCair* 1 10; *PFamTebt* 4:98; *PoxyHels* 2; cf. Packard Humanities Institute database of Greek Inscriptions and Papyri) do not contribute to the elucidation of meaning because they are fragmentary and thus very short.

[108] With the exception of Rev. 9:7 this term occurs in NT only in the Pauline Corpus: Rom. 1:23 (referring to idols which 'resemble' a mortal human being or a bird); 5:14 (a reference to the sins which were committed in the period between Adam and Moses when there was not a law in place and so these sins were not 'like' the sin of Adam which was a trespass of a command); 8:3 (the Son of God was sent in the 'likeness' of the sinful flesh; this points to the fact that the 'sinful flesh' imposed a particular 'way of existence' in the world and the Son came and shared in it); Phil. 2:7 (Christ was born in 'human likeness', meaning that he was a man).

The Language of 'Death'   77

Ath. After the writing-master, must we not address the lyre-master?

Clin. Certainly.

Ath. When assigning to the lyre-master their proper duties in regard to the teaching training in these subjects, we must, as I think, bear in mind our previous declarations.

Clin. Declarations about what?

Ath. We said, I fancy, that the sixty-year old singers of hymns to Dionysus ought to be exceptionally keen of perception regarding rhythms and harmonic compositions, in order that when dealing with musical representations of a good kind or a bad, by which the soul is emotionally affected, they may be able to pick out the *reproductions* (ὁμοιώματα) of the good kind and of the bad, and having rejected the latter, may produce the other in public, and charm the souls of the children by singing them, and so challenge them all to company them in acquiring virtue by means of these representations (μιμήσεις).[104]

Therefore, a melody, a discourse was called ὁμοίωμα because it 'represented' something (a feeling, an action, character). The issue was that this ὁμοίωμα affected the hearer/viewer, and that is why the above text speaks about the protection of the hearers/viewers by presenting them only the ὁμοιώματα of a good kind, for charming their souls.

Thus the interpretation argued for in this project is that 'the gospel is the power of God for salvation' based on the fact that when someone heard it being proclaimed (proclamation which is referred here as ὁμοίωμα) and believed it he 'was changed in the soul'. Paul uses the expression 'they were united with' what was proclaimed, they 'coalesced' with what they heard; the accent being on the 'death of Christ'. In other words, the proclamation of the gospel ('the disclosure' of God's salvation in Christ's death) is a 'representation' of Christ's death and resurrection. Paul says that both events are 'present' for being 'united with'. The relation between them is that if they 'are one' with what was proclaimed about Christ's death they 'will be one' with what was proclaimed about his resurrection. The idea is not that death is a present reality and resurrection is a future one, but that if the first is in place then the second has to be there also. This is not called 'resurrected' life but 'newness of life'. The interpretation of the ἐσόμεθα depends on the meaning given to ὁμοίωμα. If ὁμοίωμα means 'corresponding reality' (Dunn) or 'form' (Tannehill, Moo, Schreiner) the future is understood as eschatological: only then the believers will be united with the 'corresponding reality' or 'form' of the resurrection.[105]

---

[104] Plato, *Laws* (II; R. G. Bury, tr; Cambridge, Mass.; London: Harvard University Press; William Heinemann Ltd, 1984).

[105] See the arguments of Käsemann, *Romans,* 169; Dunn, *Romans,* 318; Edwards, *Romans,* 162; Moo, *Romans,* 371.

And since it is the case that music is one of the things that give pleasure, and that virtue has to do with the feeling delight and love and hatred rightly, there is obviously nothing that is more needful to learn and become habituated to than to judge correctly and to delight in virtuous characters and noble actions; but rhythms and melodies contain *representations* (ὁμοιώματα) of anger and mildness, and also of courage and temperance and all their opposites and the other moral qualities, that most closely correspond to the true nature of these qualities (and this is clear from the facts of what occurs—when we listen to such representations we change in our soul); and habituation in feeling pain and delight at representations (τοῖς ὁμοίοις) of reality is close to feeling them towards actual reality (for example, if a man delights in beholding the statue of somebody for no other reason than because of its actual form, the actual sight of the person whose statue he beholds must also of necessity give him pleasure); and it is the case that whereas the other objects of sensation contain no *representation* (ὁμοίωμα) of character, for example the objects of touch and taste (though the objects of sight do so slightly, for there are forms that represent character, but only to a small extent, and not all men participate in visual perception of such qualities; also visual works of art are not *representations* (ὁμοιώματα) of character but rather the forms and colours produced are mere indications of character, and these indications are only bodily sensations during the emotions; not but what in so far as there is a difference even in regard to the observation of these indications, the young must not look at the works of Pauson but to those of Polygnotus, and of any other moral painter or sculptor), pieces of music on the contrary do actually contain in themselves imitations of character; [1340b] and this is manifest, for even in the nature of the mere melodies there are differences, so that people when hearing them are affected differently and have not the same feelings in regard to each of them, but listen to some in a more mournful and restrained state, for instance the mode called Mixolydian, and to others in a softer state of mind, but in a midway state and with the greatest composure to another, as the Dorian mode alone of tunes seems to act, while the Phrygian makes men enthusiastic; for these things are well stated by those who have studied this form of education, as they derive the evidence for their theories from the actual facts of experience.[103]

It is clear from this text that a ὁμοίωμα (a 'representation' of anger, mildness, courage, temperance and all their opposites and other moral qualities) can change the soul of a hearer or viewer of it. There are different grades of perception and the viewers/hearers are affected differently. The next text deals exactly with this aspect of 'impact' and tries to 'exemplify' one of the comments from the quoted text ('the young must not look at the works of Pauson but to those of Polygnotus, and of any other *moral* painter or sculptor' (our italics)). The text is from Plato, *Laws*, 812b:

---

[103] Aristotle, *Politics* (H. Rackham, tr; Cambridge, Mass.; London: Harvard University Press, 1944).

interpreted as associative[99] (a translation of 6:5 being 'if we have been united with the likeness of his death, we will be also [united with the likeness] of [his] resurrection').

In Rom. 6:3-5 the reference is to the *beginning* of the Christian life (see the language of 'baptism'). The beginning of such a life is related to hearing the gospel which is proclaimed (see especially Rom. 6:17; 10:6-15; Gal. 3:1-3). The response or the attitude of those who are referred to as being Christians is that of 'believing/obeying' *what* was proclaimed (Rom. 6:17; 10:13-14; Gal. 3:3; also 1 Cor. 15:1-6). The death of Christ was part of that proclamation (Gal. 3:1-2; 1 Cor. 15:3). The evidence from Gal. 3:1 is important for understanding Rom. 6:5. That text says something about the way in which Paul proclaimed the gospel and the specific point is in relation to the way in which Christ's death was proclaimed: Christ was *portrayed* (προεγράφη) as crucified; it was a vivid verbal description.[100] The relevant point of this for our investigation is that this event was made 'present' before their eyes, or, as Betz puts it, it was 'so vividly and so impressively that his hearers imagined the matter to have happened right before their eyes.'[101]

Now the important question is whether there are any occurrences in the available Greek literature which would allow us to say that a discourse or a presentation of some action was referred to as ὁμοίωμα. If that is the case, one of the main lines of argumentation in Romans, namely, that 'the gospel is the power of God for salvation to everyone who has faith, [..] for in it the righteousness of God is revealed through faith for faith' (1:16-17), receives an important place in the argument of Romans 6. Paul says that the *act of proclamation* of the gospel is an event of revelation. The saving righteousness of God (δικαιοσύνη θεοῦ) is revealed in what he did in the death and resurrection of Christ. That proclaimed 'story/image' of God's salvation of humankind accomplished in the death and resurrection of Christ is the event with which they are 'united' in the sense that they believed it. In other words, these saving events are proclaimed and what was accomplished *then* is revealed *now* (see the present tense in 1:17).[102] Also, we note here the reference in the Rom. 6:17-18 where the releasing from the dominion of sin is the result of obedience from the heart to the 'pattern of teaching'.

Indeed there are Greek texts in which ὁμοίωμα is used with the sense of a 'representation', which refers either to a discourse, a melody, or a drama. Two texts are especially relevant for our enquiry. First, Aristotle, *Politics* 1340a-b:

---

[99] Schnackenburg, *Baptism,* 46; Bornkamm, 'Baptism,' 78; Wilckens, *die Römer,* 13; Schreiner, *Romans,* 315.

[100] Louw and Nida, *Lexicon,* 410; see the discussion in J. Louis Martyn, *Galatians* (New York: Doubleday, 1997), 283; Neil Elliot, *Liberating Paul: The Justice of God and the Politics of the Apostle* (Sheffield: Sheffield Academic Press, 1995), 93.

[101] Hans Dieter Betz, *Galatians* (Philadelphia: Fortress Press, 1979), 131.

[102] See the discussion in Dunn, *Romans,* 43; Moo, *Romans,* 69-70.

In answering the question 'why does Paul speak of the 'form' of Christ's death rather than speaking simply of his death?' Tannehill points to Phil 2:7 where ὁμοίωμα 'is used to describe the existence of Christ after self-emptying.'[95] According to Tannehill, Paul used this term in Rom. 6:5

> because the death and resurrection are connected with the two 'forms' of Christ's existence, the earthly existence of the one who was subject to the powers and the heavenly existence of the exalted Lord. The use of ὁμοίωμα in Rom. 6:5 reflects this idea of conformation to Christ (Phil. 3:21; 3:10). It adds to the thought of this verse in that it suggests that Christ's death and resurrection are continuing aspects of the 'form' of Christ and that the death and resurrection of Christ are present to the believers in transforming power, so that the believers take on the same 'form'.[96]

This line of interpretation is able to integrate the 'form' of Christ's death (by crucifixion; Rom. 6:6.) in the general line of the argument. Also it points to the theme of the section 'death to sin' by its reference to the language of transformation by the 'form' of Christ's death. What is not clear is why σύμφυτος and ὁμοίωμα have to be treated almost like synonyms; these two terms have their role in Paul's argument and that has to be defined as clearly as possible. Paul does not use μορφή, but ὁμοίωμα (the point is not the 'form' of Christ's existence (Phil. 2:7), but *something about* his death and it is not clear that the *specific* point in view in 6:5 is on the 'form' of Christ's death) and it is better first to take into consideration all the available relevant texts before choosing one background or another. An interpretation has to be able to explain satisfactorily the existence of this lexeme here in order to be accepted.

Here in Rom. 6:5 Paul speaks about Christ's death and the *historical* aspect of this event is viewed in the sense that Christ experienced it. The basic question is how is that event to be viewed here. Everyone who was not an eye-witness knew about this event because someone else had told him about it (see Rom. 10:14-15). This basic observation is our starting point for defending a different interpretation of ὁμοίωμα in 6:5 than these presented above.

In relation to the syntax of the phrase, 'taking the genitive (τοῦ θανάτου) with the preceding word is more natural'.[97] Also, σύμφυτοι is more naturally followed by τῷ ὁμοιώματι (a dative following a συν- word);[98] the dative is

---

SCM, 1969), 77, and Schlatter, *Romans,* 149.

[95] Tannehill, *Dying,* 35.

[96] Tannehill, *Dying,* 39; also Cranfield, *Romans,* 308; for a recent defence of this position see Moo, *Romans,* 369-71, and Schreiner, *Romans,* 314.

[97] F. Blass and A. Debrunner, *A Grammar of the New Testament and Other Early Christian Literature* (Robert W. Funk, tr; Cambridge; Chicago: Cambridge University Press; The University of Chicago Press, 1961), 104, § 194.

[98] Also Schnackenburg, *Baptism,* 46; Moo, *Romans,* 368; Schreiner, *Romans,* 314, 315; Cranfield, *Romans,* 307; Betz, 'Transferring,' 115.

determines the relationship between the image of something and that something itself.'[89] Betz continues:

> it seems obvious that ὁμοίωμα is an abstractum referring to baptism. [...] Given the lexicological background of the term ὁμοίωμα and its main synonyms (εἰκών, μίμημα), the usage in v.5 intends, it seems, the ritual as ritual: this ritual is a ὁμοίωμα. Indeed other terms would not be appropriate because no cult image (εἰκών) is used and no dramatic episodes (μιμήματα) are performed.[90]

In relation to this position it has to be said that it is not clear that a phrase like βαπτίσματος εἰς τὸν θάνατον (6.4) is reiterated or is in view in the form of ὁμοιώματι τοῦ θανάτου αὐτοῦ in 6:5, so that one might conclude that 'the effects of the ritual' are in view in 6:5. The choice of σύμφυτος does not point to the 'effects' of the ritual but to 'the kind of relationship' which is in view,[91] namely 'a close relationship', a 'being one with', which is available. Even the text from Dio Chrysostom to which Betz refers in the note 112 (p. 115) does not point to the 'effects' but to the fact that those men were in a close relationship with the divine:

> for inasmuch as these earlier men were not living dispersed far away from the divine being or beyond his borders apart by themselves, but had grown up (πεφυκότες) in the very centre of things, or rather had grown up in his company and had remained close to him in every way (μᾶλλον δὲ συμπεφυκότες ἐκείνῳ καὶ προσεχόμενοι πάντα τρόπον). (12:28)[92]

The 'form' line of investigation is defended by Tannehill, and his position is followed by others (Cranfield, Moo, and Schreiner). He states that 'being united with the ὁμοίωμα of Christ's death is not restricted to the past rite, but is something which is characteristic of the continuing existence of the Christian.'[93] He says that in LXX there are two basic meanings for ὁμοίωμα: 'copy' or 'image' and 'form'.

> ὁμοίωμα indicates the form of the reality itself in its outward appearance, rather than a second thing which is similar to this reality. [...] Rom. 6:5 does not refer to the union of the believers with a 'likeness' of Christ's which is distinct from that death, but rather speaks of a direct union with Christ's death.[94]

---

[89] Hans Dieter Betz, 'Transferring a Ritual: Paul's Interpretation of Baptism in Romans 6', in Troels Engberg-Pedersen, ed., *Paul in His Hellenistic Context* (Edinburgh: T&T Clark, 1994), 114:

[90] Betz, 'Transferring,' 115.

[91] See the argument in chapter 4.

[92] Dio Chrysostom, *Discourses* (XII; J. W. Cohoon, trans.; Cambridge, Mass., London: Harvard University Press, William Heinemann Ltd, 1939).

[93] Tannehill, *Dying,* 34.

[94] Tannehill, *Dying,* 35; for another position which argues for the fact that 'the 'likeness of his death' characterizes the death of Christ' see Günther Bornkamm, 'Baptism and New Life in Paul (Romans 6)', in *Early Christian Experience* (London:

Ridderbos explains it by saying that the 'likeness' is 'a redemptive-historical likeness by virtue of its oneness with Christ'[81] and in this way interpreting 'likeness' against the group of texts in which the 'corresponding transcendental realities' are in view. Fitzmyer points out that ὁμοίωμα 'denotes not merely the abstract idea of 'likeness,' but the concrete image that is made to conform to something else (cf. LXX—Exod 20:4; Deut. 4:16-18; 5:8)'.[82] The reference is 'to baptismal washing as the means of growing together; that means is baptism, a likeness to Christ's death.'[83] Furthermore, he understands the dative of ὁμοίωμα as being a dative of instrument because, he asks, 'can one grow together with a likeness?'[84] The idea of 'conformity to something else' is present because in order to speak about 'likeness' with something some 'common' features have to be in place. But the problem with the identified reference of Fitzmyer's position is that baptism was not the way in which Christ died (his death was not by drowning). Also, 6:5b points to a present aspect of that 'being one with the likeness' (see the pf. γεγόναμεν), and if the 'likeness' refers to baptism, is the believer 'still under water'[85] in order to 'grow into union with him'?[86] And ὁμοίωμα has to be supplied also in the second part of 6:5 because of the ellipsis and in this case 'the likeness of the resurrection' cannot refer to something related to a past baptismal rite (baptism is not an image of resurrection but an instrument of burial (6:4)). Käsemann's observation is helpful here especially because that particular question ('can one grow with a likeness?') asked by Fitzmyer determined him to reach that conclusion (the baptismal washing as the likeness of Christ's death). He says that: 'it is in the best interests, therefore, not to cling too closely to the LXX or to postulate a standarized usage but to let the particular context be decisive.'[87] His interpretation is that 'Paul is speaking of the death of Jesus, which is both a historical and an eschatological event, and which cannot be fixed to a single time alone but concerns the whole world. [...] ὁμοίωμα [...] distinguishes from the event of Golgotha as much as it connects with that event'.[88] Thus, he is close to Ridderbos' position.

Another scholar who argues on the line of the meaning of ritual is H. D. Betz. He points out that Paul's choice of σύμφυτος and ὁμοίωμα was intended 'to illuminate two essential problems raised by rituals in general. The first term, σύμφυτος, states the effect that the ritual has, while the second, ὁμοίωμα,

---

[81] Ridderbos, *Paul*, 208.
[82] Fitzmyer, *Romans*, 435.
[83] Fitzmyer, *Romans*, 435.
[84] Fitzmyer, *Romans*, 435.
[85] Dunn, *Romans*, 317.
[86] This is Fitzmyer's translation of 6:5a.
[87] Käsemann, *Romans*, 167.
[88] Käsemann, *Romans*, 168.

italics)[73]

But in Rom. 6:5 the reference of ὁμοίωμα is not so much to what is 'in' the Christian, even if σύμφυτος is there in 6:5a, but rather to the ὁμοίωμα *of* Christ's death with which the believers are 'united'. The text speaks of 'being one *with* the ὁμοίωμα of Christ's death' not *because* of it. Also, it is not clear that the 'palpable' element has to be introduced in the interpretation of this text.

On a similar line (of a 'corresponding reality') Dunn understands ὁμοίωμα as meaning 'the convert's experience of death to sin and life beginning to work out in himself, which Paul characterizes as a sharing in Christ's death and so as an experience which is the mirror image and actual outworking of Christ's own death to sin within the present age (6:10)'.[74] His discussion on the meaning of ὁμοίωμα concludes that it denotes 'the form of transcendent reality perceptible to man.'[75] He argues for this especially on the basis of Plato, *Parmenides* 132D and *Phaedrus* 250B, texts where the 'finite things are ὁμοιώματα in which τὰ παραδείγματα (the heavenly "ideas") are expressed;'[76] the other texts being from the LXX—Exod 20:4; Deut. 4:12,15; 5:8; etc.[77] He applies this meaning to Rom. 6:6 saying that the believer has been fused together with 'the reality of Christ's epoch-ending, sin's-dominion-breaking death, in its outworking in the here and now, Christ's death to the extent that it can be experienced and is effective within the still enduring epoch of Adam.'[78] Dunn brings together the meaning of those texts in which ὁμοίωμα is used in reference to idols (LXX—Deut. 4:16-18, 23, 25; Ps 106:20; Rom. 1:23; etc) with those referring to the form of transcendental realities by saying that 'however mistakenly, an idol was intended to give concrete representation to spiritual and transcendental realities.'[79] Thus the basic outlook of Dunn's position is the idea of 'likeness'[80] which helps him to integrate both those main kind of texts: those which refer to idols, images and those which refer to transcendental realities. It is on the meaning and relevance of these two kinds of texts that the debate developed.

---

[73] Ugo Vanni, 'Ὁμοίωμα in Paolo (Rom 1,23; 5,14; 6,5; 8,2; Fil 2,7): Un'interpretazione Esegetico-Theologica Alla Luce Dell'uso Dei LXX, 2a Parte', *Gregorianum* 58 (1977) 431-70.

[74] J. D. G. Dunn, 'Paul's Understanding of the Death of Jesus as Sacrifice', in S. W. Sykes, ed., *Sacrifice and Redemption: Durham Essays in Theology* (Cambridge: Cambridge University Press, 1991), 37.

[75] Dunn, *Romans,* 317; also James R. Edwards, *Romans* (Peabody, Mass.: Hendrickson, 1992), 161-2.

[76] Dunn, *Romans,* 317.

[77] Dunn, *Romans*, 317.

[78] Dunn, *Romans,* 317.

[79] Dunn, *Romans*, 317.

[80] Dunn, *Romans*, 316.

the 'liberation' from the powers of the old aeon. Paul can speak about a 'benefit' from that event because Χριστός is a *king* who wins a victory for his people. Those who belong[69] to him are in a particular kind of relationship with his death[70] (the event which accomplished that victory) and thus are 'liberated' from those powers. On this line the specific point in Romans 6 is in 6:5 where Paul says 'For if we have been united with the likeness of his death'; the meaning of ὁμοίωμα from this verse is important for discerning the way in which that death 'to sin' is understood to be relevant/efficacious for the believers' lives. To understand the meaning and the role of this term (ὁμοίωμα) is the purpose of the next section.

The Likeness of Christ's Death (Romans 6:5)

The meaning and reference of this term depends on the context against which it is interpreted. Every interpretation has to be able to defend a particular line of enquiry on the basis of other relevant ideas from this letter and/or from other letters from Pauline Corpus. This section is organised as follows: a) a critical analysis of the present state of research and b) in the light of this a different understanding will be proposed.

There are two main positions as far as the meaning of ὁμοίωμα is concerned: 1) 'corresponding reality' and 2) 'form'. The first position is sustained by Vanni, Dunn, Ridderbos, and Betz and the second by Tannehill, Cranfield, Moo and Schreiner.

The most detailed study is that of U. Vanni, 'Ὁμοίωμα in Paolo'. He argues for an understanding of ὁμοίωμα against the linguistic context of the LXX[71] where he says that the meaning is the 'expression-representation of a reality'.[72] Vanni interprets Rom. 6:5 as follows:

> The context of Rom. 6:5 analysed in its temporal aspects, emphasizes baptism as a past fact, eschatological life as a future fact, and the present as a commitment which unites past and future. In such a context τῷ ὁμοιώματι expresses the concrete visibility in the Christian of both death and resurrection of Christ. One can interpret the passage in this way: 'If in fact we became and remain dynamically united (*to him*) because of the palpable expression (*in the rite of baptism and then in the life that follows*) of his death, then we will certainly (*be united to him*) also (*in the palpable expression which takes place in the immediate future and culminates in the eschatological phase*) of the resurrection. (his translation and

---

[69] See συν- expressions in Rom. 6:1-11.
[70] See the discussion on σύμφυτος (Rom. 6:5) in chapter 4.
[71] Ugo Vanni, 'Ὁμοίωμα in Paolo (Rm 1,23: 5,14: 6,5: 8,3: Fil 2,7): Un'interpretazione Esegetico-Theologica Alla Luce Dell'uso Dei LXX, 1a Parte', *Gregorianum* 58 (1977) 321-45.
[72] Vanni, 'Ὁμοίωμα in Paolo, 1a Parte,' p.345.

Jews before it is for others'.[64] This usage has to be seen as a marker for a still relevant *Jewish* background against which this term has to be understood.

Focusing on our main interest, when 'the death' of Jesus Christ is in view in the Pauline Corpus[65] the usual term used in speaking about the one who experienced that death is Χριστός.[66] Specifically in Romans he never says that 'Jesus died'. Χριστός is used in 3:24-25; 5:6,8; 6:3,10; 8:34; 14:9,15. These texts are mentioned here because they point to a consistent phenomenon: when Paul discusses the Calvary event his favourite description of the one who died is Χριστός. Starting from this observation the *why* of this lexical choice can be discussed. The previous discussion about Paul's usage of Χριστός pointed out that, according to the context, Χριστός as the Anointed davidic king can be taken into consideration when the meaning of Χριστός is discussed in a particular passage, especially in Romans.

In the text studied for this project Paul speaks about the death of Christ as being a 'death to sin' (6:10). Sin is portrayed as a powerful master who enslaves people. The result of this slavery is death.[67] As Paul puts it at the end of 5:12-21, 'sin reigned in death'. Against this background Christ's death and resurrection are discussed in Romans 6:1-14 in relation to the believer's life. These events, Paul says, are relevant for the situation of the believers. Because of the Calvary/Easter event, their relation to the powers of the old aeon has been changed. As far as the identity of the one who died and was raised is concerned, Paul does not provide any other than that of Χριστός. *If* these events are understood as the death and resurrection of *the Anointed davidic king* for the 'liberation' of his people from that particular bondage, the passage makes good sense as far as the relation between his death and resurrection and their situation is concerned. God acted powerfully on his behalf when he raised him from the dead (6:3) and this event is immediately interpreted as being relevant for the possibility for the believers of 'walking in the newness of life' (what God did in his Anointed is relevant for his people). Because he is considered as the Anointed [davidic] king and his death and resurrection are spoken of as doing something to these powers of the old aeon,[68] those who are his people 'benefit' from the 'liberation' accomplished by their king. *If the king wins a battle his people are 'liberated'*.

The implication of all this for this study is that *this has to be the reason* for which, in Pauline literature, the believer 'dies' only with Χριστός — he is the Anointed [davidic] king; by his death [and resurrection] he won for his people

---

[64] Witherington, *Paul*, 134.

[65] See here especially Leander E. Keck, 'Jesus in Romans', *JBL* 108/3 (1989) 443-60.

[66] The texts are as follows: 1 Cor. 1:17,23; 5:7; 8:11; 10:16; 15:3; 2 Cor. 1:5; 5:14; Gal. 2:21; 6:12; Eph. 5:2,25; Phil. 3:18. The exceptions are 1 Cor. 2:2 and Gal. 3:1. See also the discussions in Martin Hengel, 'Jesus,' 1, 2; Kramer, *Christ*, 28-32.

[67] See the discussion in the previous section.

[68] See the argument in the previous section.

his enemies. God helped him in that and he was kept by God 'as the head of the nations' (22:44). God brought down the peoples under him (22:48), and he was exalted above his adversaries (22:49). God has shown ἔλεος τῷ χριστῷ αὐτοῦ, τῷ Δαυιδ καὶ τῷ σπέρματι αὐτοῦ ἕως αἰῶνος (22:51b LXX). This understanding of the sharing in the victories of the χριστός is a way of expressing the character of the Anointed and the relation of his people with him. They share in the victories given him by God. The victories given by God to his χριστός are their victories because they are his people (if the king is victorious the people is victorious). Those victories are the reason for praise in Rom. 15:9.

It can be said from these observations that the meaning of Χριστός as 'the Anointed [davidic] king' has to be an option which, according to the particular context, has to be taken into consideration when interpreting Paul's affirmations in Romans[60].

Paul never uses the formula 'Jesus *is* the Christ' and he does not argue for this idea.[61] This could suggest that in his communities messiahship was not an idea under debate and according to the context of each affirmation this has to be considered as a possible presupposition[62] for Paul's affirmations about Χριστός.

From the way in which Paul uses the preposition ἐν in relation to Christ it can be concluded that he never writes ἐν Ἰησοῦ, and in Romans he wrote only once ἐν κυρίῳ Ἰησοῦ (14:14). In all the other cases he writes ἐν Χριστῷ Ἰησοῦ or ἐν Χριστῷ. The preposition εἰς is always used with Χριστός and never with Ἰησοῦς or κύριος.[63] These observations point to the fact that Χριστός has to be understood, according to the context, as a title. The associated ideas with this have to be understood depending on the context in each particular case.

Also the great number of Χριστός occurrences in Paul (270 in the seven undisputed letters; Ἰησοῦ Χριστοῦ or Χριστὸς Ἰησοῦς occurs 109 times — that is more than half of all occurrences in the New Testament) requires an explanation. If it is always only a second name of Jesus there is no reason for its being used so much (for describing his identity, other terms, less controversial, can be used). A better explanation is that the apostle affirms to his increasing Gentile audience that 'salvation is from the Jews and for the

---

[60] See also the brief comments by Wright, *Climax*, 47, 48, where he says that Christ has to be seen as 'Israel's representative, Messiah.' And 'because Jesus is the Messiah, he sums up his people in himself, so what is true of him is true of them' (48) Wright also gives Christ 'incorporative significance' (49).

[61] Also Witherington, *Paul*, 133.

[62] Cf. Witherington, *Paul*, 133.

[63] See especially N.T. Wright, *The Messiah and the People of God* (unpublished PhD dissertation; Oxford, 1980), 20-27, and Wright, *Climax*, 44-6.

The Language of 'Death'

The ideas proposed by Horbury are relevant for our study because in Paul Χριστός is used without being explained and according to the discussions presented in this section there are good reasons to consider it, according to the context, as retaining the flavour of a title. Paul does not enter any arguments for proving that his understanding of Χριστός fits in a particular stream of ideas from a particular Jewish tradition as messianism is concerned.

Thus, the best thing to do to verify this state of things, as usage of this 'familiar notion which needed no explanation' is concerned, is to see if it has some relevance for a better understanding of Paul's language, and to seek whether he gives some specific allusions toward this royal 'Davidic' interpretation for Χριστός. From the evidence in Romans he does that when he attaches to his description of Χριστός the qualifier that he is 'from the seed of David' (Rom. 1:3). Also there are two other relevant echoes to discuss, namely those from Romans 15. These are important because they narrow the relevant area of investigation as far as the meaning/identity of Χριστός is concerned in this epistle. First, Romans 1:3 (τοῦ γενομένου ἐκ σπέρματος Δαυίδ) echoes the texts from 2 Sam. 7 and Ps: 2. Dahl understands Rom. 1:2-4 'as a paraphrase and interpretation of the promise to David in 2 Sam. 7, esp. vv.3 and 4a: "according to the flesh" Jesus descended from David, "according to the spirit of holiness," by virtue of God's promise and action (cf. Gal. 4:23-29), he was "designated Son of God in power".'[58] Also 'Son of God' was a designation closely associated with David and hoped-for kings of the Davidic line: 2 Sam. 7:12-14; Ps. 2:7; cf. Ps. 89:3-45; 1 Chron. 17:13; 22.10; 28:6; 4QFlor. 1:7-11; 4Q246.[59] The echo from LXX in Rom. 15:12 interprets the coming of Χριστός (as a 'servant of the circumcised on the behalf of the truth of God in order that he might confirm the promises given to the patriarchs'; see here Jer. 33:14-15) as the 'coming of the root of Jesse'. The echoes in Rom. 15:9 are either from Ps. 17:50 or 2 Sam. 22:50. The relevant point for our investigation as far as the echo from Isa. 11:10 in Rom. 15:12 is concerned is that it identifies Χριστός on the same Davidic lines (ἡ ῥίζα τοῦ Ἰεσσαί; see here texts like Jer. 23:5; 33:15; Sir. 47:22; 4QFlor 1:10-13) as Rom. 1:3 does. Also, the texts echoed in Rom. 15:9 are part of another relevant aspect for his identity as coming from the seed of David: in the context of 2 Sam. 22:50 David defeated

---

and Annti Laato, *A Star is Rising* (Atlanta, Georgia: Scholars Press, 1997). In relation to the significance of the davidic ideas see Mark L. Strauss, *The Davidic Messiah in Luke-Acts: The Promise and Its Fulfillment in Lukan Christology* (Sheffield: SAP, 1995) and Kenneth E. Pomykala, *The Davidic Dynasty Tradition in Early Judaism; Its History and Significance for Messianism* (Atlanta: Scholars Press, 1995).

[58] N. A. Dahl, 'Messianic Ideas and the Crucifixion of Jesus', D. H. Juel, rev, in James H. Charlesworth, ed., *Messiah: Developments in Earliest Judaism and Christianity* (Minneapolis: Fortress Press, 1992), 391, 392.

[59] See also the discussion in Hengel, *Cross,* 86; MacRae, 'Messiah,' 172; Witherington, *Paul,* 131.

that from the second century BC onwards the abbreviated form '(the) Anointed' was used persistently, and this means that 'it corresponded to a familiar notion which needed no explanation',[51] and this has as its referent 'above all the coming Davidic king'.[52] Here are some of his examples of the usage of this 'unexplained technical term':[53] Dan. 9:25-26 uses the term offering very little additional explanation;[54] also the 'fuller designations imply the currency of the abbreviated form (1QS 9:11, "until there shall come the prophet and the messiahs of Aaron and Israel"; also 1QSa 2:20-21; CD 12:3-13:1)'.[55] For unqualified examples see 1QSa 2:11-12; Syriac Apocalypse of Baruch 29:3; 2 Esdras 12:32; Ps. Sol. 17:32 (36); also Horbury gives texts from the NT: John 1:42; 4:25; Mark 8:29; 12:35; John 7:41-42; Acts 2:36; 9:22; 26:33; 1 John 2:22.[56] It is not the purpose of this argument to enter the debate on the relationship between Jewish messianism and Christian messianism.[57]

Freedman, ed., *Anchor Bible Dictionary* (1; New York: Doubleday, 1992), 914; C.F.D. Moule, *The Origin of Christology* (Cambridge: CUP, 1977), 31; see also the discussion in Martin Hengel, 'Jesus, the Messiah of Israel', in *Studies in Early Christology* (Edinburgh: T&T Clark, 1995), 2: 'for a Greek, χριστός referring to a person would have been meaningless.') Only the associated ideas of anointing of persons are relevant for this study the anointing of objects will not be mentioned. In the LXX χριστός is the regular term for translating the Hebrew word māšîah from the OT. The act of anointing 'was part of the investiture of kings and priests in Israel, and holders of these offices were regularly referred to as 'anointed' with reference to this symbolic act' (de Jonge, 'Christos,' 914). χριστός with reference to the priests is used in Lev. 4:5, 16; 6:15; 2 Mac.1:10. (Also de Jonge, 'Christos,' 915) and with reference to the prophets in 1 Chr. 16:22; and to the patriarchs (Ps. 104:15). (The bibliography on this subject is vast; see it at the articles on this subject in *TDNT, NIDNTT, EDNT, ABD*.)

[51] William Horbury, *Jewish Messianism and the Cult of Christ* (London: SCM Press Ltd., 1998), 8.

[52] Horbury, *Messianism,* 11; for other views see de Jonge, 'Christos'; J.H. Charlesworth, 'From Messianology to Christology: Problems and Prospects', James H. Charlesworth, ed., in *The Messiah* (Minneapolis: Fortress, 1992), 3-35; Hahn, 'Χριστός'.

[53] Horbury, *Messianism,* 9; also Moule, *Christology,* 32.

[54] The reference of this term here is debatable: in v.25 Zerubbabel or Joshua the high priest and in v.26 to a high priest; see the discussion in Horbury, *Messianism,* 9.

[55] Cf. Horbury, *Messianism,* 10.

[56] Horbury, *Messianism,* 10; see also his examples in Rabbinic Literature and Targums (10-11).

[57] The literature on this subject is vast; see especially the collections of articles edited by James H. Charlesworth, ed., *The Messiah* (Minneapolis: Fortress, 1992), Leo Landman, ed, *Messianism in the Talmudic Era* (New York: Ktav Publishing House, Inc., 1979), John Day, ed, *King and Messiah in Israel and the Ancient Near East: Proceedings of the Oxford Old Testament Seminar* (Sheffield: Sheffield Academic Press, 1998), and the monographs by Joseph Klausner, *The Messianic Idea in Israel* (W. F. Stinespring, tr; London: George Allen and Unwin Ltd, 1956), Horbury, *Messianism*

It is a subject of debate whether in Pauline literature Χριστός retains the quality of a title or it is simply a *cognomen* of Jesus. From the available data in Paul, Dahl's conclusion is a good answer to this debate: 'Christos was not established yet as a name'.[45] Paul does not lose sight of the fact that Χριστός was originally a title.[46] Paul almost never uses Χριστός with κύριος;[47] and Kramer puts it like this:

> Paul speaks of *the Lord Jesus Christ*, of *our Lord Jesus Christ*, and of *the Lord Jesus*, but not of the *Lord Christ*. Similarly, Paul uses the formulae 'in the *Lord Jesus Christ*' and 'in *Christ Jesus our Lord*', but not 'in *Christ the Lord*' (εν Χριστῷ κυρίῳ). In all these instances *Lord* and *Christ* never stand immediately side by side. In view of the variety of forms in which these expressions occur, and in view of the frequency with which they are used, this can surely not be accidental. Moreover, if we take into consideration that *Lord* is a title and that *Christ*, as a translation of 'Messiah', originally ranked as a title, it is natural that the two titles were not made to follow immediately upon one another.[48]

Furthermore, Paul never adds a genitive to this term (e.g. 'the Anointed of the Lord', or 'the Christ of God' or 'the Christ of Israel'). This observation leads some scholars to conclude that Christ is 'never or virtually never used by Paul as title in the sense of Messiah, but only as a proper name.'[49] This observation has to be interpreted in the context of its Jewish usage.[50] W. Horbury points out

---

[45] Nils Alstrup Dahl, 'The Messiahship of Jesus in Paul', in *The Crucified Messiah and Other Essays* (Minneapolis: Augsburg Publishing House, 1974), 38.

[46] Cf. J.D.G. Dunn, *Unity and Diversity in the New Testament: An Enquiry Into the Character of Earliest Christianity* (London: SCM, 1977), 43; Ben Witherington, III, *Paul's Narrative Thought World: The Tapestry of Tragedy and Triumph* (Louisville, Kentucky: Westminster/John Knox Press, 1994), 132.

[47] The exception is Col 3:24b (τῷ κυρίῳ Χριστῷ δουλεύετε·); this exception can be explained keeping in view the fact that here Paul accentuates the quality of Χριστός as Lord/king. See also W. Grundmann, 'Χριστός in Paul's Epistles', in Gerhard Friedrich, ed., Geoffrey W. Bromiley, trans. and ed, *TDNT* (9; Grand Rapids, Michigan: W. B. Eerdmans, 1974), 540-80; Witherington, *Paul,* 132.

[48] Werner Kramer, *Christ, Lord, Son of God* (London: SCM, 1966), 214; even saying this Kramer finally says that in Paul this is a custom 'as a witness to something forgotten' (214). But this conclusion is not according to the available evidence in which the cotext of each occurrence of the Χριστός has to be decisive in discerning any 'titular' echoes.

[49] George S.J. MacRae, 'Messiah and Gospel', in Jacob Neusner, William Scot Green and Ernst S. Frerichs, eds, *Judaisms and Their Messiahs at the Turn of the Christian Era* (Cambridge: Cambridge University Press, 1987), 171, also 172.

[50] The usage of χριστός (a verbal adj. derived from χρίω = 'to spread liquid over, anoint') (see τὸ χριστόν = 'unguent, salve') in LXX, NT and the writings dependent on them is a unique phenomenon in Greek literature: this term is applied to a person. (Cf. F. Hahn, 'Χριστός', in *Exegetical Dictionary of the New Testament* (3; Grand Rapids, Michigan: W. B. Eerdmans, 1993), 478-86; Marinus de Jonge, 'Christos', in David Noel

Christ in His Death

Trying to define the associated ideas behind Χριστός is a difficult task because, first, the continuity between Jewish messianism and early Christian Christology is a matter of debate, and second, this term has become a second name of Jesus of Nazareth and it is not always clear where in the Pauline Corpus it has to be understood as a 'title' and where as a 'name'. As far as this section is concerned, we need to understand *why* in Pauline literature the believer 'dies' always with Χριστός and almost never with Jesus,[41] or with the Lord,[42] or with the Son. What was so unique/relevant about this lexeme, if anything, that, when Paul wrote about the *motif* of 'dying with Christ,' he always used this term for describing *him* with whom the believers 'died'?

The texts in the Pauline literature in which this theme appears are as follows: Rom 6:4-8, Rom 7:4, Gal 2:19,[43] Col 2:20, and Phil 3:10,[44] and 2 Tim 2:11 where the referent is Χριστός Ἰησοῦς (2:10).

For discussing this relationship between 'dying with' and 'Christ' a discussion of the general issue of Χριστός in Paul with reference to Romans is needed but the main interest here will be on 'death' language. A discussion of χριστός/'the Anointed' in the ancient Jewish literature looking at the relevance of the associated ideas for our study will follow, and because in this respect at the beginning of the letter to the Romans there is an important marker ('who was descended for David according to the flesh') the 'Davidic' side of the inquiry will receive detailed attention.

Χριστός IN ROMANS

This section is not a discussion about *Christ*ology in Romans but about the role played by the term Χριστός in the language of 'death' in Romans 6.

In Pauline studies on this subject of Χριστός the reader finds some fundamental observations which have to be discussed because they give the picture of the Pauline usage of this term. These will be studied here because of their relevance for our purpose: understanding the *why* of Paul's lexical choice of Χριστός as a description of Jesus in his death.

---

[41] The text in 2 Cor 4:10 (πάντοτε τὴν νέκρωσιν τοῦ Ἰησοῦ ἐν τῷ σώματι περιφέροντες, ἵνα αἰ ἡ ζωὴ τοῦ Ἰησοῦ ἐν τῷ σώματι ἡμῶν φανερωθῇ) is the exception but it has to be understood as a way of interpreting the suffering in his apostolic ministry and not as a way of defining the relationship with the realities of the old aeon of salvation like sin, law, flesh, the elements of the world.

[42] See here Galatians 6:14, but there the language of 'dying with,' does not appear, only the language of the cross.

[43] Also Gal 5:24 (οἱ δὲ τοῦ Χριστοῦ Ἰησοῦ τὴν σάρκα ἐσταύρωσαν σὺν τοῖς παθήμασιν καὶ ταῖς ἐπιθυμίαις).

[44] In the context of Gal. 3:2-10 he is described as Χριστός.

From this argument it is not clear how Christ's *death* overcomes the power of sin.[29] This is only affirmed by Schreiner, but not explained. Also it is not sure that the relation between 6:9 and 6:10 has to be defined as Moo and Schreiner do. 6:8b speaks about 'living with Christ'. This fact is based on the reality that Christ is not dead but alive. He was raised from the dead, death no longer has dominion over him (6:9b being a summary of 6:9a). The accent is on the resurrection of Christ from the dead. The point at this stage of Paul's argument is not that death no longer rules over him because he 'died to sin', but because he was raised. So, here γάρ has to be understood as 'a marker of a new sentence, (and) often best left untranslated or reflected in the use of "and" or the conjunctive adverb "then",'[30] and not as a 'marker of cause or reason between events, though in some contexts the relation is often remote or tenuous.'[31] The discussion about Christ's 'death to sin' has to be interpreted in this context of resurrection.

The affirmation from 6:10 presupposes both the perspective on sin as that from 6:6,7 (being the christological answer to that[32]), where sin is portrayed as having 'control,' as being a 'slave Master,'[33] (also 6:12,14), and the action of Christ from the previous paragraph (5:12-21) where he confronted the dominion of death and sin. Even if Paul does not say there that Christ 'died to sin' he says that Christ came ἐκ πολλῶν παραπτωμάτων (5:16). From the affirmation of 6:9('we know that Christ, being raised from the dead, will never die again; death no longer has dominion over him.') it can be seen that before the resurrection death *had* dominion over Christ. In this way Paul describes Christ's share in the world.[34]

---

[29] Also authors like Furnish, *Theology*, 172; Ridderbos, *Paul,* 208 do not explain how the cross and the death of Christ have put an end to the bondage of sin.

[30] Louw and Nida, *Lexicon*, 811; also NRSV.

[31] Louw and Nida, *Lexicon*, 780.

[32] See Fitzmyer, *Romans*, 438.

[33] See also Ridderbos, *Paul*, 208, who says 'he once died to sin [to the detriment of] considered as an authority that exercises power'.

[34] See the discussion in Dunn, *Romans*, 323.

[35] For a clearer insight about this relationship to sin see Rom 8:3.

[36] Against Tannehill, *Dying,* 28, who says that 'he is subject [...], to sin (Rom 6:10).

[37] See also the discussion in de Boer, *Defeat of Death,* 171, 172.

[38] See discussion below and also especially chapter 5.

[39] This text is used in the studies on atonement for explaining the 'once for all' character of Christ's death; see e.g. Martin Hengel, *The Cross of the Son of God* (trans. By John Bowden; London: SCM, 1986), 235, 239; Peter Stuhlmacher, *Reconciliation, Law and Righteousness: Essays in Biblical Theology* (Philadelphia: Fortress, 1986), 99; also Wedderburn, *Baptism,* 390.

[40] See also Dunn, *Romans,* 323.

similar language used about the Christian. He says that a 'close parallel' between these situations can be maintained. This is so because

> Paul is continuing to speak of sin as a 'ruling power.' Just as death once had 'authority' over Christ because of his full identification with sinful people in the 'old age,' so that other ruling power of the old age, sin, could be said to have had 'authority' over Christ.[25] As a 'man of the old age,' he was subject to the power of sin—with the critical difference that he never succumbed to its power and actually sinned. When these salvation-historical perspectives are given their due place, we are able to give 'die to sin' the same meaning here as it had in v.2: a separation or freedom from the rule of sin. And this transfer into a new state was for Christ final and definitive: 'once for all.' The finality of Christ's separation from the power of sin shows why death can no longer rule over him—for is not death the product of sin (Rom. 6:23 etc)?[26]

His position is close to that of Barrett but Moo does not bring into discussion the element of the obedience to the Father; also he understands the 'death to sin' as having the same meaning in 6:10 and 6:2.

The question which Moo does not answer is that concerning the role of Christ's death, which is the *event* in view here, in relation to a particular understanding of sin. In Christ's case the freedom from the rule of sin is not a result of his death 'once for all' (the Calvary event) while in the life of the Christians it *is* (the 'death to sin' is shaped by this event rather than by his 'sinlessness'). Also, it is not that 'death' does 'no longer rule over him' because of his 'separation from the power of sin' (a 'death to sin'), but because of his resurrection. In other words, the point of the context is not that Christ 'lives to God' because he was 'separated from sin', but because death no longer has dominion over him (he will never die again), and this is a result of the resurrection.

Schreiner works with the relationship between sin and death based on his understanding of the relationship between 6.9 and 10. He points out (with Moo[27]) that

> v.10 advances the argument by explaining why (γάρ) the dominion of death has ended. Death no longer rules over Jesus, because he died to the power of sin. The dative τῇ ἁμαρτίᾳ should be taken here as a dative of disadvantage and perhaps also possession, as in verse 2. Paul has already said in 5:21 that 'sin reigned in death.' [...] The only way that Christ could defeat the tyranny of death, therefore, was by overcoming the power of sin. Thus verse 10 explains that Jesus overcame the mastery of death because when he died he broke the power of sin 'once for all.'[28]

---

[25] See here also Tannehill, *Dying*, 28.
[26] Moo, *Romans*, 379.
[27] Moo, *Romans*, 378.
[28] Schreiner, *Romans*, 320.

Barrett puts these together by saying that Christ 'was raised from the dead by the glory of the Father (v.4), in order that he might continue to live to God only; he never lived otherwise.'[19] This understanding of the phrase allows Barrett to say that all that was said about Christ 'is, *mutatis mutandis*, applicable to the death and life of the Christian. It follows that a Christian (a) is dead as far as sin is concerned; (b) has been raised from the dead to life; (c) in this new life belongs to God.'[20]

It is true that Paul understands Christ as being sinless (2 Cor. 5:21), but here because of ἐφάπαξ the line of interpretation has to be in relation to the event of the cross, rather than on his life seen as a continuous obedience to the Father. Paul points to the event of Christ's death as one which is 'once and for all' and which is in 'relation to' sin (sin being understood as a powerful master - 6:6b, 12, 14). The reference to Christ's life in this text is to the resurrected life which is based not so much on his obedience in the earthly life but on his resurrection. If this is so, Paul's point is not that what was said about Christ (his obedience to his Father, he died sinless) 'is, *mutatis mutandis*, applicable to the Christian,' because in this text Christ's life is not used as an example to be followed, but his death and resurrection are the ones which 'worked' something relevant for the Christian life as far as sin is concerned. Paul, by a metaphorical transfer, uses the same expression 'die to sin' (6:2,11), which he explains in 6:3-7, for defining 'the walking in newness of life' as far as sin is concerned.[21]

Dunn also says that we should not take the 'death to sin' from 6:10 in a different sense than that from 6:2.[22]

> What is in view in both cases is the effective power of sin over human life as demonstrated most emphatically in the death which none escape. Jesus, in his oneness with those who belong to this age, shared in that subordination to the power of sin in death. It is because he shared the human condition to the full that his overcoming the death which all die can effectively break the despair and fear of death, and so already break its grip on human life.[23]

In other words Dunn says that the death of Jesus is a result of a full sharing in the human condition. The unclear thing is how Christ's death overcame death. Also the idea in 6:2 is not that believers die *because* of their sin, but that they 'died *to* sin'.

Another position is that of D. Moo[24] and T. Schreiner. Moo deals with the question of the relationship between this kind of language about Christ and the

---

1991), 118.

[19] Barrett, *Romans*, 118.
[20] Barrett, *Romans*, 118.
[21] See the whole argument in chapter 5.
[22] Dunn, *Romans*, 323.
[23] Dunn, *Romans*, 323.
[24] Also Murray is near to them, J. Murray, *The Epistle to the Romans* (London: Marshall, Morgan and Scott, 1967), 224.

to in relation to powers, it is regarded as a triumph over them. Further, where a dative construction is used in relation to death it indicates not a power, but rather an area of relationship within which the death takes place. Thus if Rom. 6:10 says that Christ died to the power of sin, then it is saying something most unusual, not to say unique, in the Pauline corpus. That, of course, is not *a priori* impossible, but it is unlikely, especially if the more expected meaning of the construction makes sense in the context, that is, if we understand Rom. 6:10 to be saying that at the time he died Christ was in close relationship with sin. [...] Thus the verse is saying that at his death Jesus is thought of as associated, and in relationship with sin: not his own sin, but the sin of humankind.[12]

Later in the argument Kaye introduces the idea of 'representative of sinners'[13] as a kind of summary for his interpretation of 6:10; and, understanding sin throughout Romans as an 'act',[14] he explains the relationship between 6:2 (the 'sinner's break with sin') and 6:10 as 'an implication of [believer's] relationship with Christ in his death'.[15] Kaye does not explain either why Christ is thought of as a 'representative' or how the 'relationship with Christ in his death' has to be understood.

The positions proposed by Stuhlmacher and Fitzmyer which point to the role of the resurrection of Christ have to be presented here also. Stuhlmacher says:

The resurrected Son of God died to sin once and for all. Sin leads to the death of the sinner (5:12), but Jesus died as the righteous one in obedience to God's will (5:18). As a result, sin exercised its right once and for all on Jesus (8:3). Death had to give Jesus up to life before God.[16]

Fitzmyer's interpretation is brief and not fully developed. He states: 'Jesus came in the likeness of sinful flesh (8:3) and broke sin's domination by his own death and resurrection, and not only sin's, but even death's domination.'[17] We consider that this is the right line of interpretation but needs to be explained more (see below).

The second line of interpretation where it is argued for a similar meaning between 6:2 and 6:10 is explained in the following way. C. K. Barrett argues that Christ's death to sin has to be understood in two ways: both in the sense that 'he died rather than sin' (that is, Christ always was obedient to his Father and this was his 'death to sin') and that Christ 'died in a context of sin.'[18]

---

[12] Bruce Norman Kaye, *The Thought Structure of Romans with Special Reference to Chapter 6* (Austin, Texas: Schola Press, 1979), 49, 50.

[13] Kaye, *Structure*, 55.

[14] See the analysis in chapter 4.

[15] Kaye, *Structure*, 55.

[16] Peter Stuhlmacher, *Paul's Letter to the Romans: A Commentary* (Edinburgh: T&T Clark, 1994), 93.

[17] Fitzmyer, *Romans*, 438.

[18] C. K. Barrett, *A Commentary on the Epistle to the Romans* (London: A & C Black,

sense that he did not evade but fully reckoned with the consequence of sin.'[4] There is a kind of 'transactional language'; 'Christ gave all that can be demanded; the evil forces have no more that they can ask'.[5]

Moule does not explain how this applies to Rom. 6:2 or to 6:10. Also it is not clear why in the case of Rom. 6:10 the focus is on 'payment in full'. Keeping in view the place of this 'block' (6:8-11) in the argument of 6:1-14, the line of interpretation is not so much on the fact proposed by Moule but on that of doing something in relation to a powerful master who exercises control over humanity (see καταργέω - 6:6b, βασιλεύω - 6:12, κυριεύω - 6:14; for details see below); Christ's death had a unique role in this; it is not that 'he lives to God' on the basis of the fact that he 'paid in full' what the sin demanded, but on the fact that his death and resurrection have to be understood together as 'working' against the 'powers' of sin and death.[6] The relationship to sin is defined *not* by keeping in view 'a full payment', but a defeat. In this context one can speak about not allowing to be under the dominion of sin.

A. Schlatter is near to Moule's position when he affirms that: 'Sin necessitated his death and on account of it he endured it.'[7] Sanday and Headlam are also close when they point out that Christ died to sin in the sense that sin, which was not his but of humankind (2 Cor. 5:21), had a claim upon him; 'It was in His Death that this pressure of human sin culminated'.[8] Cranfield makes this more clear when says: 'He affected sin by his dying, in that, as the altogether sinless One who identified Himself with sinful men, He bore for them the full penalty of sin.'[9] This 'death to sin' experienced by Christ has to be understood 'in a quite different sense than in 6:2.'[10] Concerning this difference of meaning Byrne says recently: 'Christ's death to sin is different than that of all the other human beings because Christ never came personally under the sway of sin'.[11]

B. N. Kaye discusses the meaning of 6:10 in the context of other constructions used by Paul in relation to Jesus' death. His conclusion is that

> Jesus' death is basically thought of as a death on behalf of sinners, and [...] not a death in the sense of submission to a power of sin. Where Jesus' death is referred

---

[4] Moule, 'Death 'to Sin',' 153.

[5] Moule, 'Death 'to Sin',' 153.

[6] See the argument below.

[7] A. Schlatter, *Romans: The Righteousness of God* (S. S. Schatzmann, trans.; Peabody, Mass.: Hendrickson, 1995), 143.

[8] William Sanday and Arthur C. Headlam, *A Critical and Exegetical Commentary on the Epistle to the Romans* (Edinburgh: T. and T. Clark, 1902), 160.

[9] Cranfield, *Romans*, 314. On a similar line see Ulrich Wilckens, *Der Brief an die Römer* (2; Zürich, Neukirchen/Vluyn: Neukirchner, Benziger, 1980), 19.

[10] Cranfield, *Romans*, 314.

[11] Brendan Byrne, *Romans* (Collegeville, Minnesota: The Liturgical Press, 1996), 192.

be discussed,[1] because in 6:5 Paul says something about the 'likeness' of *this* death, and, keeping in view the qualifier σύμφυτος (6:5a), Paul says something about the kind of *relationship* with the 'likeness' of that death. The detailed discourse in which the elements of Christ's death, sin, and we/believers are integrated is in 6:6. Here the language used is that of 'co-crucifixion' as the means of *liberating* the σῶμα from the bondage of sin. That is why this chapter will also include a study of 'crucifixion' (the way in which Christ died) in the ancient world with reference to our text. Also for a better understanding of the 'burial' metaphor from 6:4 a study of 'burial with' language will be included.

Thus, the structure of this chapter is as follows: 1) Christ's *death* as a 'death to sin'; 2) *Christ* in his death; 3) the meaning of τῷ ὁμοιώματι τοῦ θανάτου αὐτοῦ; 4) 'crucifixion' in ancient world with reference to Rom. 6:6; 5) burial language (Rom. 6:4).[2]

Christ's Death as a *'Death to Sin'* (Romans 6:10)

A 'Death to Sin'

The language of 'death to sin' (6.10) is the starting point for Paul in formulating his metaphor of 'death to sin' in 6:2. This basic affirmation is the core of our thesis. But what is the meaning of this τῇ ἁμαρτίᾳ ἀπέθανεν? And what is the relationship between this type of language and that of 6:2?

At this point the debate is as follows. There are two main positions: (1) there are scholars who argue for a different meaning than that of 6:2 (Moule, Sanday and Headlam, Schlatter, Cranfield, Kaye, Wilckens, Stuhlmacher, Byrne), and (2) others who argue for a similar sense to that of 6:2 (Barrett, Dunn, Moo, Schreiner). The common ground for all is that Christ's death was an event which did something 'in relation to' sin. Sin was affected in some way by that event. Here are those two lines of interpretation.

(1) C. F. D. Moule says that the dative (τῇ ἁμαρτίᾳ) has to be understood as a dative of relation.[3] 'The death of Christ was thought of as the 'payment in full,' as it were, of the penalty incurred by "Adam" collectively, and, thus, the gaining of complete quittance and release for men. Jesus "died *to sin*" in the

---

[1] We decided to discuss here the meaning and reference of ὁμοίωμα and not in the 'qualifers' chapter because this term says something about the way in which Christ's death is relevant for Paul's argument.

[2] The order of this section is not very important because the results of the research will be integrated only in the fifth chapter after a study of 'qualifiers' is provided.

[3] C. F. D. Moule, 'Death 'to Sin', 'to Law' and 'to the World': A Note on Certain Datives', in *Essays in New Testament Interpretation* (Cambridge: Cambridge University Press, 1982), 152, 157; also Käsemann, Romans, 170.

Chapter 3

The Language of 'Death': *The Vehicle* of Paul's Metaphor in Romans 6:1-11

Introduction

The purpose of this chapter is to study the 'death' language in Paul's argument in defence of his thesis (ἀπεθάνομεν τῇ ἁμαρτίᾳ) in Rom. 6:2. For understanding this kind of language Paul directs his readers' attention to *Christ's death*. Here are his affirmations in which he uses the language of death: 'were baptized into his death? Therefore we have been buried with him by baptism into death,' [...] 'if we have been united with the likeness of his death', [...] 'we know that our old man was crucified with him', [...] 'if we have died with Christ'. There are also the affirmations from 6:7 ('whoever has died is freed from sin') and 6:11 ('you must consider yourselves dead to sin'). There is no direct mention of Christ's death here, but these are the main *re*iterations of the argument's thesis in 6:2 and they are to be understood in the near context; the first in that of 6:5-6 and the second in the light of 6:1-11 (8-10). The 'qualifiers' of the metaphor of 'death,' namely, βαπτίζω (6:3), σύμφυτος (6:5), and ὁ παλαιὸς ἄνθρωπος (6:6) will be studied in the next chapter.

Thus, in this chapter, in order to understand the *vehicle* of the metaphor of 'death', we will study the way in which *the death* of *Christ* is presented. Both these elements are important because they go together throughout the argument of 6:1-11 (εἰ δὲ ἀπεθάνομεν σὺν Χριστῷ, 6:8). The main questions are: on the one hand, what kind of *death* is in view? how is *Christ* understood in his death? and on the other how is this event from the life of Christ *relevant* for Paul's argument when he defends his thesis from 6:2? In relation to his *death*, in our text, Paul's main affirmation is in 6:10 where he says: 'he died to sin, once for all'. In relation to Jesus' portrayal in *his* death, the constant 'image' used by Paul is that of Χριστός (6:3, 8, 9, 11). The relevant point is that the believers, in Pauline literature, 'die' always only with Χριστός (we will present the texts). Thus, a study of the meaning of Χριστός in Romans is needed to see if there is something relevant in this repeated usage for a better understanding of the 'dying with' language for this project. From the point of view of Christ's 'death to sin,' the meaning of the phrase τῷ ὁμοιώματι τοῦ θανάτου αὐτοῦ (6:5) will words of K.J. Vanhoozer: 'by going beyond the given, metaphor encourages us to look at the world as well as to ourselves in terms of what might be'.[89]

Metaphorical interpretation takes place between these contents. An interpretation needs description of the contents in the terms of semantic components.[90] In the process of interpretation only few properties are activated while the others are put aside. We have a selection, an accentuation, an organization of aspects of the major subject (vehicle). The reader has to know the system of common things which are associated with that subject.[91] The connotations of those lexical articles at the time of using them in metaphor are important for understanding the metaphor.

In our case the associated ideas of the language of 'death' used by Paul in Rom. 6:1-11 are based on the Calvary/Easter event from the life of Jesus Christ. Jesus Christ is portrayed in a particular way when it is said about the Christians that they have 'died with' him. The event of his death is interpreted as a 'death to sin'. This event is present in a particular way in the whole discourse — this is indicated by the usage of ὁμοίωμα (6:5). The 'relationship' with that 'likeness of his death' is described using σύμφυτος. The way of Christ's death is also used by Paul in his discourse — it was by 'crucifixion'. The 'burial' of Christians is viewed as a 'burial with' Christ. The pre-Christian life of the believers is described as 'our old man'; sin is described as 'having dominion' over the body. All this complex network of ideas has to be kept in mind when an interpreter studies the metaphorical language of death here in Romans 6.

Thus, we have organized our argument in three stages: 1) a study of the associated ideas of the *vehicle* of this metaphor — language of death, 2) a study of the qualifiers from the context of the language of death, and 3) the interpretation of the metaphorical language of death by having at hand the associated ideas of Paul's language of 'death' which we were able to gather from the existing sources and the role of qualifiers in guiding toward those ideas which are relevant for discerning the point(s) of Paul's metaphors in Romans 6.

---

[89] Vanhoozer, *Biblical Narrative*, 77.
[90] Eco, *Limitele*, 167.
[91] Cf. Eco, *Limitele*, 170.

What is the role of metaphor in fixing reference? If we fix the meaning of something metaphorically we do two things: (1) we use a word which points to part of the world in such a way that we can begin to talk and think about it, (2) in the process we enable the meaning of the language, to change as it is adapted to those features of world which we hope it will help us to understand. When we open to the world with the help of the language, the world will enforce, so to speak, changes in the meaning of the words we use. Metaphor thus makes possible a dual process, of discovery and the development of our language better to speak about its object.[78]

Thus, metaphor, according to its mechanism, gives us a discovery/redescription of reality. At the same time we see it and construct it.[79] An interpreter of a metaphor needs to be in the situation of the first hearer. In those circumstances we ask why the author of a metaphor chose that *vehicle* (the unexpected element used for explication) for that *tenor* (something which is explained).[80] The components of metaphor are usually familiar but it is their combination which is strange. This unexpectedness exists because the element used for explication (vehicle) is used in a context which is alien for it.[81] This tension between the literal interpretation, which is absurd for understanding the statement, and the metaphoric meaning offers a possible understanding of this state of discovering and inventing the reality at the same time. The effectiveness of metaphor depends 'on the existence of some features common to both parts of the metaphor, but features which are not normally identified as common'.[82] The main source of this tension is, according to Ricoeur, in the copula of the verb 'to be'.[83] At the same time a metaphor does not describe 'what things really *are*, but redescribes what things are *like*'.[84] In this way reality is redescribed. Metaphorical language, according to Jüngel, says something using 'the dialectic of familiarity and strangeness'.[85] In this way it has access to the known world of the hearer but at the same time that world is 'expanded'.[86] Metaphor enlarges our understanding of the world 'by expanding the real to include the 'possible''.[87] Thus, reality is considered as 'a dynamic becoming'.[88] This expansion shows other possibilities which are at hand. In the

---

[78] Gunton, *Atonement*, 45.
[79] Vanhoozer, *Biblical Narrative*, 65.
[80] Eco, *Limitele*, 63.
[81] Peter Cotterell and Max Turner, *Linguistics and Biblical Interpretation* (Downers Grove: IVP, 1989), 300.
[82] Cotterell and Turner, *Linguistics*, 301.
[83] Vanhoozer, *Biblical Narrative*, 69.
[84] Vanhoozer, *Biblical Narrative*, 69.
[85] Jüngel, *Essays*, 68.
[86] Jüngel, *Essays*, 68.
[87] Vanhoozer, *Biblical Narrative*, 70.
[88] Vanhoozer, *Biblical Narrative*, 71.

The perceiving of the resemblances makes the metaphor possible.⁷⁰ But the perceiving of these similarities is based on creative imagination and in this sense they are new. The metaphor compels us to seek the similarity. Before the existence of that metaphor there is not such similarity.⁷¹ For example, what are the 'similarities' in view associated with σύμφυτος in Rom. 6:5? For a good discernment the interpreter has to bring together the associated ideas which were present when a term like that was used. The interpreter has to 'hear' as much as possible from what the first hearer heard.

In the process of naming one thing with the name of something else one 'denies the first thing those qualities proper to it'.⁷² Some qualities are acquired and others are lost. We are able to recognize the elements of the metaphor but they are different because of this 'new thing' which was born. In our example, 'we died to sin', we are able to identify the language of 'death' and that of 'sin' but these are used in a new way. Sin and death are close categories in Pauline literature, in that the first leads to the second (the second being a 'wage' given/paid by the first), but here the second is used in a new context which leads to a *re*orientation of meaning.

On one hand, in order to realize this hybrid it is necessary to activate some properties⁷³ of the elements implied, but on the other hand, some of them are not in view. There is a process of *interpretation* of a set of properties by others. This is governed by the 'sociocultural format of the interpreting subjects' encyclopedia',⁷⁴ and by the co-text. These ideas associated with that particular lexeme or phrase from the world of the first hearers, the elements in context and the development of the whole discourse are the necessary things for interpreting a metaphor.

In this way the elements of the encyclopedia are inserted according to the laws of context. Some semantic properties are '*interpretants*' for the others.⁷⁵ This similarity between properties is understood as a naming with the same interpretant. In a well-known example employed by Eco, 'the teeth of the maiden in the Songs of Solomon are *like* the sheep if, and only if, in that given culture the interpretation *white* is used to designate both the color of teeth and that of sheep's fleece'.⁷⁶

Being an instance of discourse, 'metaphor, like all kinds of discourse, has both a sense and a referent'.⁷⁷ What is the referential reality of metaphor? Gunton put it as follows:

---

⁷⁰ Eco, *Semiotics,* 103.
⁷¹ Eco, *Limitele,* 167.
⁷² Eco, *Semiotics*, 96.
⁷³ Eco, *Semiotics*, 97.
⁷⁴ Eco, *Semiotics*, 127.
⁷⁵ Eco, *Semiotics*, 113.
⁷⁶ Eco, *Semiotics*, 113.
⁷⁷ Vanhoozer, *Biblical Narrative,* 67.

tension between two interpretations mediated by resemblance a new significance, in the whole statement, rises.[63] At this point there is a debate concerning the perceiving or creating of the resemblance. P. Ricoeur differs from other 'interaction' theorists, such as Richards, Black and Beardsley, who say that the resemblance 'is based on latent connotation of the two things being compared',[64] in that that 'only as discourse [...] we can explain the creation of meaning'.[65] The resemblance 'is not here waiting to be discovered, but it is invented'.[66] In a metaphor the known similarities are used in an unusual way; this points to the unshared elements of knowledge that through the metaphor are made known. In this way we construct the similarities and receive an understanding of something new communicated by metaphor.

This new significance contributes to our articulation of experience,[67] which forms our world.

Concerning the form, metaphor is not restrained to a particular syntactic one because the criteria of distinguishing it are not 'merely syntactic, but semantic and pragmatic as well'.[68]

A Working Theory: Metaphor as a Contextual Phenomenon

This position is not a 'new' one, but one in which both 'faces' of metaphor 'rhetoric' and 'semantic', are *kept in balance.*

An affirmation is interpreted metaphorically when the hearer recognizes the absurdity of it if it were taken literally. In that situation we would have a semantic anomaly, or a contradiction or violation of the pragmatic norm of the reality.[69] A good example is Paul's affirmation from Rom. 6:2: the Christians 'died to sin.' If this is interpreted literally the situation is absurd because Paul speaks to living people who can 'walk in the newness of life' (another metaphor). Paul takes that 'representation' which speaks about 'the cessation of life' and applies it in a different domain. In this case there is another element implied: Paul says that this 'death' was 'with Christ.' From the event of Christ's death he selects three elements: it was a 'death to sin' (6:10), it was by 'crucifixion' (6:6) and a burial took place (6:4). For a good understanding of Paul's metaphor in 6:2 all these aspects have to be integrated, and also other qualifiers from the context which are themselves metaphors ('baptism toward his death,' 'be one with' the likeness of his death, and 'our old man') have to receive their place in interpretation.

---

[63] Ricoeur, 'Biblical Hermeneutics,' 79.
[64] Vanhoozer, *Biblical Narrative*, 64.
[65] Vanhoozer, *Biblical Narrative*, 64.
[66] Vanhoozer, *Biblical Narrative*, 64.
[67] Ricoeur, 'Biblical Hermeneutics,' 82.
[68] Soskice, *Metaphor*, 19.
[69] Cf. Eco, *Limitele*, 164.

These aspects of metaphor can be accentuated at the expense of the others. We understand them as important dimensions of this contextual phenomenon called metaphor.

Semantic Metaphor

According to this view the thing communicated by the metaphor cannot be communicated otherwise. Metaphor extends the lists of objects that can be known.[50] How does metaphor convey that knowledge?[51]

In this view, metaphor is seen as an encounter of 'different frameworks of meaning'.[52] The level of occurrence is that of discourse.[53] The important thing is the interaction of these frameworks of meaning.[54] In the words of P. Ricoeur, *'metaphor proceeds from the tension between all the terms in a metaphorical statement'* (his italics).[55] In a metaphor we meet an interaction between an underlying subject (tenor) and a mode in which it is expressed (vehicle).[56] The vehicle is always represented by an expression with content which sends to another content that could be represented by other expressions.[57] This is put by J.M. Soskice as follows: metaphor 'speaks about one thing [tenor, focus] in terms which are seen to be suggestive of another [vehicle, frame]'.[58] The relation between this interaction and a literal interpretation is viewed in terms of both presence and destruction.[59] The way in which the word is used as predicate leads to losing, or destroying the usual meaning, but the meaning of the statement presupposes the literal meaning of the predicate.[60]

The shock between these two ideas which do not go together is reduced by the resemblance.[61] This resemblance is created by the reader when he wants to understand that 'absurd' predication.[62] In metaphor those two ideas become close by these 'common' features that are activated now in metaphor. From the

---

[50] Mooij, 'Metaphor,' 68.

[51] For the debate here ('intuitionist' theory, 31; 'controversion' theory, 32-38; 'interactive' theory, 39-42; and Soskice's position, 'interanimation' theory, 43-51) and a critical analysis of it, see Soskice, *Metaphor,* 31-51.

[52] Stiver, *Philosophy*, 116.

[53] 'Ricoeur's contribution to a theory of metaphor is to be found just here, in his analysis of metaphor as a form of discourse.' Cf. Vanhoozer, *Biblical Narrative*, 63.

[54] Stiver, *Philosophy*, 116.

[55] Ricoeur, 'Biblical Hermeneutics,' 77.

[56] Soskice, *Metaphor*, 39.

[57] U. Eco, *Limitele Interpretarii* (Constanta: Editura Pontica, 1996), 176.

[58] Soskice, *Metaphor,* 15.

[59] Cf. E. Jüngel, *Theological Essays* (1; J. B. Webster, tr and ed; Edinburgh: T&T Clark, 1989), 68, and Ricoeur, 'Biblical Hermeneutics,' 78.

[60] Jüngel, *Essays,* 68.

[61] Ricoeur, 'Biblical Hermeneutics,' 78.

[62] Vanhoozer, *Biblical Narrative*, 63.

The starting point of this approach is in the way in which metaphor is understood. Metaphor is a consequence of deviancy in word usage.[36] In this deviant usage any cognitive content is lost, but an emotional one is gained.[37]

At this point we will discuss a contemporary approach which underlines the psychological power and cognitive dimension of metaphor, that of A. C. Danto. He begins his argument by showing the fact that 'the mind is moved by representations.'[38] This fact shows something very important about us and metaphors.[39] The content of those representations is the element that gives representations the power for moving[40] the mind. One known or familiar[41] representation or image shows one element of metaphor either by underlining some features or by making salient some of its attributes.[42] It is not easy to state those properties that are at issue. The important things here are the 'speed and common knowledge'[43] of the hearers. The rhetorician has to be able to activate those resemblances which are connected with the prototypes through which we conceptualize our world.[44] Thus the metaphor gives to that thing/person a 'limited identity'.[45] This 'identity' is an affirmation of its/his/her essence. The metaphor, unlike the simile, identifies the essential attributes[46] of something/someone. That this thing is achieved by metaphor shows, according to Danto, a 'cognitive dimension for metaphorical representation'.[47] This approach identifies both the function of persuasion and the function of cognition. Between these two functions there is the following kind of relation: a metaphor is a powerful way of communication because it is able to identify the essential character[48] of something/someone. But, according to Danto, metaphors 'do not tell us something we do not know'.[49]

Knowledge and Language (III; Dordrecht, Boston, London: Kluwer Academic Press, 1993), 49.

[35] Cf. Ankersmit, 'Introduction,' 4; Mooij, 'Metaphor,' 67.
[36] For details see Soskice, *Metaphor*, 27.
[37] See the analysis of this in Soskice, *Metaphor*, 27.
[38] A.C. Danto, 'Metaphor and Cognition', in F.R. Ankersmit, J.J.A. Mooij, eds, *Knowledge and Language* (III; Dordrecht, Boston, London: Kluwer Academic Press, 1993), 26.
[39] Danto, 'Metaphor,' 26.
[40] Danto, 'Metaphor,' 27.
[41] Danto, 'Metaphor,' 33.
[42] Danto, 'Metaphor,' 30.
[43] Danto, 'Metaphor,' 33.
[44] Danto, 'Metaphor,' 33.
[45] Danto, 'Metaphor,' 30.
[46] Danto, 'Metaphor,' 31; Ankersmit, 'Introduction,' 30.
[47] Danto, 'Metaphor,' 51.
[48] Danto, 'Metaphor,' 33.
[49] Danto, 'Metaphor,' 33.

figures of thought and figures of speech—and, over and above these, nobility of phrase, which again may be resolved into choice of words and the use of metaphor and elaborated diction. The fifth cause of grandeur, which embraces all those already mentioned, is the general effect of dignity and elevation.[28]

A similar position is found in 32:6 where he says that 'figurative language has a natural grandeur and that metaphors make for sublimity.'[29]

From all of these it can be observed that there is a lot of common ground between these authors. These aspects mentioned by Aristotle, in a sense, give the major tone of the discussion. All of these things are achieved with the help of metaphor but not all at the same time. Depending on the purpose of the author and on the situation, one or more things are in view.

The *impact* of using metaphor in discourse was already mentioned (see e.g. Aristotle, *Rhetoric*, 1:2:4; Quintilian, *Institutio Oratoria*, 8:6:18-19; Demetrius, *On Style*, 2:78; Cicero, *Orator*, 27:92). There are authors who accentuate this feature of metaphor and others who consider this as the only thing achieved by the metaphor. These ideas are used, generally, to deny the usefulness of a semantics of metaphor.[30] This is the result of the mathematical model for philosophy used in the modern period (T. Hobbes,[31] J. Locke), in which there is an accent on the value of univocal language, and of the logical positivist movement, in which there is 'the distinction between cognitive and emotive language, between what can be said clearly and what cannot'.[32] Figurative language does not have cognitive significance. To say something about some things is possible with the help of a particular kind of words. For expressing meaning and truth we need to purify concepts from all pictorial content. Those concepts with fuzzy edges are not appropriate for communicating the truth.[33] Because of the features of metaphorical language ('ambiguous, holistic in meaning and context dependent'[34]) the best thing about metaphor is its persuasive or emotive function.[35]

---

[28] The translation used is that from Loeb Classical Library, Longinus, *On the Sublime* (H. Hamilton Fyfe, tr; Cambridge, Mass.; London: Harvard University Press; William Heinemann Ltd., 1982).

[29] Also Heiny, 'Motives,' 13.

[30] See the discussion in Ankersmit, 'Introduction,' 4, and for a discussion on the role of 'conceptual rationalism' in the shaping the attitude toward metaphor and the ancient roots of this in Plato and Augustine see Colin Gunton, *The Actuality of Atonement* (Edinburgh: T&T Clark, 1988), 17.

[31] Hobbes locates metaphor between self-deception and lying. In a metaphor the words are used 'in other senses than they are ordained for and thereby deceive others.' T. Hobbes, Leviathan (New York: Liberal Arts Press, 1958), 39; see also the discussion in K.J. Vanhoozer, *Biblical Narrative in the Philosophy of Paul Ricoeur* (Cambridge: Cambridge University of Press, 1990), 63.

[32] Stiver, *Philosophy,* 114.

[33] For a presentation of these positions see Gunton, *Atonement,* 17-8.

[34] M.B. Hesse, 'Models, Metaphors and Truth', in F.R. Ankersmit, J.J.A. Mooij, eds,

general 'pilots' the State, and conversely that a pilot 'commands' the ship.[25]

According to Demetrius a metaphor is used for a expressing things in a clearer way, with a greater precision.

> Some things are, however expressed with greater clearness and precision by means of metaphors than by means of the precise terms themselves: as 'the battle shuddered.' No change of phrase could, by the employment of precise terms, convey the meaning with greater truth or clearness. The poet has given the designation of 'shuddering battle' to the clash of spears and the low and continuous sound which these make. In so doing he has seized upon the aforesaid 'active' metaphor and has represented the battle as 'shuddering' like a living thing. (*On Style*, 2:82)

For the author of the *Ad Herennium*, Cicero, the metaphor helps us to 'put the matter before the eyes', 'to be concise', 'to avoid obscenity', 'to magnify', 'to diminish', and 'to decorate' (4:34), 'for the sake of creating a vivid mental picture' (34:45).[26] In *Orator* Cicero says that

> All the ornaments are appropriate to this type of oration, and it possesses charm to a high degree. There have been many conspicous examples of this style in Greece, but in my judgment Demetrius of Phalerum led them all. His oratory not only proceeds in calm and peaceful flow, but is lighted up by what might be called the stars of 'transferred' words (or metaphor) and borrowed words. By 'transferred' I now mean, as often before, words transferred by resemblance from another thing in order to produce a pleasing effect, or because of lack of a 'proper' word; (27:92)[27]

The author of *On the Sublime*, Longinus, discusses metaphor in his classification of 'genuine sources of the sublime in literature' (8:1). He says:

> There are, one may say, some five genuine sources of the sublime in literature, the common groundwork, as it were, of all five being a natural faculty of expression, without which nothing can be done. The first and most powerful is the command of full-blooded ideas—I have defined this in my book on Xenophon—and the second is the inspiration of vehement emotion. These two constituents of the sublime are for the most part congenital. But the other three come partly of art, namely the proper construction of figures—these being probable of two kinds,

---

[25] The translation used is from Loeb Classical Library, Demetrius, *On Style* (W. Rhys Roberts, tr; Cambridge, Mass.; London: Harvard University Press; William Heinemann Ltd., 1982).

[26] The translation used is from Loeb Classical Library, Cicero, *Rhetorica Ad Herennium* (Harry Caplan, tr; London; Cambridge, Mass.: Harvard University Press; William Heinemann Ltd., 1954).

[27] The translation used is that from Loeb Classical Library, Cicero, *Orator* (H. M. Hubbell, tr; London; Cambridge, Mass.: William Heinemann Ltd.; Harvard University Press, 1952).

meet with most general acceptance, contenting myself merely with noting the fact that some *tropes* are employed to help out our meaning and others to adorn our style, that some arise from words used *properly* and others from words used *metaphorically*, and that the changes involved concern not merely individual words, but also our thoughts and the structure of our sentences. (*The Institutio Oratoria*, 8:6:2)[23]

Quintilian reiterates in his discourse these two aspects of improving the meaning and adorning the style. Here are some examples:

> [...] the most beautiful of *tropes*, namely, *metaphor*. It is not merely so natural a turn a speech that it is often employed unconsciously or by uneducated persons, but it is in itself so attractive and elegant that however distinguished the language in which it is embedded it shines forth with a light of its own. For if it be correctly and appropriately applied, it is quite impossible for its effect to be commonplace, mean or unpleasing. It adds to the copiousness of language by the interchange of words and by borrowing, and finally succeeds in accomplishing the supreme difficult task of providing a name for everything. A noun or a verb is transferred from the place to which it properly belongs to another where there is either no *literal* term or the *transferred* is better than the *literal*. We do this either because it is necessary or to produce a decorative effect. (*The Institutio Oratoria*, 8:6:5-6)

And

> For my own part I should not regard a phrase like 'the shepherd of the people' as admissible in pleading, although it has the authority of Homer, nor would I venture to say that winged creatures 'swim through the air,' despite the fact that this metaphor has been most effectively employed by Virgil to describe the flight of bees and of Daedalus. For metaphor should always either occupy a place already vacant, or if it fills the room of something else, should be more impressive than that which it displaces. [...] *metaphor* is designed to move the feelings, give special distinction to things and place them vividly before the eye. (*The Institutio Oratoria*, 8:6:18-19)

In his work *On Style*, Demetrius discusses metaphor in the section 'The Four Types of Style—The Elevated Style (78-88).[24] He says the following about metaphor (2:78):

> In the first place, then, metaphors must be used; for they impart a special charm and grandeur to prose style. (They have to be) [...] natural and based on a true analogy. There is a resemblance, for instance, between a general, a pilot, and a charioteer; for they are all in command. Accordingly it can safely be said that a

---

[23] The translation used is from Loeb Classical Library, Quintilian, *The Institutio Oratoria* (H.B. Butler, tr; Cambridge, Mass.; London: Harvard University Press; William Heinemann Ltd., 1966); also Heiny, 'Motives,' 13.

[24] Also Heiny, 'Motives,' 13.

manner as to render him worthy of confidence; for we feel confidence in a greater degree and more readily in persons of worth in regard to everything in general, but where there is no certainty and there is room for doubt, our confidence is not absolute. (*Rhetoric*, 1:2:4)

This strategy is part of the function of rhetoric.[16]

Aristotle defined metaphor and gave the following examples:

> Metaphor is the application of a strange term either transferred (Μεταφορὰ δέ ἐστιν ὀνόματος ἀλλοτρίου ἐπιφορὰ) from the genus and applied to the species or from the species and applied to the genus, or from one species to another or else by analogy. An example of a term transferred from genus to species is 'Here *stands* my ship.' An example of transference from species to genus is 'Indeed *ten thousand* noble things Odysseus did,' for ten thousand, which is a species of many, is here used instead of the word 'many.' An example of transference from one species to another is '*Drawing off* his life with the bronze' and '*Severing* with the tireless bronze,' where 'drawing off' is used for 'severing' and 'severing' for 'drawing off,' both being species of 'removing.'

> Metaphor by analogy means this: when B is to A as D is to C, then instead of B the poet will say D and B instead of D. [...] For instance, a cup is to Dionysus what a shield is to Ares; so he will call the cup 'Dionysus's shield' and the shield 'Ares' cup.' Or old age is to life as evening is to day; so he will call the evening 'day's old-age' or use Empedocles' phrase; an old age he will call 'the evening of life' or 'life's setting sun.' (*Poetics*, 21.7-14)[17]

Because of the way in which Aristotle defined metaphor, namely: 'the application of a strange term/name by transference' he provided 'the foundation of seeing the metaphor as [...] substitution for literal language.'[18] This 'substitution' is a matter of individual words.[19] The reasons for these substitutions are rhetorical or poetical.[20] From another perspective the metaphor is a 'deviation' from 'normal' language. This 'deviation' through 'substitution' is based on the 'underlying similarity'[21] or on the 'resemblance'[22] between figurative and literal meanings of the words which constitute the metaphor.

According to Quintilian, metaphor helps in achieving two things:

> I propose [...] to proceed to discuss those *tropes* which are most necessary and

---

[16] Cf. Ricoeur, 'Biblical Hermeneutics,' 76.

[17] The translation is that from Loeb Classical Library, Aristotle, *The Poetics* (H. Hamilton Fyfe, tr; Cambridge, Mass.; London: Harvard University Press; William Heinemann Ltd., 1982).

[18] Stiver, *Philosophy*, 113.

[19] Cf. Soskice, *Metaphor*, 5.

[20] Stiver, *Philosophy*, 113.

[21] Stiver, *Philosophy*, 113.

[22] Ricoeur, 'Biblical Hermeneutics,' 76.

> by words that signify actuality. For instance, to say that a good man is 'four-square' is a metaphor, for both these are complete, but the phrase does not express actuality, whereas, 'of one having the prime of his life in full bloom' does; similarly, 'thee, like a scared animal ranging at will' expresses actuality, and in 'Thereupon the Greeks shooting forward with their feet' the word 'shooting' contains both actuality and metaphor. (*Rhetoric*, 3:11:2)

Something which could be familiar to us gains, with the help of metaphor, new qualities. Aristotle states:

> Now we do not know the meaning of strange words, and proper terms we know already. It is metaphor, therefore, that above all produces this effect; for when Homer calls old age stubble, he teaches and informs us through the genus; for both have lost their bloom. (*Rhetoric*, 3:10:2).

By 'foreign air/distinction' he understands that quality of presenting something which challenges the audience by presenting a strange,[11] distinctive way of putting things. Thus, a metaphor helps us to speak in a clear and distinctive way (see *Rhetoric*, 3:2:8). After these Aristotle adds two other things: 'to adorn', and 'to depreciate'.[12] He says:

> We must consider, as a red cloak suits a young man, what suits an old one; for the same garment is not suitable for both. And if we wish to ornament (κοσμεῖν) our subject, we must derive our metaphor from the better species under the same genus; if to depreciate (ψέγειν) it, from the worse. Thus, to say (for you have two opposites belonging to the same genus) that the man who begs prays, or that the man who prays begs (for both are forms of asking) is an instance of doing this; as, when Iphicrates called Callias[13] a mendicant priest instead of a torch-bearer, Callias replied that Iphicrates himself could not be initiated, otherwise he would not have called him mendicant priest but torch bearer; both titles indeed have to do with a divinity, but the one is honourable, the other dishonourable. (*Rhetoric*, 3:2:10).

These are the things achieved with the help of metaphor. Aristotle 'was not concerned to give accounts of mechanisms and processes, but simply wished to provide his reader with an identifying description of metaphor,'[14] a description which will help the reader use the metaphor in presenting a case persuasively. Related to this, according to Aristotle, an important element is 'the moral character' of the speaker.[15] He says:

> The orator persuades by moral character when his speech is delivered in such a

---

[11] Cf. Heiny, 'Motives,' 12.

[12] Also Heiny, 'Motives,' 12.

[13] Head of a distinguished Athenian family which held the office of torch-bearer at the Eleusinian mysteries.

[14] Soskice, *Metaphor*, 9.

[15] Also Heiny, 'Motives,' 16.

whole 'metaphor debate' can be summarized as follows:[4] (1) 'Rhetorical' metaphor: (a) metaphor is an elevated way of saying something which also can be expressed literally. Thus, in a sense, metaphor is a 'substitute' for literal language. (b) The originality of metaphor stands not in what it says but in the impact it has. Metaphor is used for its emotive impact. (2) 'Semantic' metaphor: (a) the thing said by the metaphor cannot be communicated without the help of metaphor. This presentation has as its background those two basic alternatives concerning the nature of language: a) language is by nature metaphorical, and metaphor is that phenomenon which establishes linguistic activity and b) language is that mechanism governed by rule, in which the metaphor is a deviation, a malfunction.[5] This summary is general but it can help us to identify those two main faces of metaphor, 'rhetorical' and 'semantic,' which will lead us through the field.

Rhetorical Metaphor

The authors discussed here are Aristotle, Quintilian, Cicero, and Demetrius.[6] Aristotle, in his own context, as seen in *Poetics* and *Rhetoric*, discusses metaphor with the purpose of helping the poet to improve style.[7] In *Rhetoric*, 3:2:8[8] he formulates this as follows: 'It is metaphor above all things that gives perspicuity, pleasure, and a foreign air, and it cannot be learnt from anyone else.'[9] The clearness of a statement (perspicuity) is realised by a metaphor by putting 'the things before the eyes',[10]

---

[4] In this we will work with the following authors: Stiver, *Philosophy,* 113-23; P. Ricoeur, 'Biblical Hermeneutics', Semeia 4 (1975) 29-148; Soskice, *Metaphor,* 1-53; F.R. Ankersmit, J.J.A. Mooij, 'Introduction', in F.R. Ankersmit, J.J.A. Mooij, eds, *Knowledge and Language* (III; Dordrecht, Boston, London: Kluwer Academic Press, 1993); J.J.A. Mooij, 'Metaphor and Truth: A Liberal Approach', in F.R. Ankersmit, J.J.A. Mooij, eds, *Knowledge and Language* (III; Dordrecht, Boston, London: Kluwer Academic Press, 1993).

[5] See Eco, *Semiotics,* 88.

[6] See also the discussion in S.B. Heiny, '2 Corinthians 2:14-4:6: Motives for Metaphor', in K.H. Richards, ed., *Society of Biblical Literature 1987 Seminar Papers* (Atlanta: Scholars Press, 1987), 1-22.

[7] Cf. Soskice, *Metaphor,* 9.

[8] The translation is that from Loeb Classical Library, Aristotle, *The 'Art' of Rhetoric* (John Henry Freese, tr; Cambridge, Mass.; London: Harvard University Press; William Heinemann Ltd, 1982).

[9] καὶ τὸ σαφὲς καὶ τὸ ἡδὺ καὶ τὸ ξενικὸν ἔχει μάλιστα ἡ μεταφορά. In another translation 'Metaphor gives style clearness, charm, and distinction as nothing else can.' *The Complete Works of Aristotle* (2; Jonathan Barnes, ed.; Princeton, New Jersey: Princeton University Press, 1984).

[10] Also Heiny, 'Motives,' 12.

Chapter 2

Methodological Considerations: Understanding Metaphor

Introduction

There are important aspects of our understanding of Paul's language in Romans 6 which depend on the way in which we understand the metaphors in his argument. This section intends to offer a theoretical basis for understanding the metaphor by considering different positions in the field. We will not present an exhaustive picture of the debate among linguists because this project is not intended primarily in linguistics, but we will try to integrate those aspects from the findings of the specialists in the field which are relevant for our study.

In the last half of the twentieth century there was an increasing interest in the study of metaphor. Metaphor was taken from its state of marginalization as an 'ornament' to language, 'important to rhetoric and poetics, but not for philosophy.'[1]

The Metaphor Debate

Every discourse about metaphor means a discussion about rhetorical activity in all its complexity.[2] What are the suggestions given by the different theories of metaphor concerning this rhetorical activity related to this linguistic phenomenon? We will discuss these from the point of view of two questions: (a) *What* does the metaphor achieve? and (b) *How* does it achieve it?[3] The

---

[1] D.R. Stiver, *The Philosophy of Religious Language, Sign, Symbol, and Story* (Cambridge, Massachusetts: Blackwell Publishers, 1996), 112; for a short presentation of the metaphor against the background of philosophical debate in the 20th century, see Reed Way Dasenbrock, 'Redrawing the Lines: An Introduction', in Reed Way Dasenbrock, ed., *Redrawing the Lines: Analytic Philosophy, Deconstruction, and Literary Theory* (Minneapolis: University of Minnesota Press, 1989), 3-25.

[2] Cf. U. Eco, *Semiotics and the Philosophy of Language* (London: Macmillan, 1984), 88.

[3] Cf. Soskice, *Metaphor*, 24.

argument moves from the reality of *horror* (crucifixion as punishment of the 'old man' enslaved by sin) to the *hope* in which the walking in the newness of life already started here and the dominion of sin can be put aside.

This book gives a new understanding of Paul's language of death in Romans 6. The main element which contributes to this is the basic different outlook of interpreting the metaphors as metaphors. The scholarly positions discussed above did not explore fully this important fact. From a different point of view the areas of Christology, anthropology and cosmology, find their role in understanding these metaphors. It is necessary to have full pictures of Christ, of man and salvation as the necesary elements for a good interpretation of Paul's language. The interpreter has to explain *who* 'dies' with *whom* and *to what* as necessary elements for arguing for a particular interpretation of Pauline metaphorical language of death. These too are not fully explored by the scholars. The language of death itself is nuanced by Paul by choosing two 'moments' from the Calvary event: that of crucifixion and that of burial. The positions analysed in the review do not explore the ideas associated with these 'moments'.

Paul says that the believers are 'united' with the likeness of his death (6.5), that their old man was 'crucified' with him (6:6), and that they were 'buried with' him (6:4). All sayings about the 'dying' of believers from Pauline literature are 'with Christ'. We have to study the *why* (if anything) of this state of things. In Romans 6:1-11 Christ's death is interpreted as a *'death to sin'* (6:10); this is the insight which is 'transferred' by Paul into the area of Christian living. We will discuss the whole argument against the background offered by this depiction of Christ's death as a 'death to sin'. Paul's 'transfer' leads to other aspects which he uses for defending his thesis from 6:2. He works with the language of 'likeness,' 'crucifixion,' and 'burial', and the vehicles of these metaphors are studied in the third chapter of this work.

After the ideas associated with the language of 'death' are identified, the interpreter has to be able to identify the *point(s)* of the metaphor. Some of these ideas are in view, some are not, and a study of the *qualifiers* of the metaphor is needed for identifying the relevant ones. In our case we need to study the language of 'baptism' (6:3), 'being one with' (6:5), and 'our old man' (6:6). The 'main' qualifier, 'sin' is studied in the section on 'our old man' because it is there that Paul uses it, for the first time after the announcing of the thesis from 6:2; at that point he integrates 'sin' into this argument. These qualifiers are (we argue) metaphors in themselves so the whole process is applied to these also for their interpretation. This is done in the fourth chapter.

Then, in the fifth chapter, the identified associated ideas of the language of 'death' are interpreted alongside their qualifiers in the general line of the argument of Romans 6. There arguments will be presented in support of the thesis of this project, which is summarised here: The language of Paul's thesis from 6:2 — ἀπεθάνομεν τῇ ἁμαρτίᾳ — is transferred *from* his unique way in which he understood Christ's death as being a 'death to sin' (6:10) *into* the way in which Christians have to understand their relationship with sin as a power or master of the 'age of Adam'. *'Death'* language is nuanced by Paul in two ways according to the dual purpose in his argument 1) that the believers do not have to 'remain in' the dominion of sin and 2) that walking in newness of life is a consequence of the 'overflowing' of grace over those who belong to Christ). Christ is seen in his death as the Anointed [davidic] king. Christ's death and resurrection were proclaimed to them and they believed what God did there for their salvation; this is described metaphorically as a 'coalescence' with the 'representation' (ὁμοίωμα) of Christ's death. That 'representation' of Christ's death is a continuous reality in their lives. The aspects which are in view from the event of Christ's death, according to Paul, are those of crucifixion and burial. These 'moments' are used by Paul keeping in view the dual purpose of his argument (see above). The first is used to show the horrific consequence of a life enslaved by sin in the age of Adam — thus, they do not have to let sin to reign over them any more —, and the second, the language of 'burial with', to point to the fact that the believers became part of Christ's family and that as he was raised they started to walk in the newness of life. In other words, Paul's

our becoming what he is. This is not an *exchange* but a *sharing* experience; there is a dependence of the believer upon Christ.[233] Also, sharing in Christ's death has many meanings: in Rom. 6 this is interpreted in terms of baptism and dying to sin, but in 8:17 'we became God's children and joint heirs with Christ, only if we are prepared to share in his sufferings'.[234]

Thus, for understanding this complex idea a clear definition of relationships between different perspectives in Christology which are present in an argument is needed. Exaltation made Christ proper for applying redemption in participation terms and incarnation for achieving it. In other words we interpret 'dying with Christ' from the point of view of the resurrection. Because of the resurrection, his death created a present reality which is a constituent part of the new era of salvation.

The Argument of the Book

In the light of our purpose in this project (to understand the meaning of Paul's usage of the metaphorical language of 'death' in Romans 6) we find that the major lines developed in the history of research in this area are valid but do not answer satisfactorily the questions involved. The main reason for this is that Paul's metaphorical language was not fully explored. Every interpretation of the language of 'death' used by Paul in Romans 6 as an answer to the charge of 6:1 has to argue for a *background of ideas* against which this argument is developed. After that it has to explain the way in which this language is *developed* in order to defend the thesis of Rom. 6:2.

We will argue that because Paul uses the language of 'death' in a metaphorical way the right thing to do for interpreting it is to keep in view *how* a metaphor works. This is why our next chapter is an enquiry into that area of linguistics. We need to know what can be said about this linguistic phenomenon in which something is said about something else in terms which are suggestive of another.[235] This chapter is not a detailed discussion on metaphor but a guide which is intended to help us to identify the elements which can help an interpreter in his search for understanding metaphorical language.

Then, according to the second chapter, we need to study the *vehicle* of this metaphor, namely the language of 'death' (third chapter). This is needed because only if the interpreter is able 'to hear' as much as possible from what the first hearer heard will he be able to understand the direction toward which metaphor leads the understanding. We need to identify as many associated ideas as possible from the common presupposition pool of writer and recipient. In our case Paul's language of 'death' is *shaped* by the event of *Christ's death*.

---

[233] Hooker, 'Interchange and suffering,' 43.
[234] Hooker, 'Interchange and suffering,' 45.
[235] See J. Soskice, *Metaphor and Religious Language* (Oxford: Clarendon, 1985), 15.

the believer is not explained at other points (e.g. *who* died with Christ; *what* is explained by this).

J. D. G. Dunn and Morna D. Hooker have not written specifically on 'dying with Christ' but on 'sharing in Christ's sufferings'; we discuss them here because they pointed to important elements which need to have a place in the interpretation of the *motif* in discussion.

J. D. G. DUNN — 'DYING WITH CHRIST', THE ROLES OF CHRISTOLOGY AND ANTHROPOLOGY

Dunn's contribution to understanding 'dying with Christ' consists in the fact that he explicitly locates 'the sharing in Christ's sufferings' at the confluence of Christology and anthropology.[226] The earthly Jesus is interpreted in adamic terms, as being a 'representative man'.[227] He identified himself with man 'in his Adamic fallenness' and in his death he showed the proper end of fallen man.[228] He rose again as the eschatological Adam. This death is not only the end but also is at work in the course of the life-time of the believer.[229] But even if Dunn identifies these two main lines at work (Christology and anthropology) he does not explore them. A similar general argument can be found in his *Theology of Paul the Apostle*, in the section 'The Process of Salvation'.[230] We will analyse further Dunn's position and also the arguments as to the meaning of Christ's death, likeness of his death, burial with language, being crucified with Christ, as these appear in his commentary on Romans, in chapters 3 and 4.

M. D. HOOKER — DIFFERENT PERSPECTIVES IN CHRISTOLOGY

In her discussion of the relationship between the sufferings of Christ and those of the Christian, Morna Hooker shows the importance of the theme of participation for understanding Paul's view of redemption.[231] She points out that in order to understand what happens to us it is necessary to work with different perspectives in Christology. Christ bore the likeness of Adam and died for us as our representative but was raised in glory. 'It is not a case of Christ becoming what we are in order to become what he once was.'[232] There is a direct relationship between his humiliation, death and being raised in glory and

---

[226] J.D.G. Dunn, *Jesus and the Spirit* (London: SCM, 1975), 337; J.D.G. Dunn, *The Theology of Paul the Apostle* (Edinburgh: T&T Clark Ltd., 1998), 482-87.

[227] Dunn, *Jesus,* 337.

[228] Dunn, *Jesus,* 337.

[229] Dunn, *Jesus,* 337.

[230] Dunn, *Theology of Paul,* 482-87.

[231] Morna D. Hooker, 'Interchange and Suffering', *From Adam to Christ: Essays on Paul* (1990) 42, Cambridge: Cambridge University Press.

[232] Hooker, 'Interchange and suffering,' 42.

burial (συνετάφημεν οὖν αὐτῷ διὰ τοῦ βαπτίσματος... 6:4). The key for understanding this instrumentality of baptism is in the meaning of the metaphorical expression: τοῦ βαπτίσματος εἰς τὸν θάνατον (the question is about the reference and meaning of βάπτισμα). This expression, as well as those from 6:3, should be analysed as metaphors. Their meaning, which will be argued for, is that the rite of baptism which is alluded to by this points to the 'overwhelming action of God by which the believers are "led" toward Christ's death'; this is the instrument of 'burial with.' The language of 'burial with' does not point to the fact that 'death already occurred' (even if that is the case) but to the fact that believers become part of the family of Christ (that is why they are buried *with* him).

Also, in Furnish's explanation of 'dying with Christ' there are no clarifications in the area of Christology and anthropology. The metaphorical character of Pauline language is not explored.

W. G. KÜMMEL — A SHARE IN THE EFFECTS OF CHRIST'S DEATH

Kümmel begins his section on 'Dying with Christ' in his *Theology of the New Testament* by saying that the state of having died is real but it 'cannot be intended to denote the cessation of the earthly existence of the baptized person'.[223] It is clear from this that he observed the unusual language used by Paul but he did not explain its nature or purpose. His argument deals with the question of the relationship between Christ's death and the believer's death. He points out that:

> For Paul Christ's death and resurrection are unique occurrences of the distant past which cannot be repeated; but the Christians have died with Christ, when they believed the message of God's reconciliation, let themselves be baptised, and thus were incorporated into the body of Christ, and that at a time which was far removed from Christ's death and resurrection. Christ's death on the cross and the Christians' dying with Christ thus by no means coincide in point of time. The Christians rather have obtained in their present time a share in the past event of Christ's death and resurrection.[224]

This sharing in the past event is explained in the sense that the believer participates in the effects of that death (these are justification and reconciliation). This sharing in the effects of Christ's death is possible because 'the crucified One has risen'.[225] Kümmel does not discuss the place of the 'likeness' (Rom. 6:5) and the identity of Christ in his death. Also the 'dying' of

---

[223] W. G. Kümmel, *Theology of the New Testament* (London: SCM Press Ltd, 1973), 212.
[224] Kümmel, *Theology,* 215-6.
[225] Kümmel, *Theology,* 216.

have validity for the church.[214] The likeness of his death is understood as denoting 'the agreement as well as the distinction between what Christ's death and resurrection signify on the one hand for himself, and on the other for his own'.[215] Christ's death to sin is not the same as the church's death to sin.[216] On the other hand the 'likeness' is a redemptive-historical likeness by virtue of its oneness with Christ.[217]

We will further analyse Schnackenburg's position and also the arguments as to the meaning of Christ's death, likeness of his death, 'burial with' language in the development of the thesis in chapters 3 and 4.

V. P. Furnish — 'Dying with Christ' and Baptism

Furnish discusses 'dying with Christ' in relation to baptism. 'The believer's participation with Christ in death-resurrection is [...] determinative for Paul's understanding of Christian baptism.'[218] The 'death to sin' is explained as an implication of the fact that grace reigns (5:21), which means that the power of sin has been broken. The idea is that the power of sin is incompatible with that of grace (6:14).[219] Christ's death is the actualisation of God's power and puts an effective check on sin's tyrannical hold (6:7).[220] 'The believer's death *with* Christ has the same result. The Christian too has 'died to sin' (6:2) because his old sin-dominated self has been crucified with Christ (6:6).'[221] In the light of these elements Furnish explains the place and the meaning of baptism. He states:

> baptism itself is not the 'saving' event. Sin's power is not broken by baptism but by Christ's death and resurrection, his 'obedience' and 'righteousness' (5:18-19). In Romans 6 'we have been baptized' is not parallel with 'we have died' or 'we have been crucified' but with 'we have been buried' (6:4). Baptism is always 'into Christ Jesus' (6:3), into his death for us. The priority here is with what God has accomplished through Christ. Baptism as such does not constitute the 'event of grace' but is one aspect only of the whole event. It is only the believer who is baptized, and so baptism as 'burial' presumes that the 'death' has already occurred![222]

But Furnish's point is not entirely accurate because Paul does not speak in Romans 6 about baptism as 'burial', but about baptism as the instrument of

---

[214] Ridderbos, *Paul*, 207.
[215] Ridderbos, *Paul*, 207.
[216] Ridderbos, *Paul*, 207.
[217] Ridderbos, *Paul*, 208.
[218] V.P. Furnish, *Theology and Ethics in Paul* (Nashville: Abingdon, 1968), 171.
[219] Furnish, *Theology*, 172.
[220] Furnish, *Theology*, 172.
[221] Furnish, *Theology*, 172.
[222] Furnish, *Theology*, 174.

event' took place in two actions: in death and resurrection (4:25). The individual too, must sacramentally die and rise 'with Christ': The connecting idea is obvious: that which happened to the 'One', the Founder of the race, should also happen to 'all'.[205]

We think that this explanation given by Schnackenburg does not follow the same lines as that of Romans 6. If argued from these two sides, of Christ and of the believer for understanding 'dying with Christ', the thesis should be as follows: Christ has to be viewed as the 'anointed king' of God who died and was resurrected for doing something in relation to the dominion of sin.[206] His death was a 'death to sin' (6:10). The believers were 'united' with (believed) what was proclaimed about (ὁμοίωμα) Christ's death (6:5).[207] This is described from another angle in 6:3 as being the overwhelming action of God through which they are 'led' toward Christ's death[208] (εἰς τὸν θάνατον αὐτοῦ ἐβαπτίσθημεν). Also, this action of God is the 'instrument' through which they are 'buried with' Christ, and such language points to the fact that they became the members of the same family as Christ.[209] In other words, Paul does not work with the concept of *Pneuma* to define Christ's status or the unity of the believer with Christ, but the basic observation is that related to the *kind* of language used by him, Paul works with metaphors which have to be interpreted by keeping in view their mechanism.

H. Ridderbos points out that the specific character of the new life of the believers is given by what 'once' took place with Christ.[210] Being 'dead to sin' is understood as 'the participation of the church in the death and burial of Christ in the one-time, redemptive-historical sense of the word'.[211] Paul's appeal to baptism is explained by defining its significance. Baptism is seen as 'the incorporation into and putting on of Christ (1 Cor. 12:13; Gal. 3:27), and in thus receiving a share in his redemptive work'.[212]

'When Christ died, they died, and his death was their own. But this redemptive-historical event is appropriated sacramentally to believers, and Paul can therefore appeal for the former to the latter.'[213] Ridderbos' understanding of Rom. 6:5 ('...we have become incorporated into the likeness of his death') offers him an explanation of the way in which Christ's death and resurrection

---

[205] Schnackenburg, *Baptism*, 155.
[206] See the argument from chapter 3.
[207] See the argument in chapter 3.
[208] See the argument in chapter 4.
[209] See the argument in chapter 3.
[210] H.N. Ridderbos, *Paul: An Outline of His Theology* (Grand Rapids: Eerdmans, 1975), 206.
[211] Ridderbos, *Paul*, 206.
[212] Ridderbos, *Paul*, 207.
[213] Ridderbos, *Paul*, 207.

R. Schnackenburg and H. Ridderbos — The Sacramental 'Dying with Christ'

The position defended by Schnackenburg is close to that of Wedderburn and Wagner as to the 'origin' of the idea of 'dying with Christ', and to that of Ridderbos when he explains its development. Because he discusses both issues we analyse his position here in the second part of the review.

Schnackenburg summarises his understanding of 'dying with Christ' as inclusion in the Christ event, as follows:

> the basic idea of the sacramental dying and rising with Christ depends on the conception, peculiar to Paul yet explicable on the basis of Jewish presuppositions, that Christ represented us as second Adam and as our Representative took death on himself and attained to resurrection for our sake. When we join ourselves in faith to the new Founder of the race and in baptism become members of the 'Body of Christ', we gain a share in his death and resurrection and step with Him from death to life. This event of grace and sacrament then becomes a task for moral effort on our part (death to sin, life for God) and a rule for our entire Christian existence; in the discipleship of suffering we are to become mystically conformed to his likeness, that at the last we might attain to the eschatological resurrection and so possess in fullness the form and being of the glorified Lord.[201]

The understanding of Christ in contrast to Adam is relevant for a study of Rom. 5:12-21 but when 'dying with Christ' is in view, the Christological outlook has to be on Jesus' identity as Χριστός — the Anointed [king];[202] see the other main text of Gal. 2:19-20 for the study of 'dying with Christ' in the Pauline corpus where Christ as 'a second Adam' is not the Christological view. Actually Paul never says that the believers 'die' with him as the 'last Adam', or as 'the Son' or as 'the Lord' but always with him as Χριστός. This is the reason why this Christological outlook should be explored.

Schnackenburg also discusses the relation between the believer's 'dying with Christ' and the bloody death of our Lord on Golgotha. His approach is on two lines: of Christ and of the believer. 'From the side of Christ [...], the exalted Lord is identical with the historical Jesus. The concept of *Pneuma* makes possible an easy transition from the mode of being that Christ then had to that which He now has.'[203] From the side of the believer he enters into a real (*Pneuma-*) union with the living and present Lord, in whose name he is baptized. But for him entrance into the fellowship of Christ also goes by way of 'dying with Christ'.[204]

> Through Christ, the Founder of the new race, we were delivered from the dominion of sin and death and brought into the realm of divine life. This 'Christ

---

[201] Schnackenburg, *Baptism*, 161-2.
[202] See the discussion above and also chapter 3.
[203] Schnackenburg, *Baptism*, 155.
[204] Schnackenburg, *Baptism*, 155.

corporeity of those who are the elect to the Messianic Kingdom and render them capable of assuming the resurrection mode of existence before the general resurrection of the dead takes place.[195]

This idea of 'elect to the Messianic Kingdom' is considered as being in continuity with the Jewish eschatology in which 'only those who amid the disasters which were coming upon Israel were kept alive by God, were destined to the Messianic Kingdom (Isa. 4:3; Mal. 3:16-17; Enoch lxii:7-8, 14-15)'.[196] That 'corporeity of those who are elect' is understood by Schweitzer in the following terms:

> the essential point in their predestined relation of solidarity is that they share a corporeity, which is in a peculiar measure open to, and receptive of, the influence of the powers of the resurrection. Their common predestination to the Messianic Kingdom is a predestination to the anticipatory obtaining of the resurrection state of existence. In accordance with this the eschatological concept of the Community of the Elect (that is to say, the predestined solidarity of the Elect with one another and with the Messiah) takes on for Paul a quasi-physical character.[197]

The eschatological messianic interpretation of the death of Jesus offers Schweitzer a key element for explaining the relationship between Jesus and believers. He explains this against a Jewish idea of predestination where in 'the eschatological concept of the Community of God [...] the Elect are closely bound up with one another and with the Messiah'.[198]

In Schweitzer's exposition, the role of Jesus as Messiah is not clearly defined for establishing the unity between him at his death and the Elect. He works only with the idea of 'predestination'.

Paul speaks in Romans 6 about a real unity between Χριστός and the believers, but this real character of the unity is not understood *physically*, as Schweitzer argues.[199] The unity between the Messiah and God's people in Jewish literature is not understood in 'quasi-physical' terms. This unity is a real one and is formulated in terms of representation, understood as being between 'the king and the people who are bound together in such a way that what is true of the one is true in principle of the other' (2 Sam. 19:40-43; 20:1; cf. 1 Kings 12:16).[200] We will explore the dimensions of this 'unity' in chapter three of the present work.

---

[195] Schweitzer, *Mysticism*, 101.
[196] Schweitzer, *Mysticism*, 101.
[197] Schweitzer, *Mysticism*, 110.
[198] Schweitzer, *Mysticism*, 116.
[199] See the discussion on σύμφυτος in chapter 4.
[200] Wright, *Climax*, 46.

would have been helpful for a better definition of the role of Christ in explaining this 'motif.' This will be his major christological perspective. He interprets the cross as an eschatological and inclusive event but there is no detailed and proper discussion about *who* died on the cross.

According to Tannehill, these texts which are about dying with Christ in the present refer to a present aspect of Christian action and suffering.[191] In discussing 'the present dying with Christ' his main accent is on the relationship between the indicative and imperative in Paul's argument. He explains this by putting the whole discussion, rightly, we think, in a larger eschatological context and in the light of a particular understanding of the cross. The present state of the believer is understood in the eschatological reality of 'already/not yet' from the history of salvation; he is not under the dominion of the powers of the old aeon, but is still exposed to their influence.[192] Interpreting the cross as an eschatological and inclusive event, Tannehill says that 'the present structure of the new dominion corresponds to the events on which it is founded'.[193] This is the basis for Paul's exhortation for Christian action.

In this argument for understanding the *present* aspect of 'dying with Christ' there is no discussion of one important text: Rom. 6:5a (see the meaning of the perfect tense there). The present 'dying with Christ' for interpreting the believer's suffering is not a prominent theme in Romans (with the exception of Rom 8:17,36) and for this reason we will not analyse Tannehill's exposition at this point.

These elements of the interpretation of Christ's death, the correspondence between the structure of the new dominion and death of Christ, and the relationship of these to the believer's life discussed by Tannehill appear in a different way in the interpretations defended by A. Schweitzer, R. Schnackenburg and H. Ridderbos.

A. SCHWEITZER — PREDESTINATION, MESSIAH AND COMMUNITY

'The fundamental significance of the dying and rising again of Jesus consists (...), according to Paul, in the fact that thereby death and resurrection have been set afoot throughout the whole corporeity of the Elect to the Messianic Kingdom.'[194] This is Schweitzer's synthesis about the significance of the dying of Jesus. This is based on an eschatological understanding of redemption in Paul in which

> the powers of death and resurrection which were made manifest in Jesus, now, from the moment of his dying and rising again onwards, are at work upon the

---

[191] Tannehill, *Dying*, 75.

[192] Tannehill, *Dying*, 76.

[193] Tannehill, *Dying*, 75.

[194] Albert Schweitzer, *The Mysticism of Paul the Apostle* (William Montgomery, trans.; London: Adam & Charles Black, 1953), 110.

elements have to be integrated in every interpretation of Paul's theme of this chapter in Romans, namely that from 6:2 — ἀπεθάνομεν τῇ ἁμαρτίᾳ.

These elements used by Paul for defending his thesis were identified and interpreted differently by scholars. The next section of the review will explore the major positions in this area.

The Development of the Metaphor of 'Death'

R.C. TANNEHILL — 'DYING WITH CHRIST' AS A PAST AND A PRESENT EXPERIENCE

From an exegetical point of view the study of Tannehill is still the most detailed one in the field; this is why he is the first to be discussed in this section. His study on 'dying with Christ' covers many relevant points in searching for the meaning of this idea. He proposes a 'chronological' analysis of the motif because in the Pauline literature there are texts which refer to 'dying with Christ' as a past event, and texts which refer to dying with Christ as a present experience.[185] For logical reasons (past/present) this approach is very promising. As a past event, according to Tannehill, 'dying with Christ' 'is related to two dominions and their rulers and indicates release from one and transfer to the other. The emphasis is on the newness of Christian existence against certain dangers of falling back into the existence of the old aeon'.[186]

The two dominions and their rulers are explained in detail.[187] This eschatological position is a strong point in his argument, but when he discusses man's existence in this position he works only with the language of submission and lordship.[188] His main accent is on the meaning of σῶμα in Paul in relation to this theme: 'man as body is man-in-relation'.[189] The anthropological perspective offered by σῶμα is an important one, but not the only one. There is very little in Tannehill's argument about the human condition in that state of submission, or lordship. For example what is the *identity* of ὁ παλαιὸς ἄνθρωπος who is 'crucified with' Christ? Romans 5:12-21 has to receive an important place in defining this metaphor of 'our old man.' The metaphor of 'crucifixion' is not studied in detail for defining the means of 'release.' Also Tannehill does not explain in detail the *identity* of Jesus who died. Following Bultmann, he works with the idea of 'Christ as inclusive *anthropos*',[190] but he decided not to publish that section of his study (see his Preface); perhaps that

---

[185] Robert C. Tannehill, *Dying and Rising with Christ: A Study in Pauline Theology* (Berlin: Verlag Alfred Töpelmann, 1967), 6.
[186] Tannehill, *Dying*, 7.
[187] Tannehill, *Dying*, 14-7.
[188] Tannehill, *Dying*, 16-8.
[189] Tannehill, *Dying*, 71.
[190] Tannehill, *Dying*, 2.

not in some sacramental or quasi-magical sense, but because the baptism by which they expressed their faith in Christ also made that faith public among their friends and neighbours and exposed them to public shame. In baptism their old life was buried, and, since they were identifying themselves with Christ, buried with him, and the meaning and purpose of this costly act is that a new life of obedience should follow, made possible by the indwelling Spirit of the same Christ. So just as he died condemned by the rulers of this age and rose again, so those who identify themselves with him bring on themselves the same condemnation, and may expect the same vindication. Actual death and resurrection are still, of course, in the future, but a foretaste of them both is available immediately in the breaking off of old allegiances and the sanctifying work of the Spirit.[179]

Campbell understands ὁμοίωμα as

expressing a likeness between the death of Christ on the one hand and the believer's conversion (expressed in baptism) on the other. What makes them alike is not the action of immersion in water, but the way in which baptism involved the new believers in social rejection and public identification with the rejected Messiah. Such a social death is the best guarantee of a (moral) resurrection.[180]

He sees 'our old man' as referring to 'the people in their 'belongingness to the old era', and the enslaving power from 6.6 could be 'the power of religion or social convention.'[181]

The following observations have to be made against this 'social' interpretation of the language of 'death': it is true that Christ is portrayed in Romans 6 as 'God's anointed' but the focus is not on the fact that he is a 'rejected Messiah,' and that his followers have to break the enslaving 'power of religion and social convention,' and share in his rejection. Christ is portrayed as a representative king who died 'to sin' and was raised.[182] This language of 'death to sin' is 'transferred' by Paul into the area of Christian life; the explanation of this kind of language is the purpose of 6.3-7. The power in view is that of sin which is portrayed as a 'master of slaves.' To be under the power of sin (ὑφ' ἁμαρτίαν εἶναι) is described by Paul in Rom. 3:10-18 where the focus is *not* the 'social convention' from which the believers have to be 'liberated', but the problem is the dominion of sin which results in death. This is the 'Adam's side' of the argument from the near context of 5:12-21 which is relevant for understanding the language of 'sin' in chap. 6. In other words, when Paul speaks about 'sin' he works with two main elements: the slavery of sin in human life[183] and the death of Christ as a 'death to sin'.[184] These two

---

[179] Campbell, 'Dying,' 285.
[180] Campbell, 'Dying,' 287.
[181] Campbell, 'Dying,' 287-8.
[182] See the argument in chapter 3.
[183] See the argument in chapter 4.
[184] See the argument in chapter 3.

tradition, experience, interpretation —, this 'experience' origin thesis has its plausibility, but it has to be checked at its major claims. If Galatians was written before 2 Corinthians the whole picture looks different. The writing of Galatians is an important element in every argumentation at this point. If it was written before 2 Corinthians,[174] then Paul's understanding of the cross helped him *in explaining* these difficult experiences. The metaphor of 'crucifixion with Christ' has many dimensions and implications; among them there is one which speaks about suffering because our 'dying with him' is 'through' crucifixion. The principle affirmed in Rom 8:17 ('if, in fact, we suffer with him so that we may also be glorified with him') applies literally. These deadly circumstances provided *not* the source of the idea, but its *confirmation*.

The observation that in 2 Corinthians there is an 'undeveloped form' of this idea is not accurate. The idea formulated very briefly in 2 Cor. 5:14b ('one had died for all; therefore all have died') shows the contrary, because for a proper understanding of this statement a lot of shared knowledge is needed, which is not expressed here. The presence of this knowledge in their shared presupposition pool (even if 'dying with Christ' is not mentioned in 1 Cor) may mean that at the time of his visit to Corinth or even at that of planting the church Paul already had this idea in his tradition and/or in his proclamation.

A. Campbell argues (without mentioning Wilson) on similar lines that 'Paul's sufferings in the cause of the gospel were the origin of his speaking about dying and rising with Christ. Those who were baptised into Christ Jesus found in their experience that they were baptised into his death, and having made this costly step of faith they were not likely to continue in sin.'[175]

When he defends his thesis in relation to Romans 6:1-11 he points out that 'Paul uses the imagery of death to describe the conversion.'[176] Paul uses this language in 'an objection to his gospel,' (see Rom. 6:1).[177] Paul uses three pictures for 'pointing to the decisive break that believers have made in becoming Christians': 'dying and rising again (6:1-11), changing from one master to another (6:15-23) and marrying again (7:1-6).'[178] Campbell says that

> the reality that gives the first picture its force is not the death of Jesus, considered as a representative figure with whom by faith they identify, but the fact that in identifying with Jesus they have incurred the wrath of their old associates, and experienced the world's hatred just as he did. It was baptism that made this true,

---

[174] For an argument in this direction see Jerome Murphy-O'Connor, *Paul: A Critical Life* (Oxford: Clarendon Press, 1996), 252-56.

[175] Alastair Campbell, 'Dying with Christ: The Origin of a Metaphor?' in Stanley E. Porter and Anthony R. Cross, eds, *Baptism, the New Testament and the Church: Historical and Contemporary Studies in Honour of R.E.O. White* (Sheffield: Sheffield Academic Press, 1999), 275-6.

[176] Campbell, 'Dying,' 284.

[177] Campbell, 'Dying,' 284.

[178] Campbell, 'Dying,' 285.

baptism. Paul defines it as 'dying with Christ' in contrast to an understanding of baptism as a mere rising with Christ to a divine life.[168]

It is true that a comparative study of the use of the phrase in both contexts can help in understanding the phrase itself, but the eschatological context, having in view the apocalyptic 'already/not yet', has to be understood as the climax of the present experience of Christians with Christ, not as its origin. In Paul 'dying with Christ' is used in relation to the realities of the old aeon, its powers and influences upon the lives of Christians. It is oriented back to the cross, as a past event always relevant in this present life. Also it is true that 'dying with Christ' and the process of transformation described by it can be understood better if seen from the point of view of its climax, *e.g.* conformity with the image of the Son (Rom 8:29), but this does not say anything about the origin of the first in the last, but about the purpose of the first.

W. WILSON AND A. CAMPBELL — 'DYING WITH CHRIST' AS A PRODUCT OF PERSONAL EXPERIENCE

According to Wilson 'it is possible to prove that this doctrine [of 'dying with Christ'] is firmly rooted in [Paul's] own experience'.[169] His main point in the argument is based on his proposed chronology of the writing of 1 and 2 Corinthians and Romans in relation to Galatians. The idea of 'dying with Christ' was formed in Paul's mind 'between the time he wrote 1 Co., perhaps about the middle of his stay in Ephesus (see Ac. 19), and the time he wrote Ro., just before setting out for Jerusalem'.[170] Because this idea appears for the first time, according to Wilson, in 2 Corinthians, and here in 'a more undeveloped form',[171] this epistle was written before Romans and after these very difficult experiences. 'In this terrible experience the presence of Christ had been so strongly with him that he felt himself to be going through the very passion itself.'[172] This experience 'gave him the conception of dying with Christ'.[173] Because in Galatians there is a more developed stage in comprehending this idea, Wilson proposed a later date for this epistle, namely after the Corinthian correspondence.

This proposal shows the role of experience in understanding Paul and his development. An experience helps someone to interpret his tradition; this interpretation results in a better understanding of that tradition and, sometimes, in changing it at different aspects. Because of the truth of this dynamic —

---

[168] Schweizer, 'Dying,' 8.

[169] William E. Wilson, 'The Development of Paul's Doctrine of Dying and Rising with Christ', *The Expository Times* 42 (1930) 563.

[170] Wilson, 'Dying,' 563.

[171] Wilson, 'Dying,' 563.

[172] Wilson, 'Dying,' 564.

[173] Wilson, 'Dying,' 564.

figures upon whose actions the destinies of successive generations in some measure depend and with whom these generations either did align themselves as they did with actions of Adam or should align themselves as they were called to do with the actions of the righteous patriarchs.[161]

This understanding of 'dying with Christ'[162] from the angle of 'with' language is beneficial for our project, but it has another place (it describes the relationship between Christ and believer), not that of the origin of the idea. Wedderburn's position starts from 'with' language. This starting point is misleading, because it is not specific enough. The question is not that of the origin of *'with* Christ' language, but that of *'dying with Christ.'* In Wedderburn's argument there is little space for the role of the *death* of Christ. He makes reference to it in his discussion on Abraham as a representative, but only there, and only as observation, and he does not develop it further. The complexity of Paul's language calls for taking into discussion *all* the elements implied, namely, *Christ*, Christ in *his* death, his *death,* and the *Christians* with him in his death. Actually, an analysis of a metaphor requires a study both in the 'encyclopaedic universe' behind the chosen *vehicle*[163] of that metaphor and in the near context where, in the case of Romans 6:1-11, there are important qualifiers[164] which can help in interpreting Paul's language.

The most important element which is absent in all studies of 'dying with Christ' is a detailed analysis of the *metaphorical* character of Paul's language — 'dying with Christ' is a metaphor. What is the role of the metaphor here? How does it work? These questions remain without a clear answer.

E. SCHWEIZER — 'DYING WITH CHRIST' AND ESCHATOLOGICAL 'BEING WITH CHRIST'

For understanding the concept of living 'with Christ', Schweizer proposed the eschatological 'being with Christ'.[165] He showed that Paul uses this phrase both in eschatological contexts and in describing the present experience of Christians. More specifically, 'with Christ' appears 'only in either apocalyptic or baptismal contexts'.[166] This last one, according to Schweizer, has its origin in the first.[167] This eschatological being 'with Christ' was transferred, before and independently of Paul, to the area of ideas about the new life gained by

---

[161] Wedderburn, *Baptism*, 356.
[162] See also that of Wagner and Schweizer.
[163] See a discussion of this in chapter 3.
[164] For a discussion of these see chapter 4.
[165] Eduard Schweizer, 'Dying and Rising with Christ', *NTS* 14 (1967-68) 3.
[166] Schweizer, 'Dying,' 3.
[167] Schweizer, 'Dying,' 3.

contrast in Gal 2:19, but 'dying with Christ' is developed there; Χριστός as 'the anointed king' fits better as a Christological perspective[153] for the study of this motif in Pauline literature. Also, in Wagner's proposal, which is focused on Romans, there is no specific discussion about the way in which Christ's death and its relevance for 'dying with Christ' is interpreted.

Wedderburn proposes as the background for 'dying with Christ' the idea that Adam includes in himself all generations.[154] It is expected that Roman Christians were familiar with such Jewish ideas; the preceding argument (Rom. 5:12-21), in the case of Romans, has the role of preparing the minds for such an idea.[155] Another example which, according to Wedderburn, confirms this background is that of Abraham with whom the Christians are associated as recipients of his blessing (Gal. 3:8-9).[156] Abraham is seen as their representative. Wedderburn says that something analogous can also be found in Romans 6 where God 'associated us with Christ, [...] as co-recipients of his verdict upon human sin'.[157] Jesus, like Abraham, is 'a representative figure'. Solidarity of the race with its representative is the place from which the 'with' language of Paul arises.[158]

But the Christians are 'the seed of Abraham' (Gal 3:29) if they are *of Christ*. These are the terms in which the family of Abraham is defined. Χριστός, the anointed king, 'represents and draws together in himself the physical family of Abraham.'[159]

In Romans 6 the death of Χριστός is interpreted as a 'death to sin'; this phrase is 'transferred' by Paul into the area of Christian life when he says 'we who died to sin' (Rom 6:2). Paul works with the idea of representation, but in analysing the 'dying with Christ' language, the research has to keep in view that in the Pauline corpus, the believer 'dies' almost always only with Χριστός. This consistency has to guide the interpreter of Paul to a study of this lexeme in the available literature in trying to see the relevance, if any, of this choice (Χριστός) in coining this 'motif' ('dying with').[160]

In concluding his argument Wedderburn says:

> Paul's language of our dying with Christ then is probably his own; at least I have found no convincing enough parallel to it which might explain whence he derived it. But the ideas which he expresses by this language are not so novel; they are one with the tradition which he inherited from Israel of a series of representative

---

[153] See the discussion in chapter 3.

[154] Wedderburn, *Baptism*, 345.

[155] Wedderburn, *Baptism*, 345.

[156] Wedderburn, *Baptism*, 349.

[157] Wedderburn, *Baptism*, 349.

[158] Wedderburn, *Baptism*, 350.

[159] N.T. Wright, *The Climax of the Covenant: Christ and the Law in Pauline Theology* (Edinburgh: T. and T. Clark, 1991), 44.

[160] See a discussion in chapter 3.

to the death of the initiates as in the case of Attis, and they did not regard 'their act as being a quasi-death'.[147]

After this survey of major mystery cults it can be said that the initiates, according to the ceremonies of initiation, are assured of the power of the god/goddess in this life and the next. The sharing in his/her fate, in the case of the living, is a sharing in mourning and joy, and in the case of the dead a sharing in the different way of existence after death. The devotee does not die with a 'dying' god in any of these and also 'death' is not used to describe a way of relating to something from this life.[148]

G. Wagner and A. J. M. Wedderburn — 'Dying with Christ' and Adamic Christology

Both these scholars work, as the background of the 'dying' language in Romans 6 is concerned, with the idea of representation as this is understood by having Adam as a kind of model for Christ.

Wagner shows that σὺν Χριστῷ in Romans 6.1-11 has to be explained by the 'representative and eschatological salvation-event in Christ'.[149] The background for Romans 6 is the Adam-Christ parallel elaborated in Romans 5:12ff.[150] Christ is the new Adam and his death is a representative death for sinners.[151] Wagner also gives a place for the personal experience of Paul when he says that 'the σὺν Χριστῷ is at the bottom rooted both in Paul's theology and in his personal experience'.[152]

This ground for understanding the idea is, surely, a solid one, because it is able to explain, at least in part, the basis for the unity between Christ (as the new Adam) and the Christian. 'Adam' Christology has a place in understanding this, but not in understanding the unity between the Christians and the death of Christ. When Paul speaks about the believer and his share in Christ's death he always says that this happens with Χριστός. The Christian, in Pauline literature, never 'dies' with 'the last Adam', or with 'the Son', or with 'the Lord'. These christological perspectives are used by Paul in interpreting the identity of Jesus in his death, but not in the development of this 'motif' of 'dying with Χριστός.' As Wagner points out, the immediate context has to receive a proper place in understanding the idea under discussion, but methodologically it is not sound for a particular context to be imposed upon the understanding of others when there is no clear link between them. For example, there is no Adam/Christ

---

[147] Wedderburn, *Baptism,* 331.

[148] For similar conclusions see Wagner, *Baptism,* 268-76; Schnackenburg, *Baptism,* 139-45; Wedderburn, *Baptism,* 393-96.

[149] Wagner, *Baptism,* 290.

[150] Wagner, *Baptism,* 290.

[151] Wagner, *Baptism,* 291.

[152] Wagner, *Baptism,* 292.

sorrow while staying with Celeus and Metaneira, the rejoicing at reunion with her daughter, and finally her divine gifts of grain and mystic knowledge. In the Mysteries of Demeter, all night long, with torches kindled, they seek for Persephone and when she is found, the whole ritual closes with thanksgiving and the tossing of torches.[141]

The λεγόμενα were short liturgical statements, explanations, and perhaps invocations accompanying the δρόμενα.

The δεικνύμενα were the sacred things (ἱερά) displayed by the Hierophant while standing in front of the Anaktoron in radiant light at the climactic moment. Clement of Alexandria refers to the mystic κισται (baskets) which contained the ἱερα:

> And the formula of the Eleusinian mysteries is as follows: 'I fasted, I drank the draught (κὐκεών); I took from the chest; having done my task, I placed in the basket, and from the basket into the chest. (*Exhortation to the Greeks*, II, 18)

Ἐπόπτεια refers to the Holy Light of the Holy Night. Those initiated (μύσται) could return a year later for the higher degree of initiation attained by the ἐπόπται during the second night in the Sanctuary of Demeter. The most sacred objects were revealed to them.

The relevant aspect here is the fact that the initiates joined Demeter[142] in searching for her daughter. There is no sharing in the fate of Persephone who was abducted to the underworld. These known elements from the initiation at Eleusis show a suffering goddess who searches for her daughter. There is also a shared joy with Demeter when Kore is found. One of the benefits of the initiation was that when someone who was initiated dies he already knows the end of life: 'happy is he who, having seen these rites, goes below the hollow earth; for he knows the end of life and he knows its god-sent beginning'.[143] He can hope in the help of Demeter because he saw her already at work in the case of Kore.[144] These religious endeavours could have been of help in defeating the fear of death, but this is a different thing from what we have in Romans 6.

In the case of the Attis cult, according to one version of the myth, Attis, Cybele's beloved, being mad, castrates himself and dies;[145] his devotees 'wounded themselves to the point of shedding blood'.[146] The candidates for priesthood, imitating Attis, castrate themselves. Yet this initiation does not lead

---

[141] Cf. G. E. Mylonas, *Eleusis and Eleusinian Mysteries* (Princeton: Princeton University Press, 1961), 215.

[142] See also Wedderburn, *Baptism*, 317.

[143] Pindar, *Frag.* 102, translated by Mylonas, *Eleusis*, 285.

[144] See also Wedderburn, *Baptism*, 331.

[145] See the description of the myth in Ferguson, *Backgrounds*, 266, and Smith, 'Dying,' 523.

[146] Ferguson, *Backgrounds*, 267.

Osiris became the model for all who want to defeat death. Eliade points out that 'following the example of Osiris, and with his help, those who are dead are able to be transformed in "spirits."'[134] Osiris, being helped by Isis and Horus, inaugurates a new way of existence.[135] The important observation here is that this identification with Osiris is a part of a 'funerary ritual'.[136] It is a ritual for someone who died not for someone who is alive.

> Both the Pyramid Texts and the Coffin Texts present more than one version of the destination of the deceased: they might travel the sky with the sun-god RA or, alternatively, might pass down into the underworld of Osiris. This latter view became increasingly common from the time of the Coffin Texts onwards, setting the scene for the funerary beliefs of the New Kingdom.[137]

In this case these 'funerary beliefs' point not toward the present life but to the afterlife. In Paul's case the metaphorical language of 'death' is applied to this life. This different 'object' makes the relation of source-development unlikely. The purpose of those beliefs was to 'provide a guarantee of survival in the afterworld',[138] or in Paul's case he uses this kind of language for defining the believer's relationship with the old realities of life in the age of Adam.

In the mysteries at Eleusis[139] there were three grades of initiation: the Lesser Mysteries which were a preliminary requirement, the Greater Mysteries or τελετή, and the additional and highest degree, the ἐποπτεια. The τελετή initiation has different aspects, the δρόμενα (things enacted), the λεγόμενα (things said), and the δεικνύμενα (things shown).

In the δρόμενα the initiates may have imitated in ritual fashion the actions and feelings of Demeter in the original time.[140] These could have included the abduction of Persephone, the wanderings of Demeter, her arrival at Eleusis, her

---

who do not exist.' R. O. Faulkner, *The Ancient Egyptian Coffin Texts* (1 Spells 1-354; Warminster England: Aris & Phillips Ltd, 1973).

[134] Eliade, *History*, 100.

[135] Eliade, *History*, 100.

[136] Cf. Wedderburn, *Baptism*, 310 See also Jonathan Z. Smith, 'Dying and Rising Gods', in Mircea Eliade, ed., *The Encyclopedia of Religion* (4; New York: Macmillan, 1987), 525.

[137] Shaw and Nicholson, 'Coffin Texts,' 69.

[138] Shaw and Nicholson, 'Coffin Texts,' 69.

[139] For details see D. E. Aune, 'Religions, Greco-Roman', in Gerald F. Hawthorne, Ralph Martin and Daniel Reid, eds, *Dictionary of Paul and His Letters* (Downers Grove: IVP, 1993), 786-96; Walter Burkert, *Greek Religion* (Cambridge, Mass.: Harvard University Press, 1985), 285-90; Everett Ferguson, *Backgrounds of Early Christianity* (Grand Rapids, Michigan: Wm. B. Eerdmans, 1993), 237-42; Eliade, *History*, 290-302; Wedderburn, *Baptism*, 315-20.

[140] See Hesiod, 'The Homeric Hymn to Demeter', in *The Homeric Hymns and Homerica* (Hugh G. Evelyn-White, tr; Cambridge, Mass.; London: Harvard University Press; William Heinemann Ltd, 1982).

jackal-face and raise yourself, stand up and sit down to your thousand of bread, your thousand of beer, your thousand [of oxen, your thousand of fowl, your thousand of everything on which a god lives].

O King, be pure, that Rē may find you standing with your mother Nūt, that she may lead you on the ways of the horizon, and that you may make your abode there happily in the company of your double for ever and ever.[128]

This experience of succeeding generations in his pattern is explained by Eliade: 'Osiris, the murdered king (= the deceased pharaoh), ensures the prosperity of the kingdom ruled by his son, Horus (represented by the newly installed pharaoh)'.[129] This relation Osiris/Horus assured the continuity of the dynasty, and because Osiris also provides the fertility of vegetation, the reign of his son was flourishing.[130] The model of Osiris was at the beginning only for the kings of Egypt, but in time it was 'democratized'.[131] The so-called *Coffin Texts*, inscribed on the interior of coffins,[132] attest this. Just as the pharaoh of earlier times had claimed to participate in the fate of Osiris, so each soul now hoped to achieve a ritual assimilation to the god.

> Now you are a king's son, a prince,
> as long as your soul exists, so long will your heart be with you.
> Anubis is mindful of you in Busiris,
> your soul rejoices in Abydos where your body is happy on the High Hill.
> Your embalmer rejoices in every place.
> Ah, truly, you are the chosen one!
> you are made whole in this your dignity which is before me,
> Anubis' heart is happy over the work of his hands
> and the heart of the Lord of the Divine Hall is thrilled
> when he beholds this good god,
> Master of those that have been and Ruler over those that are to come.
> (*Coffin Texts*, I, 197-199)[133]

---

[128] Translation is from *Pyramid Texts*, 290-1.

[129] Eliade, *History*, 98.

[130] Eliade, *History*, 99.

[131] For the historical reasons for that, see Eliade, *History*, 99-100; Ian Shaw and Paul Nicholson, ed, 'Coffin Texts', in *British Museum, Dictionary of Ancient Egypt* (London: British Museum Press, 1995), 69; also Wedderburn, *Baptism*, 312.

[132] They belong to the Middle Kingdom (2250-1580 B.C).

[133] Translation by R. T. Rundle Clark, *Myth and Symbol in Ancient Egipt* (London, 1960), 134. Faulkner translates this text as follows: 'You are the son of the king, the heir, your soul shall indeed exist, so that your heart may be with you and that Anubis may remember you in Djedu. May your soul rejoice in Abydos and your corpse which is in the desert-plateau be glad, may the embalmed one rejoice wherever he is. Would that you were examined and made whole in this your mummy which is in my presence! May Anubis be glad with what is under his hands, may he who presides over the Sacred Booth be glad when he sees this good god, lord of those who exist, ruler over of those

Towards a Contextual Reading

> Horus has lifted you up in his name of '*Hnw*-bark'; he bears you up in your name of Sokar. Live, that you may go to and fro every day; be a spirit in your name of 'Horizon from which Rē goes up'; be strong, be effective, be a soul, and have power for ever and ever.[126]

The ritual assimilation of the dead pharaoh with Osiris is seen in the *Pyramid texts*. Here is the beginning of the Utterance 219 (The king is identified with Osiris) (§ 167):

> O Atum, this one here is your son Osiris whom you have caused to be restored that he may live. If he lives, this King will live; if he does not die, this King will not die; if he is not destroyed, this King will not be destroyed; if he does not mourn, this King will not mourn; if he mourns, this king will mourn.[127]

In the Utterance 677 (The king dies and rises again) (§ 2018-2028) it is said:

> The Great One has fallen on his side, (even) he who stood as a god with his power with him and his *Wrrt*-crown on his head.
>
> The King has fallen on his side, (even) the King who stood as a god with his power with him and his *Wrrt*-crown on his head, like the *Wrrt*-crown of Rē. He ascends from the horizon, he is greeted by Horus in the horizon.
>
> O King, raise yourself, receive your dignity which the Two Enneads have made for you that you may be on the throne of Osiris as successor to the Foremost of the Westerners. [Take his power, receive] his [*Wrrt*-crown].
>
> O King, how good is this, how great is this, which your father Osiris has done for you! He has given his throne to you, and you give orders to those whose seats are hidden, you lead their august ones, and [all] the spirits follow you [whoever they may be(?)].
>
> [O King, be happy] and proud, because you belong to him from whose action you will not be far removed. Rē summons you in this your name of 'Him of whom all the spirits are afraid', and the dread of you is in hearts like [the dread of Rē when he ascends from the horizon].
>
> [O] King, your shape is hidden like that of Anubis on his belly; receive your

---

[125] 'The Pyramid Texts of Ancient Egypt were carved on the walls of the pyramids of King Wenis of the end of the Fifth Dynasty and of the rulers of the Sixth Dynasty.' *Pyramid Texts*, p. v. Dynasty V. c.2560-c.2420 B.C; Dynasties VI.-VIII, c.2420-c.2240 B.C., cf. Manetho, *Aegyptiaca* (W. G. Waddell, tr; London; Cambridge, Mass.: William Heinemann Ltd.; Harvard University Press, MCMLXIV), 50, 53. See also Ian Shaw and Paul Nicholson, ed, 'Pyramid Texts', in *British Musem, Dictionary of Ancient Egypt* (London: British Museum Press, 1995), 235-6.

[126] Translation is from *The Ancient Egyptian Pyramid Texts* (R. O. Faulkner, tr; Oxford: Clarendon Press, 1969), 119.

[127] Translation is from *Pyramid Texts*, 46.

Lucius receives an answer which, partly, illuminates the meaning of the initiation which will follow. The priest says to him that the day of initiation is marked by a nod from the goddess. The whole control of the goddess over the rites is seen in the fact that she appoints the day, the priest, and the expenses for ceremony (11:21). This is so because she has in her hands both the gates of death and the guardianship of life. The act of initiation is interpreted as being 'performed in the manner of voluntary death and salvation obtained by favor' (11:21). When Lucius describes the initiation he says: 'I came to the boundary of death and, having trodden the threshold of Proserpina, I travelled through all the elements and returned' (11:23). We do not know *how* the 'boundary of death' was reached.[119] Putting together this description of initiation and the way in which Lucius speaks about it at the end of the ceremony — 'next I celebrated my birth into mysteries' (11.24) —, it is possible to understand this initiation as having the basic idea of death and rebirth.[120] This initiatory death is one which *anticipates*[121] and *prepares* the initiated for death because the priest, before initiation, says to Lucius:

> In fact, those who had finished their life's span and were already standing on the very threshold of light's end, if only they could safely be trusted with great unspoken mysteries of the cult, were drawn forth by the goddess's power and in a manner reborn through her providence and set once more upon the course of renewed life. Therefore I too, he advised, ought to submit to the heavenly ordinance... (11:21)

In this initiation to Isis there is no indication that Isis herself dies. The goddess is one who is able to protect Lucius because 'she has in her hands both the gates of death and the guardianship of life'. And Lucius was able to return from his 'journey'. In the words of Wedderburn, 'Lucius, symbolically trusting her power to convey him through the underworld and out again to life beyond, henceforth will trust her power to protect him in this world and beyond the grave'.[122] There is nothing in the description of initiation to indicate that Lucius 'dies with Isis'. In this *known* ritual, language of 'death' is not used for defining any kind of 'relationship' with something/someone.

The only god in ancient Egypt and in the mysteries who provides a pattern 'for the experience of succeeding generations'[123] is Osiris. He was killed by his brother Seth and was 'resurrected' by his son Horus. However, Osiris was resurrected only as 'a spiritual person'.[124] The *Pyramid Texts*[125] Utterance 364, § 620-621 says:

---

[119] Walter Burkert, *Mystery Cults,* 89.

[120] Also Walter Burkert, *Mystery Cults*, 99.

[121] Also Wedderburn, *Baptism*, 302.

[122] Wedderburn, *Baptism,* 310.

[123] Wedderburn, *Baptism*, 306.

[124] Mircea Eliade, *A History of Religious Ideas: From the Stone Age to the Eleusinian Mysteries* (1; Willard R. Trask, tr; London: Collins, 1979), 98.

> I drew near to the confines of death, treading the very threshold of Proserpine. I was borne through all the elements and returned to earth again. At the dead of night I saw the sun shining brightly. I approached the gods above and the gods below, and worshipped them face to face.

as referring to the concept of identification of the initiates with the destiny of the deity. This is, according to Schnelle, the common element shared with Romans 6:3-4.[115]

In analysing this relation between gods and their initiates, working with the ancient relevant texts is important. Our access to the mystery religions during the time of Paul is impeded by several obstacles. (1) Because of the secrecy of the cult, relatively little inside information has survived regarding initiation into the mysteries. (2) The sources are fragmentary (statues, altars, inscriptions, mosaics and sacrificial instruments); at this point the well-known position of A. Schweitzer is worth quoting:

> [...] those who are engaged in making these comparisons [i.e. between Pauline Christianity and the mysteries] are rather apt to give the Mystery-religions a greater definiteness and articulation of thought than they really possess, and do not always give sufficient prominence to the distinction between their own hypothetical reconstruction and the medley of statements on which it is based... They manufacture out of the various fragments of information a kind of universal Mystery-religion which never actually existed, least of all in Paul's day.[116]

And (3) the mystery religions are richly varied. Therefore, each main relevant mystery-cult has to be understood in its own terms. In what terms is the relation between the god and the initiate described? Where is the place of 'the death' of that god in this relation? What are the differences from cult to cult? What are the 'effects' of this initiation in the life of the initiate in relation with the 'death of god'? The answers to these questions can offer some elements to construct a conclusion about the possibility of the influence of mystery cults upon Pauline 'dying with Christ'.

There is only one 'first-person account of a mystery experience'.[117] This is a initiation to Isis as described by Apuleius in *Metamorphoses* 11 (2nd century AD).[118] In his longing to be initiated 'into the mysteries of holy night' (11:21),

---

[115] Udo Schnelle, *The History and Theology of the New Testament Writings* (M. Eugene Boring, trans.; London: SCM Press Ltd, 1998), 121-22.

[116] A. Schweitzer, *Paul and His Interpreters: A Critical History* (London: Black, 1912), 192-93.

[117] Walter Burkert, *Ancient Mystery Cults* (Cambridge, Mass.; London: Harvard University Press, 1987), 97.

[118] Apuleius, *Metamorphoses* (II (Books VII-XI); J. Arthur Hanson, ed and tr; Cambridge, Mass.; London: Harvard University Press, 1989); see also the analysis of A. D. Nock, *Conversion: The Old and the New in Religion from Alexander the Great to Augustine of Hippo* (Oxford: Clarendon Press, 1952), 138-56.

Christ'.[103] This is something similar with what happens in the mystery religions where 'initiations-sacraments' 'impart to the initiates a share in the fate of the cult-deity who has suffered death and reawakened to life — such as Attis, Adonis, or Osiris'.[104]

According to Lohse, the mysteries promised salvation 'through the cultic experience in which only the initiated mystai were allowed to participate'.[105] This 'cultic experience' is a participation in the fate of the deity in which they are filled with divine power.[106] This fate is one 'of suffering and dying'.[107] These ideas, according to Lohse, influenced early Christian community partly 'through the Christian community's unconscious interpretation of worship activities in accordance with the example offered by the mystery religions' and partly 'by the conscious reference to views of the mystery religions. The consequence of the cultic drama in which the myste participates — that is, his incorporation into the destiny of the cultic deity — was also the interpretation given to the Christian baptism'.[108]

Recently this thesis has been sustained also by R. Penna and U. Schnelle. Penna suggests that Romans 6 has to be understood as being a reflection not of the baptismal rite but of the historical-soteriological fact of Christ's death.[109] The whole section of 6.2-7 discusses the death to sin in the context of participation in the death of Christ.[110] The moral life of the Christian reveals the radical overcoming of sin.[111]

The original religious and cultural context with the regard to 'dying with Christ' is to be found in the mystery cults where 'we find the idea of the experience of a 'voluntary death' in the celebration of the cult'.[112]

In discussing the original religious and cultural context with regard to 'dying with Christ' Penna works with the concepts of representation and solidarity.[113] Based on these he argues for the saving efficacious character of Christ's death and participation in that event.[114]

Schnelle argues that the idea of unity between Christ and the baptised described in Romans 6:3-4 is dependent on ideas from mystery religions. He interprets Apuleius, *Metamorphoses* 11:23:8

---

[103] His italics; Bultmann, *Theology,* 140.
[104] Bultmann, *Theology,* 140.
[105] Lohse, *Environment*, 241, 242.
[106] Lohse, *Environment*, 234.
[107] Lohse, *Environment*, 243.
[108] Lohse, *Environment*, 242.
[109] Romano Penna, *Paul the Apostle: Jew and Greek Alike* (1; trans. by Thomas P. Wahl; Collegeville, Minnesota: The Liturgical Press, 1996), 138.
[110] Penna, *Paul,* 138.
[111] Penna, *Paul,* 138.
[112] Penna, *Paul,* 139.
[113] Penna, *Paul,* 138.
[114] Penna, *Paul,* 139.

ideas is that: 'what is at work here is a mystery-like feeling'.[96] At this point he suggests that the Egyptian idea of an *apotheosis by drowning*, and the description of Osiris, 'who was three days and three nights in the flood of the river' can offer a point of contact,[97] and the 'baptism in the celestial Jordan' from the Baptist sect of the Mandaeans is also important. In this background the liturgical meaning from Apuleius in relation to Paul is as follows:

> as with Apuleius the baptism is followed by the instruction about the celestial pilgrimage, the actual δρώμενον, here they are simultaneous; indeed the δρώμενον is missing. [...] We must take a strict distinction: cultic ablutions and baths of purification, as they appear in numerous religions, have nothing to do with baptism as we encounter it here; here it has to do with ζωοποιεῖν, the imparting of another life to something dead, or to something that has voluntarily died. [...] The Mandaean baptism still exhibits this basic mystery-like feature so fully that it cannot possibly stem from Christian baptism or even just from the Jewish proselyte ablutions. The same holds true for Paul in the passages cited; but Paul also is familiar with baptism as a bath for purposes of purification. 1 Cor. 6:9-11; Certainly, but the aim here is clear: the contrast to πόρνοι, κλέπται, ἅρπαγες ἧτε is supposed to be formed by καθαροί, ἅγιοι, δίκαιοι ἐγένεσθε. All the emphasis is placed on the last term, for [those who are unrighteous cannot inherit the kingdom of God]. Paul is also familiar with the more Jewish-Christian interpretation; no one disputes that. The point is that along with it he knows and employs the Hellenistic and mystery-like interpretation as well.[98]

The other influential authors of the idea that Pauline 'dying with Christ' originated by analogy with the initiation of the mystery religions[99] are R. Bultmann[100] and E. Lohse.[101] In considering the question about the way in which Christ's death releases men from the powers of this age, Bultmann points out that the answer is in the 'statements in which Paul describes Christ's death in analogy with the death of a divinity of the mystery religions.'[102] He says that *'baptism imparts participation in the death and resurrection of*

---

[96] Reitzenstein, *Mystery Religions*, 284.

[97] Reitzenstein, *Mystery Religions*, 284.

[98] Reitzenstein, *Mystery Religions*, 287-8.

[99] For detailed answers and analysis of this hypothesis, see G. Wagner, *Pauline Baptism and the Pagan Mysteries: The Problem of the Pauline Doctrine of Baptism in Romans VI.1-11, in the Light of Its Religio-Historical 'Parallels'* (London: Oliver and Boyd, 1967), 69-255; Wedderburn, *Baptism* especially chapters 2 and 5. David Seeley, *The Noble Death: Graeco-Roman Martyrology and Paul's Concept of Salvation* (Sheffield: JSOT Press, 1990), 67-83.

[100] R. Bultmann, *Theology of the New Testament* (London: SCM, 1952), 140, 298.

[101] Eduard Lohse, *The New Testament Environment* (London: SCM Press Ltd, 1976), 234, 240.

[102] Bultmann, *Theology*, 298.

from Jesus's language of death '*as* baptism'. As we will argue in chapter 3, Paul's metaphor of 'baptism' ('we have been baptized into Christ Jesus', ἐβαπτίσθημεν εἰς Χριστὸν Ἰησοῦν) in Romans 6:3 points to the saving action of God by which we are 'overwhelmed' toward that event which took place once and for all, the event of Christ's death 'to sin'. The meaning of Jesus' saying is that his death can be seen as a 'baptism' in the sense that it is a 'fatal experience.' In both situations the same *vehicle* is used but both the area in which is 'transferred' and the point of contact are different. Thus, it is not clear where it has to be worked with the notion of 'catalyst.'

R. REITZENSTEIN, R. BULTMANN, E. LOHSE, R. PENNA, U. SCHNELLE — 'DYING WITH CHRIST' AND THE MYSTERY RELIGIONS

The positions of these authors (some of them from the *religionsgeschichtliche Schule* and some of them, at this point, in that tradition) are discussed together because their positions share a common ground as the origin of Paul's 'dying with Christ' language is concerned (the order is chronological). Their position will be analysed by discussing again the relevant evidences about/from the mystery religions.

In his comparison of the story of Apuleius with other scanty evidence (mainly from Egyptian rites) about the mystery religions,[93] Reitzenstein says the following about the main events in the report of Apuleius:

> In Apuleius, after a general bath of purification, which of course must already possess religious significance, since all the *religiosi* accompany him to it, there follows a ceremonial prayer and the περιρραντισμός; then in the temple the instruction and a ten-day period of ascetic discipline; then the mystery, about the content and meaning of which it is stated. Of all this, the papyrus attests to us the visit to the underworld and the veneration of the dead, and further a veneration paid to three elements, fire, water, and air, to which are added two higher deities, the sun and the moon.[94]

Also, according to Reitzenstein, the name of the leading priest, Mithras, the following community festival and the representation of the *mystes* as a statue of the deity point to the fact that 'we are dealing with a syncretistic cult'.[95]

In explaining the references to the twofold baptismal action he discusses the texts from Mark 10:38; Rom 6:2ff; Col 2:12 in which the 'comparison of baptism and death' appears. His conclusion in relation to the background of

---

[93] Richard Reitzenstein, *Hellenistic Mystery Religions: Their Basic Ideas and Significance* (trans. by John E. Steely; Pittsburgh, Pennsylvania: The Pickwick Press, 1978), 274.

[94] Reitzenstein, *Mystery Religions,* 275.

[95] Reitzenstein, *Mystery Religions,* 282.

D. Wenham — 'Dying' Language and The Teaching of Jesus

The next position to be discussed is that of Wenham. Wenham's discussion about 'dying with Christ' is developed where, we consider, is its proper place, namely in an exposition of Paul's understanding of Christ's death.[81] He presents the main lines of Paul's understanding of Christ's death as follows: (1) the cross is understood in an eschatological context,[82] (2) it deals with human sinfulness,[83] (3) it has a redemptive significance (slavery/new exodus),[84] (4) it is an atoning sacrifice,[85] and (5) it is a 'participation' event ('something that believers come to share in').[86] Wenham does not discuss in his presentation of Paul's understanding of Christ's death the *identity* of the one who died. Also he does not explain the *what*, *why* and *how* of 'participation'.

In Wenham's exposition there is an analysis of the relationship between the teaching of Jesus, as it is preserved in the synoptics, about discipleship as 'taking up the cross' (Matt 16:24-26/Mark 8:34-37/Luke 9:23-26; Matt 10:38/Luke 14:27)[87] and 'drinking the cup that I drink' and being baptized 'with the baptism 'with which I am baptized' (Mark 10:38, 39/Matt 20:22,23).[88] He states: 'this is not the Pauline baptismal understanding of suffering with Christ, but it is a significant and strong tradition in which Jesus' suffering and death are seen as an experience in which his followers will share'.[89]

Was Paul influenced by these Jesus-traditions? In explaining 'baptism into death in Paul' Wenham points out that 'it represents the coming together of a Jewish and Christian understanding of baptism as initiation into the saved people of God with a distinctively Christian view of the death and resurrection of Jesus as the decisive saving events'.[90] Wenham's final conclusion is that 'it is impossible to prove that Paul was influenced by these[91] particular sayings of Jesus, but it is quite probable that they were at least a catalyst in his thinking'.[92]

A conclusion which includes the term 'catalyst' has to explain at what point and in what directions a 'catalyst' can suggest a development of a particular position. Wenham does not provide that. Indeed, Paul's language of 'baptism into Christ's death' and being 'buried with Christ through baptism' is different

---

[81] See chapter 3.
[82] David Wenham, *Paul: Follower of Jesus or Founder of Christianity?* (Grand Rapids: Eerdmans, 1995), 148.
[83] Wenham, *Paul*, 149.
[84] Wenham, *Paul*, 150.
[85] Wenham, *Paul*, 150-53.
[86] Wenham, *Paul*, 154.
[87] Wenham, *Paul*, 154.
[88] Wenham, *Paul*, 155.
[89] Wenham, *Paul*, 155.
[90] Wenham, *Paul*, 161.
[91] Wenham, *Paul*, 163.
[92] Wenham, *Paul*, 164.

(iii) The Pauline metaphor of death for describing a mode of living is based, at least in part, on the philosophical *commentatio mortis* theme (Aune's third point).

As we saw, the *commentatio mortis* theme is mainly developed in *Phaedo*. There, in searching for truth, beauty and the true nature of things the philosopher has a permanent obstacle, namely, the body. The soul, in order to know the truth, has to be 'separated' from the body. This 'separation' is the main task of the true philosopher. By defining 'death' as the separation of the soul from the body, Socrates says that the practice of philosophers is a 'practice of death'. Thus, death is used as a metaphor for understanding this 'true life' in search for knowledge. There is also a metaphorical usage of 'death' in Paul but his usage is much more complex and is developed against a different background. In Paul's metaphor there is no such thing as 'separation of soul from the body' but his language is based on his understanding of Christ's death as a 'death to sin.'[79] In Romans 6, the body does not disturb the soul in the believer's desire to know the truth or to acquire absolute knowledge, but the body is under the dominion of *sin*;[80] sin as a power is the 'problem' *not* 'an evil body,' and 'soul' language does not have a similar role in Paul's metaphor as it has in Plato's. They work with different approaches as far as the language of 'death' is concerned. Plato works with the language of 'separation' (the purpose being absolute separation) and Paul defines the 'relationship' with the 'old environment and its powers' in terms of 'death'; the outlook is offered by the Calvary/Easter event from Christ's life. The believer lives his/her life in a hostile environment which was inaugurated by the sin of Adam. Therefore, the differences in the anthropological and cosmological outlooks between Paul and Plato are important and the element of Christ's death, which shaped Paul's language is important as well. There is no similar element in Plato's metaphor.

The examples from Philo also show that the assimilation of ideas from the *commentatio mortis* tradition is done without a major change. There are only *added* elements such as 'service of the Father,' and life 'in the presence of Him who is immortal.'

Thus, in the light of these observations, we think that a most accurate explanation of the relationhip between these two traditions is one formulated not in terms of dependence, but of *difference*. These are to be viewed as two different traditions. The common element is only that both these traditions use the same *vehicle* which on the one hand is defined differently and on the other is 'transferred' in different contexts.

---

[79] See the argument in chapter 3.
[80] See the argument in chapter 4.

This man is advised to understand his relationship with quarrel and enmity in terms of 'death'. The meaning of this is not very clear. This could be 'you are under the pressure of these, but look at them as at death, namely, as at something fearful and miserable'. In this case a common view could be presupposed here in which an *early* death is understood as something fearful and sometimes as a sign of divine punishment.

4 Macc. 7:17-19 states as follows:

[17]Some perhaps might say, "Not every one has full command of his emotions, because not every one has prudent reason." [18]But as many as attend to religion with a whole heart, these alone are able to control the passions of the flesh, [19]since they believe that they, like our patriarchs Abraham and Isaac and Jacob, do not *die to God* (θεῷ... ἀποθνῄσκουσιν), but live in God (ζῶσιν τῷ θεῷ). [20]No contradiction therefore arises when some persons appear to be dominated by their emotions because of the weakness of their reason.[77]

This example is the closest to that of Paul. The patriarchs were not dead in relation to God, or as God is concerned, but alive.[78] That is why they were able to 'control the passions of the flesh'. The same is true for those who attend to religion with a whole heart. This text can be seen as an isolated example in which a relationship is defined in terms of death. The unfortunate thing is that this metaphorical usage is not developed, either in 4 Maccabees, or in other Jewish writtings. It is possible that this metaphor offered Paul a vivid example which was later applied by him to the relationship to sin.

Thus, it is true that 'death' is not used in ancient Jewish literature as a metaphor for a transformed life, but the examples from Proverbs and Ezekiel and especially 4 Maccabees show other possibilities of 'transfer' for the language of 'death'.

Bagster and Sons, 1844, 1851).

[77] RSV translation; H. Anderson translates 4 Mac. 7:19: 'believing that to God they do not die, as our patriarchs Abraham, Isaac, and Jacob died not, but to live to God.' Anderson, H., '4 Maccabees, A New Translation and Introduction,' *The Old Testament Pseudepigrapha* (2, Charlesworth, James H., ed., London: Darton, Longman & Todd, 1985); R.H. Charles translates 7:19: 'believing that unto God they die not, as our patriarchs, Abraham and Isaac and Jacob, died not, but that they live unto God.' R. H. Charles, ed., *The Apocrypha and Pseudepigrapha of the Old Testament in English*, (Oxford: Clarendon Press, 1963); NRSV translates 7:19: 'since they believe that they, like our patriarchs Abraham and Isaac and Jacob, do not die to God, but live to God.' *The Cambridge Annotated Study Apocrypha New Revised Standard Version*, (Kee, Howard Clark, ed., Cambridge: Cambridge University Press, 1994).

[78] See 4 Mac. 16:24-25: 'By these words the mother of the seven encouraged and persuaded each of her sons to die rather than to violate God's commandment. They knew also that those who die for the sake of God live to God, as do the Abraham and Isaac and all the patriarchs.' (ἔτι δὲ αἱ ταῦτα εἰδότες ὅτι οἱ διὰ τὸν θεὸν ἀποθνῄσκοντες ζῶσιν τῷ θεῷ ὥσπερ Αβρααμ καὶ Ισαακ καὶ Ιακωβ καὶ πάντες οἱ πατριάρχαι.)

as a power that stands opposed to God (Isa. 25:8; 1 Enoch 69:4-11). The first meaning of death ('bodily demise'; 2 Sam. 12:15; Wisdom 2:23-24) is 'metaphorically applied to the notion of perdition'.[71] For example, in 4 Ezra 7:48, the term 'death' is used metaphorically[72] in connection with a certain manner or quality of existence:

> For an evil heart has grown up in us, which has alienated us from God, and has brought us into corruption and the ways of death, and has shown us the paths of perdition and removed us far from life — and that not just a few of us but almost all who have been created!

The bodily demise and these present 'ways of death' are prefigurations of eschatological death (Ps. 88:5,11; Isa. 38:18).[73]

The 'moral' meaning is presupposed in Ezekiel 37, in explaining the 'restoration' of Israel. The restoration is described in terms 'of bringing up from the grave' (37:12,13). Israel is dead, that is, she is in the grave, and her grave will be opened. This metaphor 'of bringing up from the grave' is used negatively for describing their state and restoration.

Proverbs 25:10 (LXX)[74] and 4 Macc. 7:19 are the only examples, which we found, in Jewish ancient literature, where 'death' is used for explaining a kind of *relationship*. Prov. 25:10 states as follows:

> [8]Get not suddenly into a quarrel, lest thou repent at last. [9]Whenever thy friend shall reproach thee, retreat backward, despise him not;[10] *lest thy friend continue to reproach thee, so thy quarrel and enmity shall not depart, but shall be to thee like death.* (μή σε ὀνειδίσῃ με ὁ φίλος, ἡ δε μάχη σου καὶ ἡ ἔχθρα οὐκ ἀπέσται, ἀλλ' ἔσται σοι ἴση θανάτῳ.) [75] Favour and friendship set a man free, which do thou keep for thyself, lest thou be made liable to reproach; but take heed to thy ways peaceably.[76]

---

among them illness, persecution, despair, and nonparticipation in the life of the covenant community; (2) as a 'power' in opposition to the created order; (3) for biological cessation, usually in the sense of the end of a given individual's historical existence, and less frequently as the inevitable fate of all humans. [...] the first and third usages derived ultimately from the second: a malign power brings misfortune and death'.

[70] See also: Merill, 'מות', 886-8; de Boer, *Defeat of Death*, 90.

[71] de Boer, *Defeat of Death*, 75.

[72] de Boer, *Defeat of Death*, 75.

[73] de Boer, *Defeat of Death*, 84.

[74] Alfred Rahlfs, ed, *Septuaginta* (Stuttgart: Biblia-Druck, 1935).

[75] The Hebrew text is different. Prov. 25:10 goes like this: 'or else someone who hears you will bring shame on you, and your ill repute will have no end' (שֹׁמֵעַ וְדִבָּתְךָ לֹא תָשׁוּב פֶּן־יְחַסֶּדְךָ).

[76] The Greek text is from *Septuaginta* (Alfred Rahlfs, ed.; Stuttgart: Biblia-Druck, 1935, 1979), and the English translation is that of Lancelot C. L. Brenton, trans, *The English Translation of the Septuagint Version of the Old Testament* (London: Samuel

dead thing which was our birth-fellow, the body, or to the objects more lifeless still, glory, wealth, and offices, and honours, and all other illusions which like images or pictures are created through the deceit of false opinion by those who have never gazed upon true beauty.

Here the true serving of the Father and Creator is defined in terms of dedication to genuine philosophy. By doing this someone 'stud[ies how] to die to the life in the body'. This case given by Philo can function as an example of the way in which the *commentatio mortis*/μελέτη θανάτου tradition is 'assimilated' into a Jewish framework. This tradition is integrated without modifying its main lines and this observation is important when trying to explain the place of such tradition when studying another Jew, such as Paul.

(ii) Death as a metaphor for a morally transformed life does not appear in early Judaism (Aune's second point).

In Jewish ancient literature[67] there are three main meanings for 'death': physical, moral[68] and eschatological.[69] There is also a personification of death[70]

---

[67] For detailed studies see: Lloyd R. Bailey, *Biblical Perspectives on Death* (Overtures to Biblical Theology; Philadelphia: Fortress Press, 1979); John Bowker, *The Meanings of Death* (Cambridge: Cambridge University Press, 1993); Martinus C. de Boer, *The Defeat of Death: Apocalyptic Eschatology in 1 Corinthians 15 and Romans 5* (Sheffield: JSOT Press, 1988); Eugene H. Merill, 'מות', *NIDOTTE* II 886-8; Johs. Pedersen, *Israel, Its Life and Culture* (I-II; London, Copenhagen: Oxford University Press, Branner Og Korch, 1926), 453-96; W. Schmithals, 'θάνατος', *NIDNTT* II 430-41; Nicholas J. Tromp, *Primitive Conceptions of Death and the Nether World in the Old Testament* (Rome: Pontifical Biblical Institute, 1969); Gerhard von Rad, ''Righteousness' and 'Life' in the Cultic Language of the Psalms', in *The Problem of Hexateuch and Other Essays* (E. W. Trueman Dicken, trans.; London: SCM Press Ltd, 1984). For a recent synthesis on Sheol see Georges Minois, *Istoria Infernurilor* (Alexandra Cunita, trans.; Bucuresti: Humanitas, 1998), 54-70.

[68] Note here the debate presented in Tromp, *Primitive Conceptions,* 129-38 about the meaning of those individual laments from Psalter in which the psalmist often claims to be in Sheol, when he is still alive; to be delivered from the abode of death, while he is not there. The two main participants are Christoph Barth (*Die Errettung vom Tode in den individuellen Klage-und Dankliedern des Altes Testaments*, Zollikon, 1947) and Nicholas Tromp. Barth defines life as human existence on earth worth being lived (53-66), and death as being the lack of this fullness; he says that illness, calamity and restraint belong to the essence of death. If someone is in need or in a dangerous situation, then he is in Sheol. Tromp agrees with Barth that the psalmists are in Sheol, but in the sense of being in 'the domain of Death, and not in the domain of dead' (137). In this case 'death' is a metaphor for a dangerous situation; that is why this brief discussion is not developed in the main text. For another analysis of Barth's understanding see von Rad, ''Righteousness' and 'Life' in the Cultic Language of the Psalms,' 255-6.

[69] Cf. de Boer, *Defeat of Death,* 84. For a different understanding see Bailey, *Perspectives,* 39 'The term death used in the literature of the OT has at least three senses: (1) as a metaphor for those things which detract from life as Yahweh intends it,

In this letter the ideas are similar to those in *Ep.* 24. A man of an old age has to 'think of death' for not being surprised when it will come. In this way that man lives a life 'free' of fear.

Thus in Seneca we do not have as in *Phaedo* the metaphor of death (as separation of soul from the body) for understanding 'the true life' of philosopher. Here we have one of the main Stoic principles at work: 'We should strip the mask, not only from men, but from things, and restore to each object its own aspect' (24:13). When someone applies this, even to the fear of death, he receives 'peace of mind'.

Although not discussed by Aune, in Philo there are texts in which he is in the *Phaedo* tradition where death is used as a metaphor[63] for understanding the true philosophical life.

In *De Agricultura* (13:104-105)[64] Philo speaks about those who 'have genuinely devoted themselves to the pursuit of wisdom, and entered into no association than that with the beautiful and have renounced everything else whatever.' This is an echo from *Phaedo* 64, 65, 67. A clearer affirmation is found in *De Gigantibus* (3:13-15).[65]

> Now some of the souls have descended into bodies, but others have never deigned to be brought into union with any of the parts of earth. They are consecrated and devoted to the service of the Father and Creator whose wont it is to employ them as ministers and helpers, to have charge and care of mortal man. But the others descending into the body as though into a stream have sometimes been caught in the swirl of its rushing torrent and swallowed up thereby, at other times have been able to stem the current, have risen to the surface and then soared upwards back to the place from whence they came. These last, then, are *the souls of those who have given themselves to genuine philosophy, who from first to last study to die to the life in the body,*[66] (αὗται με οὖν εἰσι ψυχαι τῶν ἀνόθως φιλοσοφησάντων, ἐξ ἀρχῆς ἄχρι τέλους μελετῶσαι τὸν μετὰ σωμάτων ἀποθνῄσκειν βίον) that a higher existence immortal and incorporeal, in the presence of Him who is Himself immortal and uncreate, may be their portion. But the souls which have sunk beneath the stream, are the souls of the others who have held no count of wisdom. They have abandoned themselves to the unstable things of chance, none of which has aught to do with our noblest part, the soul or mind, but all are related to the

---

[63] For other metaphorical meanings of death in Philo see D. Zeller, 'The Life and Death of the Soul in Philo of Alexandria: The Use and Origin of a Metaphor', *The Studia Philonica Annual* 7 (1995) 19-55.

[64] The text and translation are from The Loeb Classical Library, Philo, *On Husbandry (De Agricultura)* (III; F. H. Colson and G. H. Whitaker, trans.; London, Cambridge, Mass.: William Heinemann Ltd, Harvard University Press, 1968).

[65] The text and translation are from the Loeb Classical Library, Philo, *On the Giants (De Gigantibus)* (II; F. H. Colson and G. H. Whitaker, trans.; London, Cambridge, Mass.: William Heinemann Ltd, Harvard University Press, 1968).

[66] Our italics.

In Seneca's *Epistles* 24, 26[62] there is a discussion about the right attitude when someone faces a threat, and about the subject of old age. In *Ep.* 24 (On Despising Death), the purpose of Seneca is to conduct Lucilius 'to the peace of mind' (24:2) at a time when he is 'anxious about the result of a lawsuit, with which and angry opponent is threatening (him)' (24:1). The course of the argument is as follows: 'assume that what you fear may happen will certainly happen in any event. (24:2) [...] If you lose this case, can anything more severe happen to you than being sent into exile or led to prison? Is there a worst fate that any man may fear than being burned or being killed?' (24:3) After this Seneca gives him a list of men who were not frightened in the face of death, to encourage him 'to face that which is thought to be most terrible' (24:9). Death, simply, has to be despised. Discussing Scipio, who pierced his body with a sword in order not to fall into the hands of his enemies (24:10), Seneca says that 'it was a great deed to conquer Carthage, but a greater deed to conquer death' (*Multum fuit Carthaginem vincere, sed amplius mortem*) (24:11). In other words 'death is so little to be feared' (24:12). As a principle, always 'hope for that which is utterly just, and prepare yourself against that which is utterly unjust' (24:12). 'We should strip the mask, not only from men, but from things, and restore to each object its own aspect' (24:13). Seneca asks Lucilius to do this thing even with death (24:14). 'Away with all stuff, which makes us to numb with terror!' (24:14). 'Say to yourself that our petty bodies are mortal and frail' (*Dic mortabile tibi et fragile corpusculum esse*) (24:16). 'Every day a little of our life is taken away from us' (24:20). In this sense 'we die every day' (*cotidie morimur*) (24:20). When death finally comes 'it merely of itself completes the death-process. We reach death at that moment, but we have been a long time on the way' (24:21). 'The death of which you are afraid is the last, but not the only death' (24:22).

In all this we can see that, according to Seneca, death is 'a way of life' *not* as an understanding of 'a new life' but as an observation that man is *mortal* and *frail*, that is, 'he dies daily'. With this 'restoring [every] object in its own aspect' Seneca helped Lucilius to receive peace of mind knowing that death/mortality is a *condition* of this life.

In *Ep.* 26 Seneca writes 'on the subject of old age' (26:3). Death is seen as a thing which 'will deliver the final judgment in [each] case' (26:6). Man never knows where death awaits him, so he has to be ready for it everywhere (26:8). This 'being ready' is expressed as 'learning thoroughly how to die' or 'think on death' (*meditare mortem*) (26:10). This 'thinking on death' is 'thinking on freedom' (26:10), for that man 'who has learned to die has unlearned slavery; he is above any external power, or, at any rate, he is beyond it' (26:10).

---

[62] The translation used is that from The Loeb Classical Library, Seneca, *Ad Lucilium Epistulae Morales*.

nearest to knowledge when we avoid, so far as possible, intercourse and communion with the body, except what is absolutely necessary, and are not filled with its nature, *but keep ourselves pure from it until God himself sets us free* (ἀλλὰ καθαρεύωμεν ἀπ' αὐτοῦ, ἕως ἂν ὁ θεὸς αὐτὸς ἀπολύσῃ ἡμᾶς). (66d-67a)[55]

In this present life the true philosopher prepares himself for that event. He will always be eager to release and separate the soul from the body (67d). In other words 'the true philosophers practise dying' (οἱ ὀρθῶς φιλοσοφοῦντες ἀποθνῄσκειν μετελῶσι) (67e). That philosopher who understands philosophical life in this way will have the 'courage' (68c)[56] in the face of death because this was the thing for which he longed and also will have 'self-restraint' (this is 'characteristic of those alone who despise the body and pass their lives in philosophy') (68d). From the point of view of the practice of the philosophical aspiration, the entire theory of 'death' could be reduced to three words: search - obstacle - possession.[57]

A true student of philosophy will always try to keep his soul apart from the influence of the body.[58] The soul is 'entirely fastened and welded to the body and is compelled to regard realities through the body as through prison bars, not with its own unhindered vision, and is wallowing in utter ignorance' (82e).[59] He has to avoid living in the fashions of the body, and say farewell to all these (82d). This is 'the practice of death' (μελέτη θανάτου) (81a).

Thus, here, in *Phaedo*, the philosophical goal is that of knowing the truth. This knowledge is attained by the soul. In reaching that goal there is a permanent obstacle, the body. While man is in the body, the obstacle of the body remains insurmountable.[60] The true philosopher will try to separate the soul from the body (this is the meaning of death) in order to be able to know the truth as well as he can. Thus 'the practice of death' is a delivery from that obstacle. Also this way of life will be a 'preparation for death' (ἐπιτηδεύουσιν... ἀποθνῄσκειν) because 'it would be absurd to be troubled when the thing comes for which they have so long been preparing and looking forward.'[61] (64a).

---

[55] Another example is when Socrates talks about the soul as being 'most enthralled by the body' (83d). How each pleasure and pain 'is a sort of nail which nails and rivets the soul to the body' (83e). This is so because then the body makes the soul to believe that what is true for itself is true also for her (83e). For this reason 'the true lovers of knowledge are temperate and brave' (83e).

[56] Arthur J. Droge and James D. Tabor, *A Noble Death: Suicide and Martyrdom Among Christians and Jews in Antiquity* (New York: HarperSanFrancisco, 1992), 20.

[57] Cf. Di Giuseppe, *La teoria de la morte,* 113.

[58] Di Giuseppe, *La teoria de la morte,* 113.

[59] I.F. Stone, *The Trial of Socrates* (London: Jonathan Cape, 1988), 195-6.

[60] Di Giuseppe, *La teoria de la morte,* 114.

[61] Translation is from *The Collected Dialogues of Plato Including the Letters*, (Edith Hamilton; Huntington, Cairns, eds., Princeton: Princeton University Press, 1989).

He defines death as a 'separation of the soul and the body' (τὴν τῆς ψυχῆς ἀπὸ τοῦ σώματος ἀπαλλαγήν) (64c). This is attained totally only at death.

The true philosopher has to despise (64e) 'the so-called pleasures' such as eating, drinking, (64c) love (64d) and also 'other cares of the body' (64d). 'Such a man would not devote himself to the body, but would, so far as he was able, turn away from the body and concern himself with the soul' (64e).[53] The soul is able to search the reality when 'none of these things troubles it, neither hearing nor sight, nor pain nor any pleasure, but it is, so far as possible, alone by itself, and takes leave of the body, and avoiding, so far as it can, all association or contact with the body, reaches out toward the reality' (65c).

The body is a 'hindrance' (65a) or an inaccurate witness (65b) in the philosopher's search for truth, beauty and the true nature of things.[54] The philosopher is not able to attain pure truth because of the body (65c).

> Would not that man do this most perfectly who approaches each thing, so far as possible, with the reason alone, not introducing sight into his reasoning nor dragging in any of the other senses along with his thinking, but who employs pure, absolute reason in his attempt to search out the pure, absolute essence of things, and who removes himself, so far as possible, from eyes and ears, and, in a word, from his whole body, because he feels that its companionship disturbs the soul and hinders it from attaining truth and wisdom? (66a)

The philosopher will not be satisfied while he is in the body for his soul is contaminated by the body — 'such an evil' (τοιούτου κακοῦ) (66b). The body will always be a 'source of endless trouble' (requirement of food, in danger of diseases, an obstacle in search for the truth) (66c). If the philosopher wants 'to know anything absolutely' he 'must be free from the body and must behold the actual realities with the eye of the soul alone' (66d). This thing will be attained after death (66e) because as long has he has the body he will never completely attain what he desires, that is, the truth (66b). He is a slave in its service (66d). Socrates describes this conflict and final release as follows:

> But the worst of all is that if we do get a bit of leisure and turn to philosophy, the body is constantly breaking in upon our studies and disturbing us with noise and confusion, so that it prevents our beholding the truth, and in fact we perceive that, if we are ever to know anything absolutely, we must be free from the body and must behold the actual realities with the eye of the soul alone. And then, as our argument shows, when we are dead we are likely to possess the wisdom which we desire and claim to be enamoured of, but not while we live. For, if pure knowledge is impossible while the body is with us, one of two things must follow, either it cannot be acquired at all or only when we are dead; for then the soul will be by itself apart from the body, but not before. And while we live, we shall, I think, be

---

[53] See also Di Giuseppe, *La teoria de la morte*, 114.
[54] Ilham Dilman, *Philosophy and the Philosophical Life: A Study in Plato's Phaedo* (London: Macmillan, 1992), 21, 70.

It will be shown critically that in Aune's thesis an important author is missing, namely, Philo, and that another, Seneca, is misinterpreted.

In ancient times, someone was regarded as a philosopher not according to the originality and richness of his invented or developed philosophical discourse, but according to his way of life.[45] First of all a philosopher has to become a better man. A philosophical discourse is a genuine one only if it becomes a way of life. This holds true for Platonic and Aristotelian traditions where the climax of a philosophical life is a living according to the spirit. This is also true about the Cynics and the Stoics.[46] The essence of a philosophical life is the existential choice of a particular way of life.[47]

According to Plato this choice is the most important thing. This is shown in the story of Er from *Republic* 618 b-c.[48] A person has 'to distinguish the life that is good from that which is bad, and always and everywhere to choose the best that the conditions allow.' The philosophical way of life means a turning toward the intellectual and spiritual life. It is a 'conversion of the soul' (518d). This 'shifting or conversion' is 'an art' (518d). This 'turning' toward the spirit presupposes a considerable effort,[49] which has to be renewed daily. This effort is explained by different 'practices'. In Plato's writings there are 'spiritual practices' for instructing the soul for being in conformity with the universe and being identified with the divinity[50] (e.g., 'preparing for sleep', *Republic,* 571-572; 'being able to go through a disaster without rebellion', *Republic,* 604 b-c).

The best-known practice is that of 'preparing for death' which is explained in Plato, *Phaedo*.[51] There, Socrates defines the study of philosophy as being a preparation for 'dying and being dead' (ἐπιτηδεύουσιν ἢ ἀποθνῄσκειν τε καὶ τεθνάναι) (64a).

The study of philosophy was the major purpose in Socrates' life (60e-61a). That man who has the spirit of philosophy will be willing to die (61c),[52] 'would desire to follow after the dying' (61d); Socrates will explain what that means.

---

[45] Pierre Hadot, *Ce Este Filosofia Antica?* (George Bondor and Claudiu Tipurita, trans.; Iasi: Polirom, 1997), 198.

[46] Hadot, *Filosofia antica*, 193.

[47] Hadot, *Filosofia antica,* 199.

[48] The translation is that from Loeb Classical Library, Plato, *The Republic* (Paul Shorey, tr; Cambridge, Mass.; London: Harvard University Press; William Heinemann Ltd, 1987).

[49] Cf. Hadot, *Filosofia antica,* 94.

[50] Cf. Hadot, *Filosofia antica,* 94.

[51] The translation, where not mentioned otherwise, is that from Loeb Classical Library Plato, *Euthyphro, Apology, Crito, Phaedo, Phaedrus* (I; Harold North Fowler, trans.; Cambridge, Mass., London: Harvard University Press, William Heinemann Ltd, 1982).

[52] Cf. Ricardo Di Giuseppe, *La teoria della morte nel Fedone platonico* (Napoli: Societa Editrice Il Mulino, 1993), 111.

to withdraw the soul from the concern of the body.³⁵ This idea, developed/explained only in Plato, *Phaedo*³⁶ is also found, according to Aune, in Stoic literature (Seneca, *Ep.* 24; 26; 70; 65),³⁷ in Ps. Plato *Axiochus* 366A,³⁸ and in several Cynic letters (in Ps-Socrates *Ep.* 14:8; Ps-Diogenes *Ep.* 39).³⁹ Death 'as a metaphor for the morally transformed life occurs neither in early Judaism nor in Hellenism apart from the *commentatio mortis* theme'.⁴⁰

Also Paul used frequently 'the language and imagery of death and dying to describe a mode of living in which the liberating effects of the death of Jesus are actualized in the present moral experience of the Christian'.⁴¹ Aune says that 'it is possible that Paul's use of the metaphor of death as the basis for ethical behaviour, is based, at least in part, on the popular philosophical *commentatio mortis* theme in both its cognitive and behavioural dimensions'.⁴² The death 'to sin' from Romans 6:2 is based, according to Aune, on baptism, which is 'understood as a vicarious ritual experience of the death and resurrection of Christ'.⁴³ In Paul's discussion about how the death of Christ can be appropriated he uses cognitive language: 'knowing that...' Rom 6:6; 'knowing that...' Rom 6:8-9; 'Consider yourselves...' Rom 6:11; 'set their minds on...' Rom 8:5-6.⁴⁴

Our critical analysis of David Aune's essay will focus on his main proposals: (i) that the *commentatio mortis* theme is found only in the Hellenistic traditions quoted above, (ii) that death as a metaphor for a morally transformed life does not appear in early Judaism (he does not prove it, he only affirms it), and (iii) that the Pauline metaphor of death for describing a mode of living is based, at least in part, on the popular philosophical *commentatio mortis* theme.

(i) The *commentatio mortis* theme is found only in the Hellenistic traditions quoted above.

For a better discussion of the place of this theme in ancient literature a background of this usage of 'death' will be sketched; then a detailed study of *Phaedo* in relation to our theme, and then a presentation of our understanding of Seneca's position and also the witness from Philo. A comparison with Pauline usage will be discussed with the analysis of point (iii) of Aune's essay.

---

³⁵ Aune, 'Human Nature,' 305.
³⁶ Aune, 'Human Nature,' 305.
³⁷ Seneca, *Ad Lucilium Epistulae Morales* (IV; Richard M. Gummere, trans.; Cambridge, Mass., London: Harvard University Press, William Heinemann Ltd, 1979).
³⁸ Ps. Plato, *The Axiochus: On Death and Immortality* (E. H. Blankeney, trans.; London: Frederick Muller Ltd, 1937).
³⁹ Aune, 'Human Nature,' 307.
⁴⁰ Aune, 'Human Nature,' 310.
⁴¹ Aune, 'Human Nature,' 310.
⁴² Aune, 'Human Nature,' 310.
⁴³ Aune, 'Human Nature,' 311.
⁴⁴ Aune, 'Human Nature,' 312.

language of 'death' in Romans 6. David E. Aune sketched some general ideas in his essay 'Human Nature and Ethics in Hellenistic Philosophical Traditions and Paul: Some Issues and Problems',[32] which will be taken into account. The most known area of research where 'dying' language of Romans 6 is studied is that of 'dying with Christ'. All relevant studies on 'dying with Christ' are discussed in the review.

The review is organised in two main sections: first, those authors who have written on the question of the place of origin of this type of language (hellenistic ideas, the teaching of Jesus, early Christian ideas and experience), and secondly, authors who have written about the way in which Paul develops/explains this language of 'death' in Romans 6 (different ideas which receive importance for explaining this *motif*). The authors which include in their research work on both these aspects are discussed in the second group. It is also convenient to integrate the questions of 'background' at this point of the argument because these questions are deeply relevant to the wider secondary discussion which we here review. This review will help us focus our particular interest by comparing and analysing critically the work in those areas. Also in the light of the history of research — its strengths and weaknesses — the *what* and *why* of this project will become clear.

The Place of Origin of the Metaphorical Language of 'Death'

D. E. AUNE — THE METAPHOR OF 'DEATH' AND THE *COMMENTATIO MORTIS* TRADITION

The first author to be discussed is D. E. Aune. His work is the most important for this section because he tried to offer a new particular 'context' for interpreting Paul's metaphorical language in Romans 6. Because of this we will engage extensively with him. Aune offers a strong argument for a hellenistic philosophical background to understand Romans 6. Here is the line of his proposal.

According to Aune, in ancient times the idea of *commentatio mortis* (the preparation while in the body for the true life which is possible only when the soul is separated from the body at death; Plato, *Phaedo*, 81a)[33] was relatively widespread.[34] According to this 'practice' the true philosopher will always seek

---

[32] David E. Aune, 'Human Nature and Ethics in Hellenistic Philosophical Traditions and Paul: Some Issues and Problems', in Troels Engberg-Pedersen, ed., *Paul in His Hellenistic Context* (Studies of The New Testament and Its World; Edinburgh: T&T Clark, 1994), 291-312.

[33] Aune, 'Human Nature,' 305.

[34] Aune, 'Human Nature,' 307.

6:14. Rom 6:14b is the base for the imperatives from 6:12-14a.[28] The 'liberation' from the dominion of sin is not an effect of the 'dominion' of the law but of being 'overwhelmed' by (God's) grace (to which the rite of baptism alludes)[29] — see 6:2b. Thus the whole argument is brought to an end, the emphasis being on the 'charge' of 6:1. The abundance of grace does not lead to sin but to participation (as a weapon[30]) in the 'war' of δικαιοσύνη. Grace will not lead to sin because the death of Christ is the major event in the manifestation of grace and the 'walking in the newness of life' is thought of as being shaped by this event with the result, as far as the relation with sin is concerned, of being 'dead to sin'.[31]

This argument by Paul in Romans 6 was and continues to be the subject of many studies. A review of those which are relevant to our subject will be presented below for knowing the strength and weakness of different positions in the field. In this way can be established the need for such a project and possibilities for new insights.

A Critical Review of Scholarship

There is a huge amount of literature on Romans 6. Because of this we were confronted with the following dilemma: either to discuss here all relevant positions on the meaning of the important Pauline affirmations from our text ('we died to sin' (6:2), 'we were baptized into his death' (6:3), 'we have been buried with him by baptism into his death' (6:4), 'we have been united with the likeness of his death' (6:5), 'our old man was crucified with him' (6:6), 'you must consider yourselves dead to sin' (6:11)), or to analyse here only those scholars who have written specifically on 'dying' language in Romans 6 and to present all the other positions on the meaning of the phrases presented above in our argument in the sections where we argued for a particular understanding of these. Because of the focus of this project on metaphorical language of 'death' and because this review is even so extensively long (we will discuss 20 scholars) we decided to follow the second route; thus here the work of those scholars who wrote on the 'dying' language in Romans 6 will be analysed but the conclusions of the review will be made knowing the state of research from all relevant studies.

According to our knowledge there is no study in the area of Pauline studies, which explores, in a detailed way, the metaphorical character of Paul's

---

[28] Cf. Louw, Semantic Discourse, 76.

[29] See the argument in chapter 4.

[30] Also Schreiner, *Romans*, 300.

[31] Moo puts it as follows: Christ died to sin (vv.8-10), we died with Christ (vv.3-7), therefore we died to sin (v.2). Douglas J. Moo, *The Epistle to the Romans* (Grand Rapids, Michigan / Cambridge: Wm. B. Eerdmans Publishing Co., 1996), 355, note 12.

6:3-7 is an explanation which clearly defines the terms of 6:1-2.[20] This explanation is developed on two lines, as the discussion of 6:1-2 indicates, namely those of 'grace' and 'sin'. In 6:3, by the metaphorical language of 'baptism',[21] Paul points to the 'overwhelming' action of God over us in 'pushing/leading' us 'toward' Christ's *death*, the event where 'the grace of God' was given abundantly (5:15b, 17b). In 6:4-11 the death of Christ receives the place of reference for the 'sin' side of the argument. Christ's death in this passage is understood as a 'death to sin' (τῇ ἁμαρτίᾳ ἀπέθανεν, 6:10), which is a singular expression in the whole New Testament.[22] This perspective is behind his language of 'death' in 6:1-11.[23]

The argument is continued[24] in the other two main blocks: 6:8-11 and 6:12-14. The lines of development follow different strategies: one is conditional (εἰ...) and the other is imperative (μὴ οὖν βασιλευέτω...).[25] If ἀπεθάνομεν σὺν Χριστῷ results in συζήσομεν αὐτῷ (which is defined specifically as ζῇ τῷ θεῷ), then it is imperative (λογίζεσθε) to consider yourselves 'dead to sin' and 'alive to God' (6:11).

In 6:8-11 the implication of 6:8 is repeated in 6:11 (ἀπεθάνομεν σὺν Χριστῷ/ ὑμεῖς λογίζεσθε ἑαυτοὺς [εἶναι] νεκροὺς με τῇ ἁμαρτίᾳ; συζήσομεν αὐτῷ/ ζῶντας δὲ τῷ θεῷ). 6:9-10 presents the justification[26] for the affirmations from 6:8,11. This christological outlook has its focus on the role of the death and resurrection of Christ in understanding the realities of sin and death.[27] 6:9b is a summary of 6:9a and 6:10b is an important equivalent (from a different perspective) of 6:10a.

Rom 6:14a is a reiteration of 6:12a, and 6:13 is a reiteration of 6:12 and 6:14. Rom 6:13a is a negative reverse, and 6:13b a positive one, of 6:12 and

---

[19] Also Käsemann, *Romans*, 170.

[20] Käsemann, *Romans*, 165 and Bornkamm, 'Baptism,' 74-5 understand 6:2-4, 5-7 and vv:8-10 as parallel to one another.

[21] See the arguments in chapter 4.

[22] It occurs only once in the LXX in the Achan narrative Josh. 22:20 where the dative is causal.

[23] See the discussion in chapter 3.

[24] Also Cranfield, *Romans*, 296, understands vv.2-11 as a repudiation of the false inference of v.1.

[25] Cf. J. P. Louw, *A Semantic Discourse Analysis of Romans. Commentary* (2; Pretoria: Dept. of Greek University of Pretoria, 1979), 76; Cranfield, *Romans,* 297, understands 6.12-13 as a conclusion of the preceding argument.

[26] Elliot puts it like this: 'the conviction that 'we shall also live with him (6.8) is justified by the assertion that 'death no longer has dominion over him' (6:9); he lives 'to God' (6:10). 'So also you consider yourselves dead to sin but alive to God in Christ Jesus' (6:11); 'no longer let sin have dominion' (6:12-13a) but 'present yourselves to God' (6:13b)'. Elliot, *Rhetoric,* 240.

[27] See the argument in chapter 3.

Christ Jesus were baptized into his death' from 6:2 is based. Paul describes this event using familiar language (baptism), but he uses it metaphorically.[12] Rom. 6:3 is explained in 6:4-5, where 6:5 is a summary of 6:4.

Romans 6:2 describes 'sin' as an accompanying element (life 'in' it/death 'to' it) which has to be understood in the context of the affirmations from 5:21 ('sin exercised dominion in death'), 6:12 ('do not let sin exercise dominion in your mortal bodies') and 6:14 ('sin will not have dominion over you') as a powerful personified agent[13] which exercises 'control'. 6:3 points to a 'goal'[14] (εἰς...) and 6:4 is formulated with οὖν which marks a particular emphasis (συνετάφημεν... αὐτῷ).[15] The purpose of this fact (ἵνα) is formulated in terms of a comparison ὥσπερ/οὕτως; thus the 'walking in the newness of life' is shaped by the death and resurrection of Christ. In Rom. 6:6,7 (see especially the reference to 'releasing' from the dominion of sin) the argument from 6:3-5 (where 6:5 is understood as a confirmation (εἰ γὰρ...) of 6:4)[16] is related to that from 6:1-2.[17] This fact of 'releasing' from sin explains the answer to the charge of 6:1 in 6:2. Rom 6:6b (ὅτι...) gives the content of 6:6a and 6:6c (ἵνα...) is the result of 6:6b. Rom 6:6d (τοῦ μηκέτι δουλεύειν...) is another purpose clause which has an explicative role for 6:6c and it is a version of the answer to the question in 6:1.[18] Rom 6:7 is a supporting[19] summary of 6:6. In this way Rom

---

Verlag, 1973), 284; Käsemann, *Romans,* 165; Fitzmyer, *Romans,* 430; Otto Kuss, *Der Römerbrief* (1; Regensburg: Verlag Friedrich Pustet, 1963), 296; Cranfield, *Romans,* 298; Brendan Byrne, *Romans* (Collegeville, Minnesota: The Liturgical Press, 1996), 189.

[12] For the argument here see chapter 4; also Dunn, *Baptism,* 141; A.J.M. Wedderburn, *Baptism and Resurrection: Studies in Pauline Theology Against Its Graeco-Roman Background* (Tübingen: Mohr, 1987), 59.

[13] Also Fitzmyer, *Romans,* 430; Käsemann, *Romans,* 163.

[14] Cf. Johannes Louw and Eugene A. Nida, eds, *Greek-English Lexicon of the New Testament Based on Semantic Domains* (New York: United Bible Societies, 1988, 1989), 79, 76.

[15] Cf. Louw and Nida, *Lexicon,* 812; Cranfield understands it as a clause by which Paul 'draws out and clarifies the meaning of the last clause of v.3.' Cranfield, *Romans,* 304.

[16] Cf. Cranfield, *Romans,* 306.

[17] The ἵνα clause in 6:4 'recalls the objection of v.1.' Fitzmyer, *Romans,* 434; Käsemann, *Romans,* 167 says that vv.2-4 are repeated for clarification in vv.5-7. It is not so much that 6:6 'starts a new section and reverts back to the theme of verse 2 by emphazing the death of the old person' (Thomas R. Schreiner, *Romans* (Grand Rapids, Michigan: Baker Books, 1998), 299), because 6:6 has to be understood together with 6:7 as a part of the 6:3-7 'section' bringing the idea pointed by σύμφυτος ('be one with') in relation to the 6:1-2. Also 6:6-7 is not a thematical reiteration of 6:3-4a by emphasing that believers died with Christ, (Schreiner, *Romans,* 299) but rather a clarification of the implied elements presented behind Paul's thesis from 6:2 as his answer to the charge of 6:1.

[18] Cf. Fitzmyer, *Romans,* 436.

shown more clearly if we take the affirmations from 6:12-14 as a part of it. Also the rhetorical question of 6:15 continues Paul's argument by shifting the emphasis. Thus, an analysis of the structure of this larger unit is necessary.

Paul's saying from 5:20 can be distorted.[2] An example of this is in 3:8.[3] This is why his rhetorical question in 6:1 is formulated as it is, 'What then are we to say?' (τί οὖν ἐροῦμεν) revealing that what he has just said is controversial and requires elucidation.[4] His question looks back to what precedes,[5] and points to a conclusion that might be drawn from the previous argument,[6] but then its answer from 6:1b points to a false[7] conclusion: ἐπιμένωμεν τῇ ἁμαρτίᾳ, ἵνα ἡ χάρις πλεονάσῃ. Paul does not say that there will not be more grace where sin increases but that this principle from the history of salvation cannot be applied by believers. The reason for this is given in the exposition which follows.[8]

Briefly,[9] the argument goes like this: 6:1 puts the terms[10] of exposition in the form of a question and 6:2 is the answer to it. This second part of 6:2 needs to be explained;[11] this is the role of 6:3-7. 'All of us who have been baptized into

---

Barrett, Byrne, Cranfield, Edwards, Leenhardt, Moo, Nygren and Wilckens at v.14.

[2] Also Joseph A. Fitzmyer, *Romans* (New York: Doubleday, 1993), 432; C.E.B. Cranfield, *A Critical and Exegetical Commentary of the Epistle to the Romans* (Vols 1 and 2; Edinburgh: T. & T. Clark, 1975 & 1979), 296.

[3] See also Ernst Käsemann, *Commentary on Romans* (Grand Rapids, Michigan: Eerdmans, 1980), 165; Fitzmyer, *Romans*, 430; Neil Elliot, *The Rhetoric of Romans: Argumentative Constraint and Strategy and Paul's Dialogue with Judaism* (Sheffield: JSOT, 1990), 237; F. Watson, *Paul, Judaism and the Gentiles: A Sociological Approach* (Cambridge: CUP, 1986), 147; Cranfield, *Romans*, 297.

[4] So also J.D.G. Dunn, *Romans* (Waco: Word, 1988), 306; Fitzmyer, *Romans*, 432.

[5] Also Elliot, *Rhetoric*, 236.

[6] Elliot, *Rhetoric*, 238.

[7] Also Elliot, *Rhetoric*, 238; Cranfield, *Romans*, 296.

[8] It is not so much that in Rom. 6:1-11 Paul 'picks up the contrast of death and life from 5.21', but he develops his argument as a detailed answer (which is enounced briefly — ἀπεθάνομεν τῇ ἁμαρτίᾳ) to the charge of 6:1; also Käsemann, *Romans*, 165.

[9] Details of the argument are discussed in the argument of the thesis where relevant.

[10] Also Udo Schnelle, *The Human Condition: Anthropology in the Teachings of Jesus, Paul, and John* (Edinburgh: T&T Clark, 1996), 74; A. Nygren, *Commentary on Romans* (Philadelphia: Fortress, 1949), 239; Rudolf Schnackenburg, *Baptism in the Thought of St. Paul: A Study in Pauline Theology* (trans. by G. R. Beasley-Murray; Oxford: Basil Blackwell, 1964), 31; Günther Bornkamm, 'Baptism and New Life in Paul (Romans 6)', in *Early Christian Experience* (London: SCM, 1969), 79; Ulrich Wilckens, *Der Brief und die Römer* (2; Zurich, Neukirchen/Vluyn: Neukirchener, Benziger, 1980), 7; Peter Stuhlmacher, *Paul's Letter to the Romans: A Commentary* (Edinburgh: T&T Clark, 1994), 100.

[11] Also J.D.G. Dunn, *Baptism in the Holy Spirit: A Re-Examination of the New Testament Teaching on the Gift of the Spirit in Relation to Pentecostalism Today* (London: SCM, 1970), 140; B. N. Kaye, 'βαπτίζειν εἰς with Special Reference to Romans 6', in Elizabeth A. Livingstone, ed., *Studia Evangelica* VI (Berlin: Akademie

Chapter 1

Towards a Contextual Reading of the Metaphorical Language of 'Death' in Romans 6:1-11

The Subject of Research

Paul's message about 'the grace of God in one man Jesus Christ' was accused of leading to an easy approach to the question of sin in the life of believers. If the principle which says that 'where sin increased, grace abounded all the more (Rom 5:20b) is true, then why not 'do evil so that good may come' (Rom 3:8)? or 'should we continue in sin in order that grace may abound'(Rom 6:1)? Paul's immediate answer is an emphatic 'by no means'. His specific answer is formulated as a thesis to be demonstrated /defended: 'How can we who died to sin go on living in it?' Understanding this metaphorical language of 'death' [of his thesis] is the subject of this project.

For this purpose, this first chapter is organized as follows: (a) we will discuss, briefly, the line of Paul's argument in Romans 6:1-14; (b) a critical review of the relevant literature on the subject of the meaning of the language of 'death' here in Romans 6; and (c) the way in which this project is developed for defending our thesis concerning the meaning of the metaphorical language of 'death' in Romans 6.

The Structure of Romans 6:1-14

This brief presentation of the line of Paul's argument has the role of an introduction into the world of Paul's ideas as these are interrelated in Romans 6.

Rom 6:1-11 should be understood in relation to 6:12-14,[1] because the contrast 'grace'/'sin' is carried to a conclusion in 6:14, and the portrait of sin is

---

[1] The structure division of chapter 6 is a subject of debate: the question is the place of 6:12-14 in the argument; is it related to 6:1-11 or to 6:14-23? If it is understood in relation to 6:14-23, the 'imperative' side of the argument is kept together (even if in this section there are 'indicatives' too) and the 'indicative' side of 6:1-11 is left by itself. Black, Dunn, Käsemann, Kuss, and Murray divide chapter 6 at v:12 and Achtemeier,

Abbreviations

ABD	*Anchor Bible Dictionary*
BAGD	W. Bauer, W.F. Ardnt, F.W. Gingrich and F.W. Danker, *Greek-English Lexicon of the New Testament and Other Early Christian Literature*
BDF	F. Blass, A. Debrunner şi R.W. Funk, *A Greek Grammar of the New Testament and Other Early Christian Literature*
Bib	*Biblica*
CBQ	*Catholic Biblical Quarterly*
EDNT	*Exegetical Dictionary of the New Testament*
EvQ	*Evangelical Quarterly*
ExpTim	*Expository Times*
HTR	*Harvard Theological Review*
JBL	*Journal of Biblical Literature*
JETS	*Journal of Evangelical Theological Society*
JTS	*Journal of Theological Studies*
LCL	Loeb Classical Library
MT	Masoretic Text
NIDNTT	*New International Dictionary of the New Testament Theology*
NIDOTTE	*New International Dictionary of the Old Testament Theology and Exegesis*
NIV	New International Version
NRSV	New Revised Standard Version
NovT	*Novum Testamentum*
NTS	*New Testament Studies*
RB	*Revue biblique*
REB	Revised English Bible
RSV	Revised Standard Version
SBL	*Society of Biblical Literature*
TDNT	*Theological Dictionary of the New Testament*
ThZ	*Theologische Zeitschrift*
TrinJ	*Trinity Journal*
TS	*Theological Studies*
TynB	*Tyndale Bulletin*
VoxEv	*Vox Evangelica*
WTJ	*Westminster Theological Journal*

PREFACE

This book is a version of my PhD thesis defended in May 2001 at London Bible College; it is an analysis of the metaphorical language of death in Romans 6:1-11.

I am thankful to God for helping me to write it. I thank to my supervisors: Prof. Max Turner who was my first supervisor in the first year, and to Dr Stephen Motyer who was that kind of *Doktorvater* who trusted me and had the courage to let me almost alone in this project; from time to time he gave me that necessary push for not loosing speed in the process. Also I want to thank to Dr Bruce Winter, the Warden of Tyndale House, Cambridge, where I wrote the final draft of the thesis, for his useful insights and to Prof. James Edwards for his time in discussing different things from Romans.

I am thankful to my wife Simona, who has worked in the same time at her thesis 'Trading Silence for Words of Praise– The Status of Woman in Eastern Orthodoxy as Reflected in the Works of Paul Evdokimov', London Bible College, June, 2003, for her love and time management, and to our daughters Andra and Dora for their love and patience to their parents.

The Metaphor of 'Baptism' (Romans 6:3)	95
σύμφυτος Metaphor (Romans 6:5)	109
ὁ παλαιὸς ἄνθρωπος Metaphor (Romans 6.6)	116
A Presentation of the Proposed Meanings for	
ὁ παλαιὸς ἄνθρωπος	117
Towards an Understanding of the Meaning of	
ὁ παλαιὸς ἄνθρωπος	119
THE RELATIONSHIP BETWEEN	
ROMANS 6:1-11 AND ROMANS 5:12-21	120
ADAM'S SIN AND HUMANKIND'S SIN IN	
ROMANS 5:12-21	120
σῶμα IN ROMANS 6:6	133
THE INTEGRATION OF THE DATA IN RELATION	
TO ROMANS 6:6	137

Chapter 5
ἀπεθάνομεν τῇ ἁμαρτίᾳ: Interpreting the Metaphorical Language of 'Death' in Romans 6:1-11   139

The Question of Origin	139
The Question of Development/Explanation	141
Bibliography	**145**
Index	**157**

R. SCHNACKENBURG AND H. RIDDERBOS –
THE SACRAMENTAL 'DYING WITH CHRIST' 36
V.P. FURNISH – 'DYING WITH CHRIST' AND BAPTISM 38
W.G. KÜMMEL – A SHARE IN THE EFFECTS OF
CHRIST'S DEATH 39
J.D.G. DUNN – 'DYING WITH CHRIST', THE ROLES OF
CHRISTOLOGY AND ANTHROPOLOGY 40
M.D. HOOKER – DIFFERENT PERSPECTIVES IN
CHRISTOLOGY 40
The Argument of the Book 41

Chapter 2
Methodological Considerations: Understanding Metaphor 44

Introduction 44
The Metaphor Debate 44
Rhetorical Metaphor 45
Semantic Metaphor 52
A Working Theory: Metaphor as a Contextual Phenomenon 53

Chapter 3
The Language of 'Death': *The Vehicle* of Paul's Metaphor in Romans 6:1-11 57

Introduction 57
Christ's Death as a *'Death to Sin'* (Romans 6:10) 58
A 'Death to Sin' 58
Christ in His Death 64
Χριστός IN ROMANS 64
The Likeness of Christ's Death (Romans 6:5) 70
The 'Crucifixion' Language (Romans 6:6) 79
The 'Burial' Language (Romans 6:4) 90

Chapter 4
The Qualifiers of the Metaphor of 'Death' in Romans 6:1-11 94

Introduction 94

Contents

Preface	xiii
Abbreviations	xv

Chapter 1
Towards a Contextual Reading of the Metaphorical
Language of 'Death' in Romans 6:1-11 1

The Subject of Research	1
The Structure of Romans 6:1-14	1
A Critical Review of Scholarship	5
The Place of Origin of the Metaphorical Language of 'Death'	6
D.E. AUNE - THE METAPHOR OF 'DEATH' AND THE *COMMENTATIO MORTIS* TRADITION	6
D. WENHAM – 'DYING' LANGUAGE AND THE TEACHING OF JESUS	17
R. REITZENSTEIN, R. BULTMANN, E. LOHSE, R. PENNA, U. SCHNELLE – 'DYING WITH CHRIST' AND THE MYSTERY RELIGIONS	18
G. WAGNER AND A.J.M. WEDDERBURN – 'DYING WITH CHRIST' AND ADAMIC CHRISTOLOGY	27
E. SCHWEIZER – 'DYING WITH CHRIST' AND ESCHATOLOGICAL 'BEING WITH CHRIST'	29
W. WILSON AND A. CAMBELL – 'DYING WITH CHRIST' AS A PRODUCT OF PERSONAL EXPERIENCE	30
The Development of the Metaphor of 'Death'	33
R.C. TANNEHILL – 'DYING WITH CHRIST' AS A PAST AND A PRESENT EXPERIENCE	33
A. SCHWEITZER – PREDESTINATION, MESSIAH AND COMMUNITY	34

To Simona and our daughters

Series Editors

I. Howard Marshall, Honorary Research Professor of New Testament, University of Aberdeen, Scotland, UK

Richard J. Bauckham, Professor of New Testament Studies and Bishop Wardlaw Professor, University of St Andrews, Scotland, UK

Craig Blomberg, Distinguished Professor of New Testament, Denver Seminary, Colorado, USA

Robert P. Gordon, Regius Professor of Hebrew, University of Cambridge, UK

Tremper Longman III, Robert H. Gundry Professor and Chair of the Department of Biblical Studies, Westmont College, Santa Barbara, California, USA

PATERNOSTER BIBLICAL MONOGRAPHS

Series Preface

One of the major objectives of Paternoster is to serve biblical scholarship by providing a channel for the publication of theses and other monographs of high quality at affordable prices. Paternoster stands within the broad evangelical tradition of Christianity. Our authors would describe themselves as Christians who recognise the authority of the Bible, maintain the centrality of the gospel message and assent to the classical credal statements of Christian belief. There is diversity within this constituency; advances in scholarship are possible only if there is freedom for frank debate on controversial issues and for the publication of new and sometimes provocative proposals. What is offered in this series is the best of writing by committed Christians who are concerned to develop well-founded biblical scholarship in a spirit of loyalty to the historic faith.

Wipf and Stock Publishers
199 W 8th Ave, Suite 3
Eugene, OR 97401

Between Horror and Hope
Paul's Metaphorical Language of Death in Romans 6:1-11
By Sabou, Sorin
Copyright©2005 Paternoster
ISBN: 1-59752-766-1
Publication date 6/10/2006
Previously published by Paternoster, 2005

This Edition Published by Wipf and Stock Publishers
by arrangement with Paternoster

Paternoster
9 Holdom Avenue
Bletchley
Milton Keyes, MK1 1QR
PATERNOSTER Great Britain

Scripture quotations (unless otherwise noted) are taken from New Revised Standard Version Bible, copyright 1989, Division of Christian Education of the National Council of the Churches of Christ in the United States of America. Used by permission. All rights reserved.

PATERNOSTER BIBLICAL MONOGRAPHS

Between Horror and Hope

Paul's Metaphorical Language of Death in Romans 6:1-11

Sorin Sabou

Wipf & Stock
PUBLISHERS
Eugene, Oregon